THE BEST OF
CORWIN

EDUCATIONAL TECHNOLOGY
for *School Leaders*

The Best of Corwin Series

Classroom Management
Jane Bluestein, Editor

Differentiated Instruction
Gayle H. Gregory, Editor

Differentiated Instruction in Literacy, Math, and Science
Leslie Laud, Editor

Educational Neuroscience
David A. Sousa, Editor

Educational Technology for School Leaders
Lynne M. Schrum, Editor

Equity
Randall B. Lindsey, Editor

Inclusive Practices
Toby J. Karten, Editor

Response to Intervention
Cara F. Shores, Editor

EDUCATIONAL TECHNOLOGY
for School Leaders

LYNNE SCHRUM

Editor

With contributions by

Marc Prensky · Frank S. Kelly · Ted McCain · Ian Jukes

Lynne Schrum · Barbara B. Levin · Alan November · Jessica K. Parker

William Kist · Lori Langer de Ramirez · Aimée M. Bissonette

Sameer Hinduja · Justin W. Patchin · Jill Jolene Myers

Donna S. McCaw · Leaunda S. Hemphill

CORWIN
A SAGE Company

CORWIN
A SAGE Company

FOR INFORMATION:

Corwin
A SAGE Company
2455 Teller Road
Thousand Oaks, California 91320
(800) 233-9936
Fax: (800) 417-2466
www.corwin.com

SAGE Ltd.
1 Oliver's Yard
55 City Road
London EC1Y 1SP
United Kingdom

SAGE India Pvt. Ltd.
B 1/I 1 Mohan Cooperative
Industrial Area
Mathura Road, New Delhi 110 044
India

SAGE Asia-Pacific Pte. Ltd.
33 Pekin Street #02-01
Far East Square
Singapore 048763

Printed in the United States of America

Library of Congress Cataloging-in-Publication Data

A catalog record of this book is available from the Library of Congress.

978-1-4522-1727-7

Acquisitions Editor: Debra Stollenwerk
Associate Editor: Desirée A. Bartlett
Editorial Assistant: Kimberly Greenberg
Production Editor: Melanie Birdsall
Typesetter: C&M Digitals (P) Ltd.
Cover Designer: Rose Storey
Graphic Designer: Nicole Franck
Permissions Editor: Adele Hutchinson

This book is printed on acid-free paper.

11 12 13 14 15 10 9 8 7 6 5 4 3 2 1

Contents

PART III. SAFETY AND POLICY MATTERS

Preface

Lynne Schrum

Currently, school leaders, educators, and communities are eager to improve student achievement, engagement, and general outcomes for their students and the larger educational system. It is an enormous task and complicated by many factors, including the realities that our students today are not the ones for whom our schools were created, that our society has become more complex, that funding has been cut and resources are limited, and that metrics for evaluating school progress have narrowed.

According to the literature over the past few decades, "the principal is key to building a better school . . . a strong and supportive principal can enable a faculty to succeed in the most challenging conditions" (Drago-Severson, 2004, p. xvii). Darling-Hammond, Meyerson, LaPointe, and Orr agree: "The critical role of principals in developing successful schools has been well established" (2010, p. 179). How do school leaders prepare themselves for the enormous tasks they face, and in particular, to develop or shift to an educational environment that reflects the increasingly pervasive role of technology in society and work, and the need to prepare students for the realities of the 21st century?

We know the reality of our learners' lives; most students are well connected and use multiple digital technologies. Web 2.0 tools, which offer greater potential to increase interactivity and perhaps better address the digital divide, have become almost commonplace, and typically involve voluntary participation (Alexander, 2008). Technology has had a positive impact on education, even if it has not yet resulted in wholesale educational transformation, but there are larger issues that have not yet been addressed. For example, disparity in educational outcomes still exist, too many of our youth still drop out of school and do not reach their potential, and students are often disengaged from content and learning.

Research informs us that technology leadership matters for promoting teachers' uses of technology (Anderson & Dexter 2005) and that school administrators need to become increasingly involved in the technology projects in their schools to model and support its use (Dawson & Rakes,

2003; Stuart, Mills, & Remus, 2009; Williams, 2008). Many suggest school leaders need to effectively and quickly make shifts in their knowledge, skills, and practices (McLeod & Richardson, 2011; Schrum, Galizio, & Ledesma, 2011).

To assist in the challenges faced by all school leaders, Corwin has published thousands of books for teachers and school leaders, including many seminal works that brought together important academic research, creative new ideas, and concrete, practical strategies to help improve the professional lives of educators. Now, Corwin launches its Best of Corwin series to showcase key chapters from a variety of critically acclaimed Corwin publications to give readers a useful overview of multiple perspectives on important education issues and topics, like equity, technology, differentiated instruction, and others. We hope these selected pieces will provide educators with helpful "mini-encyclopedias" on these critical topics, and that the ideas, perspectives, and strategies contained in them will be of both immediate and long-term value.

OVERVIEW OF THIS BOOK

The Best of Corwin: Educational Technology for School Leaders comprises some of the most important chapters devoted to an understanding of 21st-century students and challenges, technology and curriculum, and an overview of the types of questions a school leader may face. Some themes will appear and reappear throughout the chapters:

- We must redefine literacy and knowledge today.
- Students benefit when choices are provided and authentic questions are asked.
- Teachers need support for learning to teach in new ways.
- We must move away from implying or expecting the "one right answer" to every question.
- Although our challenges are great, our need to tackle them is greater.

It is clear that if a school leader is not well-informed regarding the breadth and depth of 21st-century skills and ways to approach them, it is possible that students and teachers may disengage and that moving toward a vision of change may not happen. Yet it is also true that while the school leader is essential, she or he is only one part of a leadership system needed to implement change and reform (Gerard, Bowyer, & Linn, 2010). So this book was created not only for those of you who are school leaders but also for other stakeholder groups as well (teacher leaders, professional learning communities, technology coordinators, school boards, and parent groups in general). In fact, this may be useful for all who are critically involved in preparing students today for life, post-secondary education, and careers.

Part I. Our 21st-Century Schools

The four chapters in this section of the book provide a broad introduction to the students who now enter our doors—student expectations and the need for a new educational environment. This section suggests how the nature of schools, as we have conceptualized them for the past century, must change to adapt to the future our graduates will face. The chapters also provide insight into what a leader needs to know to support the changes required, and ways to draw on the entire community of resources to implement these changes.

Part II. Technology-Powered Classrooms

Four chapters comprise this section of the book; this part's goal is to offer an exploration of what is possible using digitally enhanced curriculum. The chapters explore how students relate to digital media and suggest ways to leverage that connection for true engaged learning activities. The authors look beyond our classrooms and anticipate ways to partner with individuals and communities throughout the world and provide ideas for differentiated learning to reach all students. And because every school is not completely wired (yet) and resources are too often scarce, we included a chapter that recommends methods to take advantage of digital resources' power in low-tech situations.

Part III. Safety and Policy Matters

The final section of the book offers insights into some of the realities faced by schools and their leaders when moving toward more digital deployment in classrooms. These are especially vital if a school or district is considering implementing a BYOD (bring your own device) policy. The three chapters in this section provide suggestions for communicating expectations to the school community, as well as leading discussions on preventing and responding to cyberbullying. Having information on these topics will help school leaders assure they are implementing intentional and proactive strategies rather than reacting to unexpected events.

We hope this Best of Corwin book answers some of your questions on these topics; we also hope some of these chapters will encourage you to investigate the topics further. Enjoy!

Introduction

Lynne Schrum

This volume is an overview of the concept of differentiated instruction, featuring excerpts from ten works by recognized experts. The following is a synopsis of what you will find in each chapter.

PART I. OUR 21ST-CENTURY SCHOOLS

Chapter 1. Partnering: A Pedagogy for the New Educational Landscape

Marc Prensky

In Chapter 1, Marc Prensky explores why students require new ways of teaching and learning. He presents the concept of partnering, which is really collaborative, and investigative learning, in which students and teachers approach student learning by *working together*, each assuming critical and active roles in a true dialectic relationship. By describing student and teacher roles and responsibilities, he is establishing a rich educational environment in which learners are active and teachers create opportunities to learn, explore, and question, and setting the stage for teachers working with parents and the larger community. His suggestions provide a roadmap for getting started, making changes in the ways of using technology, and planning and implementing instruction. More than anything, we see that in a partnering educational environment, technology supports students in personalizing their educational experiences and tackling important and authentic tasks. As an example, teachers *ask* rather than tell and students *find out* rather than take notes. Prensky encourages teachers not to fear change: "It can be quite invigorating and exciting to rethink your job from a new perspective."

Chapter 2. No More Cookie-Cutter High Schools

Frank S. Kelly, Ted McCain, and Ian Jukes

Chapter 2 explores the ways high schools need to customize, individualize, and meet the needs of communities, population, and trends. The authors offer suggestions for making substantial changes and how to sustain those changes. In addition, they offer ideas for promoting ongoing and effective vision development over time; in fact, they support the notion that moving through the steps of visioning is part of the problem many schools experience! Most important, the chapter explores ways in which high schools can provide more choices to their learners, just as the real world has evolved to allow customization of many aspects of our lives. Technology can assist in creating these choices, but, realistically, there must be an effort to meet the changing nature of our global world. As the authors postulate, "the most important issue facing schools today is the reluctance of those in control of education to let go of what they are used to, whatever their roles in the system."

Chapter 3. Strategic Leadership: Encouraging and Assessing Technology Integration

Lynne Schrum and Barbara B. Levin

Chapter 3 introduces two models for understanding and leading change for school improvement—the concerns-based adoption model and the adoption of innovation theory—within the construct of integrating technology to improve student achievement and engagement. This chapter explains how to manage and sustain that change and how to handle professional development that actually takes hold and becomes institutionalized through professional learning communities. Further, Lynne Schrum and Barbara Levin offer guidance for school leaders who must mentor and support teachers in the integration of technology into their lessons, rather than employing it as an add-on or reward for completing assignments. The chapter also explores and describes roles and responsibilities of the technology coordinator, technology planning committee, and teacher leaders so that the school works together toward a common vision.

Chapter 4. Emerging Roles Within the Knowledge Community

Alan November

In Chapter 4, Alan November explores what it means to be a teacher within an environment in which students are digital natives and far more proficient at using technology to accomplish educational goals; he suggests "reverse mentoring," in which we allow our students to show us what they know. He provides a variety of resources available within the knowledge community—a community that no longer stops at the school walls or even at the country's borders—and suggests ways educators can use technology to enhance and expand relationships with the community, become active participants in real problems, gather and use resources, and engage with experts near and far. He proposes opportunities for teachers to work together to promote collaborative learning activities, link with families, and also become sensitive to cultural perspectives.

PART II. TECHNOLOGY-POWERED CLASSROOMS

Chapter 5. Understanding Youth and Digital Media

Jessica K. Parker

Jessica Parker starts this chapter by asking extremely important questions: What do learning, literacy, and knowledge look like in the 21st century? How are they different from the familiar definitions of these terms from the last century? She encourages us to consider that there is no one right way to answer these questions, just as there is no one way to transform a school or the curriculum. The chapter delves into the nature of new media, new media environments, and the characteristics of those media that must be used and developed in our learners' educational experiences. Parker presents ways educators can reach the learners now entering our schools and lessen the disconnect between what students do during our six hours with them and what they do the rest of their waking hours as well as offering ways to embrace and adapt the new media for the purpose of teaching and learning.

Chapter 6. "Short": Social Networking in a Low-Tech Environment

William Kist

William Kist's chapter offers numerous ways to employ the interaction and interest of technology-rich environments in low-tech circumstances. Chapter 6 includes many interactive ideas for students while weaving in ways to use the technology tools that the students are likely familiar with, like blogs, and taking advantage of the benefits of a one-to-one computer situation. For example, he encourages students of almost any age to participate in a literacy autobiography in which genres are introduced and discussed. This allows students to think about all the ways we define *literacy,* prompting discussion about *digital literacy.* While many of the examples are targeted to the language arts classroom, the strategies are useful in all content areas and adaptable for all ages.

Chapter 7. Why Use Web 2.0 Tools With ELLs?

Lori Langer de Ramirez

In Chapter 7, Lori Langer de Ramirez explores how educators can strengthen the vocabulary and, in particular, the academic language that frequently takes extra time to develop in English language learners (ELLs). These students may often acquire social language long before the more academic spoken and written language evolves; happily, this chapter suggests that Web 2.0 tools offer extra opportunities to help ELLs meaningfully explore this language in their own time, offering the possibility and creation of their own knowledge and involving collaboration among students in authentic activities. Her experiences show that with an audience (and, frequently, an international audience), students may develop academic language more quickly. In addition, Web 2.0 tools support the TESOL standards for these learners—as well as TESOL's three technology standards—through a variety of tasks, assignments, and interactions these tools also support.

Chapter 8. Assessment in the Partnership Pedagogy

Marc Prensky

Marc Prensky addresses an issue of interest to school leaders, educators, and parents in today's world of high-stakes testing: What (if any) changes to assessment are valuable and appropriate in a technology-rich environment with partnering as a pedagogical framework? His many suggestions push the notion of assessment far beyond formative and summative tasks, many of which end up being artificial in practice. He encourages self-assessment, peer assessment, and iterative examination of work. Chapter 8 also describes how students may go out and find "real" assessment connections; for example, a student learning a foreign language may want to post an audio file and have a native speaker assess it on multiple dimensions. One guiding question might be, "Is each student, teacher, and administrator moving in positive directions and developing essential skills?" This chapter offers ways that a school and its many participants can examine progress and growth.

PART III. SAFETY AND POLICY MATTERS

Chapter 9. Policies, Procedures, and Contracts: Communicating Expectations to Teachers, Students, and Parents

Aimée M. Bissonette

Recognizing the need faced by all educational entities for policies and procedures to govern the effective use of technology resources and tools,

Chapter 9 introduces the reader to acceptable use policies (AUPs) and the notion of contract law as it applies to the safety, protection, and responsibilities of the stakeholders (students, parents, educators, school leaders, district, and the community). Aimée Bissonette, in a user-friendly and helpful manner, offers guiding questions to prompt the reader to consider topics that may not even be on your radar and to ensure that the various constituent groups understand their roles and responsibilities. For example, she offers suggestions and ideas for helping parents' understand the legal, ethical, and educational aspects to using technology. Most helpful are the step-by-step suggestions for collaboratively developing a school AUP. The samples and ideas will be extremely helpful as more districts institute one-to-one computing, or "any device" policies which give students new access and therefore, accountability. A sample AUP is also included.

Chapter 10. Preventing Cyberbullying

Sameer Hinduja and Justin W. Patchin

Chapter 10 focuses on the need to address cyberbullying very early in students' school lives (between fifth and seventh grades). The authors propose a process for preventing cyberbullying that includes strategies for gathering data about the issue in a school or district, specific approaches for introducing the topic within classrooms, and ways to involve the important participants (students, teachers, parents, law enforcement, and society) in related discussions, activities, and schoolwide implementation. In other words, the authors support the notion of shining a bright light on the issues and involving everyone as the best way to diminish the impact or potential development of cyberbullying. Readers will find practical scenarios that allow students to think about cyberbullying from all perspectives, identify solutions, and role-play ideas for addressing the issues. This chapter offers plans for how to recognize cyberbullying, suggestions for improving overall school climate, and ideas for all stakeholders about dealing with cyberbullying. Also included are sample contracts regarding Internet and family cell phone use.

Chapter 11. Top Ten Rules That Govern
School Authority Over Student Cyber Expressions

Jill Joline Myers, Donna S. McCaw, and Leaunda S. Hemphill

Once cyberbullying has occurred, it is critical for school leaders to address it. Chapter 11 provides clear rules to assist in this task, tackling school leaders' serious concerns about students' legal rights in relation to the need to protect students. What are the rules about censoring what students see, hear, or create in this new environment? Do schools have control over what students do digitally when they are not on school grounds? And exactly what types of regulations can a school reasonably impose? The chapter provides answers to these and other questions school leaders and the broader educational community might consider. The answers are based in common sense and extremely helpful for a community to open dialogue, explicate expectations, and identify consequences, as these rules must be used together in a strong, coherent system.

About the Editor

Lynne Schrum is a professor and director of teacher education in the College of Education and Human Development at George Mason University. Her research and teaching focus on appropriate uses of information technology, online and distance learning, and preparing teachers for the 21st century. She has written four books and numerous articles on these subjects; the most recent is *New Tools, New Schools: Getting Started with Web 2.0*. Schrum is currently on AERA's Council, editor of the *Journal of Research on Technology in Education* (JRTE) (2002–2011), and is a past-president of the International Society for Technology in Education (ISTE).

About the Contributors

Aimée M. Bissonette, JD, is a lawyer, teacher, and writer. She has written extensively for trade publications and conducts training sessions for corporate, educational, and nonprofit groups (nationally and internationally) on the topics of copyright, rights negotiation and licensing, and the legal issues associated with technology in schools. She has written website copy for two websites on intellectual property and copyright law, and has written and co-produced a satellite broadcast for the Minnesota State Colleges and Universities titled *Copyright Considerations for Higher Education*. She practices law with Little Buffalo Law & Consulting in Minneapolis, MN.

Over the past 20 years, **Leaunda S. Hemphill** has consulted with higher education and K–12 faculty on the use of effective instruction in computer-based and online environments. As an associate professor at Western Illinois University, she teaches instructional design and K–12 technology integration courses in the instructional design and technology department. She also teaches online student assessment for Illinois Online Network. She regularly conducts professional development workshops for state and international organizations. Her research includes evaluating online instruction and interactivity, and integrating emerging online technologies and virtual environments into the classroom.

Sameer Hinduja is an assistant professor in the Department of Criminology and Criminal Justice at Florida Atlantic University. For the past several years, Hinduja and his coauthor Justin W. Patchin have been exploring the online behaviors of adolescents, including social networking and cyberbullying. They travel across the United States training teachers, parents, and others about how to keep their kids safe online. They administer a website as an information clearinghouse for those interested in learning more about cyberbullying. He received his PhD in criminal justice from Michigan State University.

Ian Jukes has been a teacher, administrator, writer, consultant, university instructor, and keynote speaker. He is the director of the InfoSavvy Group, an international consulting group that provides leadership and program development in the areas of assessment and evaluation, curriculum design and publication, professional development, change management, hardware and software acquisition, and information services as well as conference keynotes and workshop presentations. Over the past decade, Jukes has worked with clients in more than 30 countries. In August 2002, Consulting Magazine Online named him one of the top ten educational speakers in America. Jukes has written six books, nine educational series, and had more than 100 articles published in various journals. He is also the publisher of an online electronic newsletter, the Committed Sardine Blog, which is electronically distributed to more than 20,000 people in 60 countries. His two most recently published books are *Net.Savvy: Building Information Literacy for the Classroom* (Corwin, 2000), co-authored with Anita Dosaj and Bruce Macdonald, and *Windows on the Future* (Corwin, 2000), co-authored with Ted McCain. His focus is on the compelling need to restructure educational institutions so that they become relevant to the current and future needs of children. His rambunctious, irreverent, and highly charged presentations and articles emphasize many of the practical issues related to ensuring that change is meaningful. His self-avowed mission in life is to ensure that children are properly prepared for the future rather than society's past, and his material focuses on many of the pragmatic issues related to educational restructuring.

An architect, **Frank S. Kelly** is senior vice president and director of planning/programming for the SHW Group, an architectural, planning, and engineering firm focused on architecture for education. SHW's practice extends across much of the country, with offices in Texas, Michigan, and Virginia.

Kelly taught design in the School of Architecture at the University of Tennessee and has worked with architectural classes at both Texas A&M and Rice University. With particular interest in the relationship between instruction and facilities, much of his architectural experience has focused on the planning, programming, and design of K–12 schools. He frequently lectures at school conferences related to instruction and has written a number of articles for education journals. His projects have been recognized by design awards from the architectural profession and educational organizations. In 1984, he was elected to the American Institute of Architect's College of Fellows for his work in design.

William Kist is an associate professor at Kent State University, where he teaches literacy education courses. A former high school English teacher, Kist has presented nationally and internationally, with over 40 articles and book chapters to his credit; his profiles of pioneering teachers were the essence of his book *New Literacies in Action* (2005). In November, 2007, Kist began a three-year term as director of the Commission on Media for the National Council of Teachers of English. Kist continues to work in video and film and has earned a regional Emmy nomination for Outstanding Music Composition.

Lori Langer de Ramirez began her career as a teacher of Spanish, French, and ESL. She is currently the chairperson of the ESL and World Language Department for Herricks Public Schools.

Langer de Ramirez is the author of *Take Action: Lesson Plans for the Multicultural Classroom and Voices of Diversity: Stories, Activities and Resources for the Multicultural Classroom* (Pearson), as well as several Spanish-language books and texts (*Cuéntame: Folklore y Fábulas* and *Mi abuela ya no está*). She has contributed to many textbooks and written numerous articles about second-language pedagogy and methodology. Her interactive website (www.miscositas.com) offers teachers over 40 virtual picturebooks, videos, wiki and blog links, and other curricular materials for teaching Chinese, English, French, Indonesian, Italian, Spanish, and Thai.

In the past decade, Langer de Ramirez has presented over 50 workshops, staff development trainings, and addresses at local, regional, and national conferences and in schools throughout the United States (Connecticut, Illinois, Iowa, Massachusetts, New Jersey, New Mexico, New York, Pennsylvania, Tennessee, Texas, Virginia, Washington DC) and abroad (Puerto Rico, Thailand, Venezuela).

She is the recipient of the Nelson Brooks Award for Excellence in the Teaching of Culture; several National Endowment for the Humanities grants for study in Mexico, Colombia, and Senegal; and a Fulbright Award to India and Nepal. Her areas of research and curriculum development are multicultural and diversity education, folktales in the language classroom, and technology in language teaching. She holds a master's degree in applied linguistics and a doctorate in curriculum and teaching from Teachers College, Columbia University.

Barbara B. Levin is a professor in the Department of Curriculum and Instruction at the University of North Carolina at Greensboro (UNCG). Her research interests include studying teachers' pedagogical beliefs and the development of teacher thinking across the career span, integrating technology into the K–16 curriculum, and using case-based pedagogies and problem-based learning in teacher education. Levin is an associate editor of *Teacher Education Quarterly* and has authored or coauthored numerous journal articles and three books, including *Who Learns What From Cases and How? The Research Base on Teaching With Cases* (1999), *Energizing Teacher Education and Professional Development With Problem-Based Learning* (2001), and *Case Studies of Teacher Development: An In-Depth Look at How Thinking About Pedagogy Develops Over Time* (2003). Levin completed a PhD in educational psychology at the University of California at Berkeley in 1993. Prior to that, she taught elementary school students and was a computer specialist for 17 years.

Ted McCain is an educator who has taught high school students at Maple Ridge Secondary School for 25 years and has considered it his primary calling to help prepare teenagers for success as they move into adult life. McCain has received the Prime Minister's Award for Teaching Excellence, a prestigious Canadian national award, for his work in developing a real-world technology curriculum for students in Grades 11 and 12 that prepares them for employment in the areas of design and computer networking. McCain was recognized for his work in creating an innovative "4-D" approach to solving problems, the unique use of role playing in the classroom, and the idea of progressive withdrawal as a way to foster independence in his students. McCain has also taught computer networking, graphic design, and desktop publishing for Okanagan College/University. McCain has written or cowritten six books on the future, effective teaching, educational technology, and graphic design. McCain currently works with the Thornburg Center for Professional Development in Chicago as an associate director. In this role, McCain has expanded his work as an educational futurist and focuses on the impact on students and learning from the astounding changes brought about by technological development. He is passionate in his belief that schools must change so they can effectively prepare students for the rest of their lives.

Donna S. McCaw's three decades in public schools include experience in special education services and school counseling as well as positions as school principal and director of curriculum. She currently serves as professor of Educational Leadership at Western Illinois University. In that capacity she teaches at the master's and doctoral levels. Her specialties include issues and challenges surrounding effective 21st century leadership. In addition to a love of teaching, she has a commitment to work with public schools. Consequently, through her school consulting work, she spends much time guiding and directing improvement processes.

Jill Joline Myers has extensive experience dealing with juvenile offenders through the criminal court system. In two decades as a state prosecuting attorney, she dealt with a wide spectrum of inappropriate and illegal behaviors, from school truancy to terrorism. As an associate professor at Western Illinois University teaching criminal justice courses, she is aware of the need for a straightforward, transparent, consistent, and nonbiased sanctioning process. Her research agenda includes civil liability of state agents, violence reduction strategies, and cyber bullying. She regularly instructs state and federal agencies on constitutional issues.

Alan November began his education career as a science and math teacher and a residential dorm counselor on an island reform school in Boston Harbor. November went on as a teacher and administrator in the Boston Public Schools, Lexington and Wellesley (Massachusetts) Public Schools, and the Glenbrook High Schools in Illinois. He has also taught in the graduate schools of education at the University of Massachusetts-Amherst, and Seton Hall in New Jersey. He was the cofounder of the Institute for

Education Leadership and Technology at Stanford University. He has presented in all 50 states, every province of Canada, across Europe, Asia, Central America, and South Africa. He is most proud of being named one of the first Christa McAuliffe Educators in the United States. November is the author of the best-selling book *Empowering Students With Technology*. Each July, November leads the international Building Learning Communities summer conference near Boston.

Jessica K. Parker is currently an assistant professor at Sonoma State University, and she studies how high schools integrate multimedia literacy into academic literacy learning. She has taught middle school, high school and college students for over a decade and has also created and taught professional development courses for teachers. She has published teacher-researcher articles in *English Journal,* and has presented at national conventions such as AERA, National Media Education Conference, NCTE Assembly for Research, and many others. Jessica completed her undergraduate and graduate work at the University of California, Berkeley; she has a BA in Media Studies and a MA and a PhD in Education.

Justin W. Patchin is an assistant professor of criminal justice at the University of Wisconsin-Eau Claire. For the past several years, Patchin and coauthor Sameer Hinduja have been exploring the online behaviors of adolescents, including social networking and cyberbullying. They travel across the United States training teachers, parents, and others about how to keep their kids safe online. They administer a website as an information clearinghouse for those interested in learning more about cyberbullying. Patchin earned his PhD in criminal justice from Michigan State University.

Marc Prensky is an internationally acclaimed speaker, writer, consultant, futurist, visionary, and inventor in the critical areas of education and learning. He is the author of several critically acclaimed books and over 60 articles on education and learning, including multiple articles in *Educational Leadership, Educause, Edutopia,* and *Educational Technology.*

Marc's presentations around the world challenge and inspire audiences by opening up their minds to new ideas and approaches to education. One of his critically important perspectives is to look at education through the eyes of the students—during his talks, he interviews hundreds of students every year.

Marc's professional focus has been on reinventing the learning process, combining the motivation of student passion, technology, games, and other highly engaging activities with the driest content of formal education. He is the founder of two companies: *Games2train,* an e-learning company whose clients include IBM, Bank of America, Microsoft, Pfizer, the U.S. Department of Defense, and Florida's and Los Angeles's Virtual Schools; and Spree Learning, an online educational games company.

Marc is one of the world's leading experts on the connection between games and learning, and was called by *Strategy + Business* magazine "that rare visionary who implements."He has designed and built over 50 software games in his career, including worldwide, multiuser games and simulations that run on all platforms, from the Internet to cell phones. *MoneyU* (www.moneyu.com), his latest project, is an innovative, engaging, and effective game for teaching financial literacy to high school and college students. Marc is also the creator of www.spreelearninggames.com and www.socialimpactgames.com.His products and ideas are innovative, provocative, and challenging, and they clearly show the way of the future.

The New York Times, The Wall Street Journal, Newsweek, TIME, Fortune, and the *Economist* have all recognized Marc's work. He has appeared on FOX News, MSNBC, CNBC, PBS's Computer Currents, the Canadian and Australian Broadcasting Corporations, and the BBC. Marc also writes a column for *Educational Technology.* He was named as one of training's top "New Breed of Visionaries" by Training magazine and was cited as a "guiding star of the new parenting movement" by *Parental Intelligence Newsletter.*

Marc's background includes master's degrees from Yale, Middlebury, and Harvard Business School (with distinction). He has taught at all levels, from elementary to college. He is a concert musician and has acted on Broadway. He spent six years as a corporate strategist and product development director with the Boston Consulting Group and worked in human resources and technology on Wall Street.

Part I

Our 21st-Century Schools

1

Partnering

A Pedagogy for the New Educational Landscape

Marc Prensky

Guiding Questions

1. What works in the classroom today? What needs changing?
2. Can we see students differently? Can we achieve mutual respect?
3. What is partnering? What are the teachers' and the students' roles?

Consciously or not, all of today's teachers are preparing their students not only for the world they will face the day they leave school (a world we know), but also for a future in which, within the students' working lifetimes, technology will become over one trillion times more powerful (a world we can hardly imagine). Every year of these students' lives, the world's information will explode anew: Tools will get smaller, faster, better, and cheaper; people will have access to more of these tools (and will change their behavior because of them); and schools and teachers will no doubt struggle to keep up. Given all these changes, and the new realities of students' out-of-school environment, how can teachers best prepare students for their long-term future—as well as for tomorrow—while at the same time preserving the important legacy of the past? This is not an easy question.

But the consensus among experts is clear.[1] The way for us to succeed under such conditions is not to focus only on the changing technology, but rather to conceptualize learning in a new way, with adults and young people each taking on new and different roles from the past.

Young people (students) need to focus on using new tools, finding information, making meaning, and creating. Adults (teachers) must focus on questioning, coaching and guiding, providing context, ensuring rigor and meaning, and ensuring quality results.

This 21st century way of working together to produce and ensure student learning is what I call *partnering*. Learning to do it is the subject of this book.

MOVING AHEAD

Today's overwhelming (and, to various extents, outmoded) educational division of labor is for teachers to lecture, talk, and explain, and for students to listen, take notes, read the text, and memorize. This is often known as *direct instruction*. Unfortunately, direct instruction is becoming increasingly ineffective; that too many of their teachers just talk and talk and talk is today's students' number-one complaint. And unfortunately, the students' response is almost always to tune out.

So the era in which this type of teaching—lecturing, presenting, explaining to all, or telling—worked has pretty much come to an end. To the extent that teachers are a tool for learning, those who teach mainly by telling are becoming a less effective tool in the 21st century.

Yet most teachers were trained to tell. Most of them learned (and learned well) by being lectured to. Many teachers like explaining and think they are good at it. And they may, in fact, be good at it. But this method is no longer relevant, because students are no longer listening. I often liken this to Federal Express: you can have the best delivery system in the world, but if no one is home to receive the package, it doesn't much matter. Too often, today's students are not there to receive what their teachers are delivering. They are off somewhere else, often in the electronic world of 21st century music, socializing, or exploring. The goal of this book is to help teachers bring them back.

What Is Working

Most students recognize and applaud their creative, energetic teachers—especially the ones who respect them and care about their opinions. But when I ask students "What in your entire school experience has engaged you the most?" the most frequent answer I get is "School trips." While trips have always been popular, I think this answer reflects the urgency that today's students feel to connect to the real world. Why? Because another frequent answer is "Connecting with other kids our age in other places electronically" (e.g., through a secure e-mail service such as ePals).

Inside their classrooms, what students say they find most engaging is group work (except when slackers are allowed to get away with not contributing), discussions, sharing their own ideas, and hearing the ideas of their classmates (and of the teacher when expressed as the ideas of an equal).

While they typically say they enjoy using technology, the single thing most valued by students is being respected by their teachers as individuals and not treated as kids who don't know much and thus have to learn. "We're not stupid" is a universal lament.

Seeing Students Differently

Some teachers bemoan current students' capabilities, compared to students of the past. But there is another way to see students, a better, more positive way for the 21st century. We too often treat kids as if they were still (using a 19th century metaphor) trains on a track when actually today's kids are a lot more like rockets (a much more up-to-date metaphor).

Which, by the way, makes educators (again metaphorically) rocket scientists! (Who knew?)

Why should we think of today's kids as rockets? At first blush, it's their speed; they operate faster than any generation that has come before. Although little may have changed in the rate kids grow up emotionally, there has been enormous change in what today's kids learn and know at early ages, and therefore, many think, in the rate they grow up intellectually.[2] Many kids are on the Internet by the age of two or three. I recently found that a NASA moon simulation I used in graduate school works just as well with fourth graders. Although today's parents and educators struggle with getting kids to learn in the old sense, the fuel they offer kids (i.e., the curriculum and materials) is often way behind what today's kids need. "Age appropriate" has totally outrun us. Even students of Piaget suggest it is time for a new look.[3] While some want kids to slow down and "just be kids," like before, speed is clearly a reality for young people in the 21st century.

But Wait . . . There's More

What makes today's kids rockets is not just this increased speed. They are headed to faraway destinations, places that those who launch them often can't even see. They have been designed by their 21st century upbringing—especially by the Internet and the complex games many play—to explore and find out for themselves what works. Like rockets, they often cannot be controlled at every moment, but are initially aimed, as far as possible, in the right direction, with mid-course corrections to be made as necessary. And because both kids and rockets are difficult to repair in flight, they must be made as self-sufficient as possible.

As with all rockets, kids' fuel mix is volatile. Some go faster and farther than others. Some lose their guidance or their ability to follow direction. Some go off course or stop functioning unexpectedly. Some even blow up. But as we get better at making them, many more hit their mark, and it is our job as rocket scientists to help them do so.

Huge Potential

Perhaps most important, today's rockets—and kids—can potentially go much farther and do things far beyond what any such voyager could do in the past. With the arrival of widely distributed and easy-to-use digital tools, kids already, on a daily basis, accomplish things that still seem like far-off science fiction to many of us adults. They communicate instantaneously with, play complex games with, and learn from peers around the globe; ePals, a secure electronic interchange site for kids, reaches every country and territory. Kids regularly make videos and post them for the world to see and comment on. They organize themselves socially and politically across the planet.

Educators as Rocket Scientists

So what does this metaphor imply for those whose job is to educate today's young people? It tells us that we must conceive of what educators do in a new way—not just as teachers, but as rocket designers, building and sending off the best rockets we possibly can. This includes not filling students with the educational fuel of the past, because that fuel just doesn't make today's kids go. We need new fuel, new designs, new boosters, and new payloads. Rocket scientists understand that their rockets will likely encounter many unforeseen events and trials, so they work hard to build into the rockets enough intelligence to get the job done with minimum outside help. They build into the rockets the ability to self-monitor, self-assess, and self-correct as much as possible. They create the ability for their rockets to use whatever devices and instrumentation are available to regularly gather data and then analyze it, even as they are speeding along. They perform rigid quality control, not of what the rockets' brains know— that's updatable on the fly—but of what they can do with the information they encounter. And while they may preprogram a target, they know that the target will likely change midcourse and that there are likely to be other changes during the course of the rocket's life.

A Useful Perspective

Seeing our students and ourselves in this new way encourages educators to set the bar for student achievement extremely high, far higher than we typically do currently. I have often heard educators say they are "blown away" by what their students have accomplished. We should not be blown away by our students; we should be expecting even more from them.

Of course, rockets are high maintenance and often require more of designers' effort and skills to build and keep up. They are also useless on the ground, so that is not where we should be preparing them to stay (many of the "ground skills" have been taken over by machines and are no longer needed).

Exploration or Destruction?

Depending on the payload installed at the beginning of the journey, students (like real rockets) can be powerful forces for exploration and change or potential weapons of destruction. Educators, along with parents and peers, install the payload. Then we send them off to fly into the future, hoping we have prepared them well for what they will meet. To make the payload positive, installing ethical behavior—the ability to figure out the right thing to do and how to get it done—ought to be our number-one concern. We need to best configure students' brains so they can constantly learn, create, program, adopt, adapt, and relate positively to whatever and whomever they meet, and in whatever way they meet them, which increasingly means through technology.

Conceptual, Not Technical Changes

It is with this positive view of 21st century students in mind that we turn to partnering. We want young people, like rockets, to "boldly go where no one has gone before,"[4] and partnering offers the best prospects for getting them there. Surprisingly, perhaps, the most important changes required of educators are not technological, but rather conceptual—thinking of themselves less as guardians of the past and more as partners, guiding their living, breathing rockets toward the future. No one advocates throwing away the past completely. But unless we start preparing our students to fly much further than before and land safely, we won't be doing them much good. If we don't soon start putting some new and different fuel and payload into the rockets that are in our charge, then they will never get off the ground.

HOW PARTNERING WORKS

The term *partnering* can mean different things to different people. After all, a teacher's talking while the students take notes is a kind of partnership. But that's not at all the type of partnership I am talking about here. Let me specify precisely what partnering means in this book's context: letting students focus on the part of the learning process that they can do best, and letting teachers focus on the part of the learning process that they can do best.

Letting the students do what they can do best means giving students primary responsibility for the following:

- Finding and following their passion
- Using whatever technology is available
- Researching and finding information
- Answering questions and sharing their thoughts and opinions
- Practicing, when properly motivated (e.g., through games)
- Creating presentations in text and multimedia

Letting teachers do what they can do best means giving teachers primary responsibility for the following:

- Creating and asking the right questions
- Giving students guidance
- Putting material in context
- Explaining one-on-one
- Creating rigor
- Ensuring quality

Partnering is the very opposite of teaching by telling. In fact, in the partnering pedagogy, the teacher's goal is to do no telling at all (at least to the whole class). Rather than lecture, or even explain, the teacher needs only give students, in a variety of interesting ways, questions to be answered and, in certain cases, suggestions of possible tools and places to start and proceed. In partnering the onus is then completely on the students (alone or in groups) to search, make hypotheses, find answers, and create presentations, which are then reviewed by the teacher and the class and vetted for their correctness, context, rigor, and quality. The required curriculum gets covered because the questions the students answer are the ones they need to know. And as we will see, there exist levels of partnering to fit different types of students, different situations, and different backgrounds.

PARTNERING TIP

How you can eliminate telling, or direct instruction (and what to replace it with), is a great topic for you to discuss with your class, in a specific time that you set aside. Ask your class if they think you talk too much, or more than you need to. Then ask them for suggestions on how you could reduce the amount of time you tell. You will likely be surprised by their answers.

Such a major shift in pedagogy—from telling to partnering—is clearly not a change that either teachers or students will make overnight. It is, in reality, a gradual shift that can take years to perfect. But as thousands of teachers will attest, it can happen. And it must happen for 21st century students to get the education they need and deserve. The good news is that there are now a great many teachers—in every subject and at every level—happily and effectively partnering with their students every day, and you can use them as models.

Partnering Basics: A Simple Example

The best example of partnering that I have ever heard came from a teacher during one of my student panels. The teacher asked the students on the panel this question: "Suppose there are three causes of something that you, the students, have to learn about. Which of the following would you prefer: that I say, "There were three causes of [whatever]. I will now lecture and tell you what they were—please take notes," or that I say, "There were three main causes of [whatever]. You all have 15 minutes to find out what they were, and then we'll discuss what you've found."

To nobody's great surprise, whenever students are asked this question they almost universally prefer the second alternative. Most of today's students, no matter what their age or grade level, prefer to take an active role and find things out for themselves, rather than be told them by the teacher.

Do Some Things Require Lectures?

Yet whenever I say, "No lectures," I get people who push back with "Some things require lectures." So please take a minute right now to reflect on what, in your subject area, you think might not be possible to teach without lecturing, telling, or explaining in front of the class. Now ask yourself this question: "Could I reframe this topic or information instead as answers to a series of questions, questions that I might ask, say, on a test to see if the students understood the topic or material?"

At its simplest, partnering is just giving the students those questions to research, explore, and find answers to, and then for the class to discuss and review. I believe partnering can be done in any subject with any material. But it does require a new perspective.

Is Partnering New?

At this point you may be saying to yourself, "Partnering is nothing new. It's just what used to be called [put your answer here]." If so, you are absolutely right. To a great extent, partnering falls into the great pedagogical tradition known, variously, as

- student-centered learning,
- problem-based learning,
- project-based learning,
- case-based learning,
- inquiry-based learning,
- active learning,
- constructivism, or co-constructing
- learning by doing.

John Dewey famously espoused this form of pedagogy in the early 20th century,[5] and it has probably been used, in one form or another, since Socrates. (One early reader of this book pointed out nicely the lineage from Pestalozzi to Frances Parker to Dewey to Bruner.) Other names for this pedagogy exist as well. The Massachusetts Institute of Technology calls its version technology-enhanced active learning (TEAL). A teacher recently wrote me about process-oriented guided inquiry learning (POGIL). Challenge-based learning is another variation from Apple that was recently described in a report from the New Media Consortium.[6] Quest-based learning is being tried in a New York City experimental school. All of these are continually being revised and updated.[7]

But while each of these pedagogies has its own proponents, principles, and peculiarities, they are all, at their core, very similar. In a sense, they are merely brands, if you will, of the same general type of learning. The common thread is that students learn on their own, alone or in groups, by answering questions and solving problems with their teacher's help, coaching, and guidance.

I prefer the term *partnering* to any of the others because it emphasizes that the roles of each group, teachers and students, are different, but equal. Partnering underscores that each party must draw on its own particular strengths to improve the learning process as a whole. I also like what partnering has to say about the role of technology: that it is the job of the students, and not the teacher, to use it, and the job of the teacher to assess the quality of that use. But this last term may only reflect that digital technology didn't exist when some of these other brands were established—I think it really applies to all.

Again, what matters is not the name or brand of partnering you choose—that will depend on you, your students, and your context, such as the school, or state, you teach in. What does matter is that you move in the partnering direction. Figure 1.1 points out some of the different ways that work in the partnering pedagogy is split between the students and the teacher.

Partnering and the Curriculum

One concern frequently raised by teachers is that they are constrained by a mandated curriculum, which somehow conflicts with partnering. Certainly, at least in public schools, there is for every subject and level a required set of (increasingly skills-based) standards to be taught. But remember that those standards specify only *what* to teach, not how to do it.

Partnering can, and does, work with today's required curricula. But it demands a rethinking of those curricula on the part of teachers from the "this is the material to be learned" approach of textbooks to an approach of "guiding questions to which students need to find answers." Interestingly, textbooks—most of which reflect the old, telling pedagogy—have gotten things completely backward from the point of view of partnering (and, generally, student interest). Textbooks put the answers (i.e., the content) up front and the questions in the back. Partnering reverses this, putting the questions first, which, as it turns out, is far more motivating to students. Asking "Why?" upfront (Why do we have seasons? Why do opposites attract? Why does English have so many nonstandard past tenses? Why do we forget, or make bad decisions? Why did people from Europe come to America?) is far more likely to make kids think than are lectures on seasonality, polarity, irregular verbs, psychology, or discovery and immigration.

But what students have to know (and what they will, of course, be tested on in the standardized tests), remains the same regardless of the pedagogy. Partnering teachers find that the process of students actively answering the questions leads almost universally to higher engagement (I've never heard a partnering teacher say that his or her students were *less* engaged.) The increased engagement, in turn, typically produces better retention of material and higher test scores, as in the case of the primary school teacher who saw his students' descriptive writing scores go up an entire testing level.[8] Many teachers describe similar phenomena.

Figure 1.1   How Partnering Work Is Shared

Teacher	Student
Doesn't tell, *asks*!	Doesn't take notes, *finds out*!
Suggests topics and tools	Researches and creates output
Learns about technology from students	Learns about quality and rigor from teacher
Evaluates students' output for rigor and quality; supplies context	Refines and improves output, adding rigor, context, and quality

Technology in Partnering: The Enabler and Personalizer

And what, in the partnering pedagogy, is the role of technology? Technology's role is to support the partnering pedagogy and to enable each student to personalize his or her learning process. All students and teachers know that students get the greatest reward for their efforts when things are individualized and customized for each student. What's always been needed in our classrooms is a way to deal with each student individually or, at the most, in extremely small groups in a way that is truly implementable and effective. Up until now, though, the combination of large class sizes and few resources outside of textbooks, outdated reference books, and limited library and teacher time have made total individualization and differentiation difficult, if not impossible, for most teachers to pull off.

The greatest single boon of the arrival—albeit slowly and unevenly—of digital technology in our schools is that it will, in the long run, enable teachers and students to partner in this much more personal and individual way, that is, for each student to learn on his or her own, with the teachers' coaching and guidance. It will permit students not just to "learn at their own pace," as is often heard, but to learn more or less in whatever ways they prefer, as long as they are in pursuit of the necessary and required goals.

Just adding technology, however, will not make this happen. In fact, in some cases, laptops have already been added *and* removed for having "failed."[9] But the failure in those cases was neither of the students nor of the technology, but rather of the pedagogy. In order for technology to be used successfully in classrooms, it *must* be combined with a new type of pedagogy—partnering. Partnering works with technology because it allows technology to be used, especially by students, to its fullest extent.

Rather than teachers interrupting their lecture for a technology "exercise," partnering enables students to be engaged, from the start of every class, in discovering on their own (and sharing with each other) what the material is and how it works, in finding examples in multiple media, in creating and sharing their own examples, and in communicating with peers and writers around the globe.

ESTABLISHING ROLES AND MUTUAL RESPECT

For any type of partnering to succeed, however, it is key that mutual respect between students and teachers be established. To some readers this may sound obvious, or like something that is already there, but that is not always the case. My discussions with both students and teachers have taught me that there is not nearly enough respect in our schools and in teaching. And it goes both ways—students' respect for teachers and vice versa. Respect is, of course, a key element of any teaching and learning, but it is especially important for teaching and learning via partnering.

The key requirement for respect in a partnering context is that it be mutual; each partner must truly respect the other. I'm quite sure that all teachers want and expect their students to respect them, and all teachers would say, if asked, that they respect their students. But that is often not what happens in reality. Frustrated teachers say (or think) things like "My students can't concentrate" or "My kids have the attention span of a gnat"—things that are just not true overall. (Although these things may be true in the context of school, most students concentrate just fine on topics and activities that interest them.)

I've heard many teachers comment (mostly when students are not around) about their students' lack of caring, interest, motivation, even ability. When students overhear teachers saying these things (and other things that, outside of the school context, are similarly untrue), they feel disrespected—and rightfully so. And in reaction they often turn around and disrespect their teachers right back, frequently by pointing out the teachers' technological illiteracy.

Such mutual *dis*respect almost entirely prevents effective learning and partnering. For learning to take place, disrespect must be rooted out wherever it exists, on both sides of the teacher's desk. For successful partnering, teachers and students alike must realize and accept that we have entered an era in which both students and teachers have something of equal importance to contribute to the learning process. Each side must respect and learn from what the other has to offer.

Some teachers have used the strategy of putting up a large sign in the classroom that says, "We are all learners, we are all teachers," and some schools have even gone so far as to adopt this as their official motto. These words can be reinforced and internalized by giving students the chance, whenever appropriate, to teach the teacher (for example, about technology) and by the teacher being a willing and eager learner.

Student Roles in Partnering

The metaphor I introduced earlier of students as rockets, needing to be properly fueled by teachers, programmed with self-directing capabilities, and sent to new and distant places is far more respectful of students than the old pedagogy's view of students as empty vessels to be filled with knowledge (or blank slates to be written upon). Making students more active and equal participants in the learning process is a sign of respect—respect that students everywhere are looking for. But what, specifically, are the students' roles in partnering?

Student as Researcher

One important role is that of researcher. When we adopt the partnering pedagogy of no longer telling students what they need to know, but instead requiring them to find it out for themselves (and then to share it with their peers and with the teacher for evaluation), that immediately puts students in this new and very different role. One bonus of doing this is that the role of researcher, being a professional one, carries with it a level of respect not always accorded to mere "students." For this reason, some schools have actually chosen to officially rename their students as "researchers." Consider the case of a student in Texas, a former dropout, who commented, "That is almost all I do—look things up on the computer." She was quite happy to spend most of her school day in this way.

Take a minute to picture yourself working in such a school. It might be more akin to working at a magazine or a library, where you expect a very professional job from all your partners or colleagues. Obviously, if you get less than you expect from someone, you would give that person feedback, but preferably in a way that would help him improve next time. The atmosphere would be much more equal and collegial, which is exactly the goal in the partnering pedagogy.

Student as Technology User and Expert

A second key role for students in the partnering pedagogy is that of the technology user and expert. Students typically love this role and use as many technologies as they are given access to. I have watched different groups of students in a class simultaneously using video, audio podcasts, games, blogs, and other social networking tools to answer the same guiding question posed by the teacher. Such guiding questions (which I discuss much more in Chapter 5) could range from "How would you like your teachers to use technology in class?" to "How do people persuade each other?" to "What is the evidence for evolution?"

Obviously, no student knows everything there is to know about technology. Some know a lot, and some know surprisingly little. (That doesn't, by the way, make them any less digital natives, a distinction which is more about attitude than knowledge.) Many teachers, of course, are extremely technology savvy. But whether students or teachers know a lot or a little, in partnering it is key for teachers to reserve the role of using the technology for students. Even when some (or even most) students in a class do not know about the technology, teachers should never use technology *for* them. Rather, teachers should only suggest what students might use (and solicit students' suggestions) and then get them to use it for themselves and teach each other (possibly modeling some examples of effective use up front). This is true whether we are talking about interactive white boards, computers, podcasts, blogs, or any other technology.

In the partnering view, even when teachers know a lot about technology and like it, they should not make things for students; they should rather help and supervise students in using technology to make things for themselves (and, in some cases, for the teachers to use). In fact, many partnering teachers have designated the most tech-savvy students in their classes as technology assistants to create things that are needed and to deal immediately with any problems with equipment or with lack of knowledge on the part of the teacher or other students.

Student as Thinker and Sense Maker

Another key role for students in the partnering pedagogy is thinker and sense maker. Most teachers would probably say students are supposed to have that role today, but it's often not clear to the students that they do, or what this entails. When partnering, the role of thinker and sense maker needs to be made much more explicit.

Our students do think, of course. To say they don't (or can't) is to disrespect them. But the way they think, and what they think about, is often not what teachers would prefer. It is important in all teaching, and especially in partnering, to let students know frequently that thinking more logically and more critically is one of their primary roles. That is one reason that peer-to-peer communication, both orally and in writing, is so important to the partnering pedagogy; it lets students see and evaluate just how logically and critically they and their peers think. Teachers with students writing for publicly available blogs have reported an immediate improvement in both writing and thinking quality on the part of students once they know their work will be seen by others.[10] To emphasize this thinking role, Ted Nellen, a New York City Teacher of the Year, calls all of his students "scholars."

Student as World Changer

The fourth student role relates to learning being *real*, and not just relevant. Real learning (as I discussed in the Introduction and will do in more detail in Chapter 4) involves students immediately using what they learn to do something and/or change something in the world. It is crucial that students be made aware that using what they learn to effect positive change in the world, large or small, is one of their important roles in school. For example, some middle school students outside Atlanta, Georgia, made a video on genetically modified food that changed their parents' shopping habits. Another group in the same school used what they learned to raise money to help cure malaria in Africa.[11] Many schools also use what students learn to help their local communities.

Student as Self-Teacher

The fifth role of the student (and the role that is perhaps most different in the partnering pedagogy) is that of self-teacher. That students can teach themselves might sound strange at first. But consider how you would learn about something new—say, a disease that someone in your family had suddenly contracted. While you could opt to go to a class and have someone tell you, most likely you would choose to learn on our own. You would do research in books or on the Internet, ask friends and colleagues for information and guidance, and consult experts when possible. It is really important that students learn these same skills and become self-reliant when it comes to learning, rather than depending on a teacher or anyone else. The best way for them to do so is to be expected to do it repeatedly, with feedback, until they get really good at it. For this reason, the role of self-teacher might be the most important student role of all. One student who learned that his grandmother had cancer was able to find online, by himself, using skills he had learned, not only the best hospital for her to go to, but the name of the doctor with the best success rate in dealing with the particular cancer she had.

It is extremely important to understand, however, that students learning to teach themselves doesn't mean that the teacher's role goes away, or even that it gets diminished. On the contrary. In the partnering pedagogy, the teacher's job retains its importance, but its roles change dramatically. We will look at the teacher's many roles in the partnering pedagogy in the next section. Perhaps unexpectedly, it turns out that these new roles for the teacher are far more important and useful to students than the old role of teller.

Other Student Roles

Some additional roles for students in partnering include, from time to time, journalist, writer, scientist, engineer, and politician. They also include being the "doer" of the many verbs I will discuss later. I will have more practical things to say about all of these roles in Chapter 3.

Teacher Roles in Partnering

Some of the many roles a teacher plays in partnering will be comfortable and familiar to almost any teacher. Others, though, may be new and will require some learning and practice.

Teacher as Coach and Guide

In the roles of coach and guide, the partnering teacher sets daily and longer-term goals for the class as a whole and then sets each student free (within appropriate limits) to reach those goals in his or her own way, providing assistance when requested or clearly needed. The role of guide implies taking students on a journey; the role of coach implies each student having an individual helper. Neither coach nor guide is a new role for teachers, but each is one that, in the partnering pedagogy, they can spend much more time on. And these roles allow teachers to provide a much more personalized, or differentiated, education for their students.

In general, today's students much prefer getting there on their own to being micromanaged. But not all students can find their way with equal ease. Some find it more difficult than others to work by themselves. This is especially true when confronting partnering for the first time: it is new for students as well as teachers. Part of the coach's role is to monitor each student's work and progress, and to give assistance where it is needed—not by reverting to telling in the old style, but by gently nudging students back on track with useful questions and suggestions for how to proceed (and never doing it for them). For example, a coach might refer a student having trouble to a website, a YouTube video, an online animation, or even a game, if available.

Some educators, particularly those working in difficult inner-city schools, say, "I'm sure this would work in the suburbs, but our kids need much more structure." No doubt they do. And teachers do need to be able to scaffold the new way of learning for all kids. But as many teachers have demonstrated (mostly in charter schools), *all* kids can learn to partner and take on the responsibilities involved in their part of the learning process. Depending on where students start, guiding some of them into partnering can be a long and complex process. But as with everything in partnering, it is done student by student, rather than with classes as a whole.

Teacher as Goal Setter and Questioner

In the partnering pedagogy, freed from telling and preparing and giving lectures, the teacher has a number of other important roles to play. One is setting goals for students' learning. These goals are almost always best expressed as guiding questions for students to answer, which are typically open-ended and include both overarching questions and more detailed ones. The larger questions are followed more specifically by the kinds of questions that students would or might be asked on a test. Many teachers now hand out or post their guiding questions as they start a term or unit. The premise is that if the students can answer all those questions, they ought to do pretty well on any exam.

Questioner is a truly important role for the teacher in the partnering pedagogy. Despite teacher training and the professionally developed questions created for standardized tests by Educational Testing Service and other organizations, the art of good questioning has to a large extent fallen into disuse in schools. An important lesson for partnering students is that four-answer multiple-choice questions do not reflect the real questions in the world. The art of Socratic questioning (i.e., asking challenging questions designed to get people to reflect and reconsider their point of view) is an important skill for partnering teachers to relearn and practice.

Much of the work in the problem-based learning variation of partnering has been to develop rich questions that can serve as the basis for extended projects. Some districts and states (such as West Virginia) have been leaders in collecting these questions and connecting them to standards. But although many predesigned questions are now available online and in books, turning any content into good guiding questions is a skill that each partnering teacher needs to perfect over time. I consider this skill in more detail in Chapter 5.

Teacher as Learning Designer

Another important role for the teacher in the partnering pedagogy is as designer of original learning-creating experiences. No one wants class days that are repetitive; teachers as well as students are hungry for variety and frequent, positive change. In the role of designer, starting from where he or she wants students to wind up in their understanding, the partnering teacher crafts the questions, problems, and suggested activities that will lead students to understanding.

Designing is a role that should not be unfamiliar to most teachers, as it is somewhat akin to lesson planning. But in the partnering pedagogy designing takes on very different forms. For example, there are no presentations or worksheets to design. Rather than all students following the teacher on the same designed path, partnering students need to be coached and guided toward the goal along a variety of individual paths. This makes the learning designer role of the partnering teacher one of increased complexity and importance. When planning, a teacher needs to reflect on and prepare for various ways in which students might come to an understanding of what is being taught, particularly in view of students' individual passions. So a teacher focusing on the Gettysburg Address, for example, might think up ways to approach it from many student perspectives such as conciseness (comparison to Twitter), politics (comparison to recent speeches), arts (comparison to Oscar acceptance speeches), music (comparison to memorable lyrics), visual images (what pictures does it evoke?), oral interpretations and readings, and so on. There is even a website that illustrates what the address might have looked like as a PowerPoint (http://norvig.com/Gettysburg/).

Abandoning Total Control for Controlled Activity

An important thing for teachers to know and understand about partnering is that it generally involves activity and movement on the part of students. To a casual observer, a partnering class may not seem controlled or disciplined in the traditional sense. A partnering class looks and feels different from a traditional class. For example, one typically does not see students sitting in rows listening to a lecture or filling in worksheets. Rather, one is likely to see desks and chairs arranged in a variety of configurations, students working in groups of different sizes, and groups and individuals using all the technology that is available.

Given the increased level of student movement and conversation in a partnering classroom, it is important to underscore that partnering does not mean chaos in the classroom—that is never acceptable—but rather controlled activity, where each student's movement around the room has a learning purpose. In a partnering class students might be all over the place, some working at their desks or computers, some working or discussing in groups, some at the library or shooting a video. (For this to be allowed, administrators, too, must become comfortable with partnering, and more and more of them are. I have heard principals welcome the idea of having students in the halls, or even outside, shooting videos—just as long as their activity has a clear connection to their learning.)

> **Check It Out!**
>
> For an example of a useful (and fun) student project done in the halls, see the student-made video about not videoing other students and posting it on YouTube, found at www.youtube.com/watch?v=kJEnVzMXK1E.

For teachers new to partnering, who have been taught that control is crucial and lack of order is a sign of students not learning, a higher level of classroom activity may take some getting used to. But when done right, this increased activity is good because it directs students' often high energies in a positive learning direction. While at first it might be hard for a teacher (or administrator) to learn to tolerate this, I recommend having faith and patience, because the end result is worth it.

One high school teacher told me an illustrative story of how she let her class of girls use her room in an "off" period to design their senior class project while the teacher worked at her desk.

> The girls were off the walls, yelling, talking, running in and out of the room. But by the end of the hour, they had designed a fantastic senior project. Still, when I thought about it, I realized that if that had been my class I couldn't have tolerated that level of chaos in the classroom, even if I were sure that the end result would be great.

This insight led the teacher to begin to change the level of what she could tolerate in class.

At every level, kids today do not want to—and in many cases cannot—sit quietly in neat little rows. They need to be much freer, and they often do their best work when free to relate in ways that are much "wilder" than in the past. More and more teachers and parents are realizing that they benefit from tolerating more of this. Teachers often get better results by taking a much more flexible view of control (while still being sure that students are always learning and on track and that a class does not devolve into actual chaos).

What most allows this increased classroom flexibility to happen, and to happen without chaos, is mutual respect, with teachers respecting students' need for freedom in how they work and students respecting their teachers' need for real learning to take place. Achieving this ideal state and balance for each partnering classroom is not something that happens automatically; it is a teaching skill that must be learned and practiced. Remember, though, that it is possible to have an animated, even noisy, classroom and still be in control.

PARTNERING TIP

If the concept of a less tightly controlled class is a tough one for you, you might try it first with a single partnering project, first talking with your students to mutually set rules and parameters, and afterward assessing the results. You can then expand from there as you and the students become more comfortable with the process. As a group, you might decide, for example, that no permission from you is needed for students to use technology in the classroom or talk to each other when working in groups, but that non-work-related comments or disturbing the work of others is inappropriate and will cause a student to lose group or technology privileges.

Teacher as Context Provider

Yet another important role of the partnering teacher is context provider. While students in their role as researchers are often good at finding content, they are often less capable of putting that content in the proper context. My favorite example of the importance of context is the following test answer by a student:

While most of us laugh at this response, it is important to realize that, in a searching context, it would be perfectly correct. It is wrong (and funny) because we know it is in a math context. Every subject has a context from which individual facts and ideas derive their true meaning. Whether helping students understand the role of Wikipedia in a research context or the existence of hate mongering in a free speech context, providing context is a

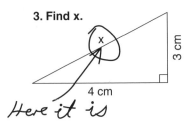

key role of the partnering teacher. As with most things in partnering, this role is best accomplished through asking (e.g., through Socratic questioning) rather than through explaining or telling. Students can be asked what things are right or acceptable in some contexts but not in others. This would be a great lead-in, for example, to an English class discussion of types of writing and speech, and their contextual appropriateness.

Teacher as Rigor Provider and Quality Assurer

The last two major roles of the teacher in the partnering pedagogy are rigor provider and quality assurer, which are closely related although not precisely the same. What they have in common is setting the bar really high for student accomplishment. I strongly believe that, in general, we set the bar far too low for students and that they are capable of (and want to do) much, much more than we generally ask or require of them.

The place where I first truly learned the meaning of rigor was in my freshman literature class in college. I had not done much writing of literature papers in my public high school career, so I was very much at sea in writing my first required paper. I ended up handing in only a single, difficultly produced page. When the instructor handed back the papers the following week, I kept my eyes lowered, fully expecting an F. The instructor stopped at my desk. "Prensky," I still remember him saying to me, "I'm not even going to grade this. You go out and learn how to write a literature paper and then turn it in, and then I'll grade it." Somehow I did, and I learned that there is a minimum floor that work must rise above in order to be considered acceptable.

Rigor is that floor. In partnering, when you give students a task to do, you don't give those who are below the level of acceptability an F—you just don't accept anything less than that floor.

Quality, on the other hand, is something else. Quality is what separates a merely acceptable effort from a really good one. Of course, we have a system of As, Bs, Cs, and Ds (or 0–100) for administrative purposes, but for partnering students those grades alone are not good enough. Letter or number grades exist only in school, not in life. A boss or supervisor will rarely if ever give you a letter or number grade, but will certainly have a minimum standard and will almost always reward you for high-quality work. So students need to have a good understanding of what high-quality work is. Therefore, for partnering teachers, assessing quality—not just by assigning letter grades but by explaining to students why something they do is or isn't high quality and helping (and requiring) them to iterate until it is—is perhaps the most important part of the job.

Of course, doing that—and not just giving a letter grade—is a very time-consuming and intensive task, especially with large class sizes. That is why a successful implementation of partnering pedagogy needs to include a large amount of peer-to-peer teaching, learning, and evaluation, as we shall see in the next section.

An important issue arises when assessing quality in student projects done in media that are unfamiliar to a teacher. How do you judge what is a high-quality machinima, game, or mashup? I have occasionally had teachers show me, with great pride, student work that most kids would totally dismiss as unworthy of even a D. In such cases you will need to rely on your student partners to teach and guide you. Between their knowledge of the media and your own experience, you should be able to arrive at fair quality assessments no matter what the medium.

Peer Roles in Partnering

Many of today's students, given a choice, would prefer to learn not from their teachers but from their peers. I have been told this by hundreds of kids. Some people might find it upsetting that today's kids often trust their peers' opinions (and even abilities) more than those of their teachers. But this is not necessarily a bad thing, particularly if monitored by the teacher. Although a teacher's contextual framework is likely to be much deeper than a friend's, one's friends share the same references, the same generation of TV, movies, songs, and so on. In students' terms, they all speak the same language.

If it is used to the teachers' (and students') advantage and if monitored well, peer-to-peer teaching and learning can be a great ally to partnering teachers. It is a tool that teachers could benefit from much more than they currently do. Not only do students enjoy learning from their peers, but a great many students really like it when teachers give them the opportunity to teach other students. One strategy that has worked well for some partnering teachers is to directly teach only a few kids in a class and make those kids responsible for teaching the rest, in whatever ways they all want. Giving students this opportunity is yet another way of showing respect. For these reasons, peer-to-peer learning is an important part of the partnering pedagogy.

A striking example of the power of peer-to-peer learning in action is the phenomenal music teaching program from Venezuela known as *El Systema*. In this program, poor kids from all over Venezuela—often street kids—are trained to be truly fine classical musicians in local, regional, and national orchestras, mostly through peer-to-peer teaching and learning.

Check It Out!

You can learn more about El Systema and see it in action—along with its amazing results—by watching the videos on the program at www.ted.com.

One of El Systema's major principles is that as soon as kids learn something, they have to teach it to someone else. This is not all that different from the surgeon's model of "watch one, do one, teach one."

There are many ways of using the power of peer-to-peer learning in partnering, and partnering teachers are constantly figuring out new ones. For example, peer-to-peer is an excellent (and possibly the best) way to spread the knowledge and use of technology among students and bridge any digital divide that may exist in your classroom. Also, because of the power of peer-to-peer learning, for some partnering tasks, such as understanding or evaluating a particular text or finding a solution to a problem, putting two or three students in front of a single computer may be as good as, or even better than, having each student work individually.

The School Principal as Leader, Facilitator, and Partner

The participation of the school principal (and the school administration) in the partnering pedagogy is crucial, in the multiple roles of leader, facilitator, and yet another partner. Although it is not impossible for partnering to survive and flourish without strong administrative support, it is difficult.

Many teachers have told me that they have wanted to try, or even did try, to use some or all of the partnering pedagogy described in this book, but were frustrated by the lack of support from the administration in their school. Yet I hear just as often from principals who are frustrated and often have trouble when attempting to get their teachers to try these new methods.

Clearly, to be most successful, teachers and administrators must work in partnership. In the long run, teachers must be supported by their administration in order to succeed in partnering with their students. An administrator who formally observes or just walks into a class where the teacher is coaching and not telling, where students are teaching themselves and each other with various amounts of controlled activity going on, and where students are presenting and critiquing in a truly vigorous give-and-take manner needs to understand that all of this is producing learning that is as good as or better than that which results from traditional direct instruction.

Things will go much more smoothly if principals and other administrators do understand and accept this new approach and are willing to support their teachers in transition and guide them to the new partnering pedagogy. But a principal or administrator who believes in partnering can and should do more than just support and encourage. He or she should be evaluating teachers on where they currently are along the continuum from telling to partnering (see Figure 9.1) and providing assistance to those who are moving more slowly, or not at all. Such assistance can come in the form of pairing teachers who are further along the continuum with those who are less advanced, pairing teachers with advanced students, and offering teachers professional development. But—and this is crucial—administrators should make sure that any professional development or training offered focuses not (at least at first) on using various technologies, but rather on shifting teachers' thinking and actions to the partnership mentality and pedagogy. Unless and until this is done, the technology training is unlikely to prove fruitful.

Parents as Partners

There is one more group that is key to the success of the partnering pedagogy, and that is parents. Unless they are properly initiated and engaged in the partnering process, parents can often be a point of resistance to the changes it brings. In particular, many parents expect (or at least say they expect) their students to be taught as they were, that is, by telling. Unless their understanding of the partnering process is complete, parents may view what they hear their children are doing, or what they see them doing if they come to class, as a reason to complain.

In most cases, though, this distrust goes away with time, as kids arrive home much more excited about school than in the past and talk positively about their accomplishments. "[Now] when we sit down to dinner," says one parent, "the kids talk nonstop for twenty minutes, telling us what they did and what they saw. This is literally every day!"[12] It also helps when the kids' grades and attendance rise accordingly.

Most parents know instinctively that the 21st century is different; they see the changes all around them. What they really want is to be assured that their children are being well prepared for their future lives and jobs. Partnering teachers need to help parents understand that colleges and employers are also changing their expectations. Teachers need to let parents know that the teaching is changing to keep up with these new expectations, emphasizing what students can do as much as what they know and giving young people many more future-oriented capabilities and skills than just listening and taking notes. It is terribly important that parents understand this, not just for the partnering pedagogy, but especially for students. Having this dialogue with parents is the responsibility of the entire school, faculty, and administration.

In that dialogue, parents should be encouraged, just as educators should, to respect their kids as users of technology, even when that technology baffles or alarms them (as is often the case with video and computer games). Like teachers, parents need to be encouraged to talk with their kids frequently, to ask them about what they are doing, both school-related and not, and to praise them for their creative accomplishments, both in and out of school.

It helps enormously when a school or district employs technology as a means to reach out to parents. Wi-Fi coverage of students' homes, as well as dedicated websites for parents (with feedback from them), is now, with judicious use of grants, within almost every district's financial reach. For a great example of what can be done with relatively little, look at Lemon Grove, an economically below-average school district in Southern California (www.lemongroveschools1.net). Its Wi-Fi system to schools and homes, created entirely with government grants, is so robust that the district was able to pass along some of the upkeep costs to the local police and fire departments, who use it as a backup.

GETTING MOTIVATED TO PARTNER WITH YOUR STUDENTS

Hopefully, you have already begun the move to partnering. But if not, how can you, as a teacher, get motivated to make big changes? And, even more important, how do you stay motivated to continue changing and not fall back to old, familiar ways at the first sign of trouble? The best way, I think, is not to make the changes in secret, but to be as open as possible—with your students, your administrators, and your colleagues—about what you are trying to do. After all, the goal is to improve your students' experience, your own experience, and the test scores.

The easiest and most effective way of doing this is to enlist the help of those who have gone before you and succeeded. These can be colleagues you know, and hopefully there are at least a few where you teach. But help can also come from people you don't know, people whom you will meet online by joining support groups, such as Listservs, blogs, and Ning groups (see Chapter 7) and by searching YouTube and TeacherTube. Many teachers, several quite experienced, have e-mailed me to say how much these partnering ideas have reinspired them and brought them back to the original level of excitement they felt when they started teaching.

It is also crucial to enlist your supervisors, your students, and their parents in your own personal change process. Often, when they understand your goals, they will be quite supportive.

Have Courage, but Also Have Fun

For most people, doing anything for the first time elicits some fear. You probably felt fear the first time you stood in front of a class as a student or first-time teacher. When you feel such fear and need the courage to proceed anyway, it often helps to remember the lion in *The Wizard of Oz*—you don't need the medal, because the courage is inside you all the time.

But also keep in mind that change is not all fear and pain. In fact, it can be quite invigorating and exciting to rethink your job from a new perspective. Thinking not in terms of material or content but in terms of the questions the material answers is often liberating to long-time teachers.

And do not think that teaching in this new way will necessarily make your job harder. A very important lesson I have learned from the partnering I do regularly in workshops with students and teachers is that there are times when the best thing I can do to enhance everyone's learning is actually nothing at all. After I offer guiding questions and the teams or individuals get to work, I ask frequently if anyone needs my help. But I often get no requests for assistance from the busy learners. So I walk around watching, asking what people are doing, and usually they are right on track. In those moments of teaching when no one "needs" me, I have learned to smile to myself and think, "What a nice job I have."

My hope is that, as you change your pedagogy, this same thought will occur, more and more often, to you as well.

In the remainder of the book, I'll discuss how to apply partnering step by step. I will do this not by presenting you with preset lessons and plans, but rather by considering general principles of partnering and providing numerous examples and practical suggestions. That is the equivalent of teaching you to fish—you'll eat for a lifetime.

2

No More Cookie-Cutter High Schools

Frank S. Kelly, Ted McCain, and Ian Jukes

Given the exponential pace of change and the state of our schools today, we must rethink what a high school should be each time we plan a new school. We simply cannot continue to allow the industrialized, cookie-cutter approach of the early 20th century to fail to serve the diverse and evolving needs of 21st-century students.

- Each high school must be customized to address the needs of the community in which it operates. What works in one community may not work in another.
- No single teaching and learning approach can serve the needs of every student. Schools need to tailor teaching and learning to individual students.
- Schools must offer more choice—where students attend, and what, how, and when they learn.
- Significant change is difficult to effect and still more difficult to sustain.
- Although there are challenges and potential risks to changing, the greater and more certain danger is continuing to operate high schools that fail a third or more of our students and leave many others ill prepared for postsecondary schooling and work.

In the chapters that follow, we explore ideas for high school design that go beyond the typical school we have today. But we must remind you that the focus cannot be on the material we will present there. In fact, those ideas don't begin to make sense until you have first developed a vision for what you want a school to be. A vision for the kind of instruction you see meeting the needs of students and the community both now and in the future. A vision that results from following the process we outlined earlier.

In the past, there was a single approach to high school design that naturally developed from the mass-production mentality of the assembly line oriented Industrial Age. Although it was a great step forward in providing high school education to large numbers of students, it could not and never did meet the needs of every student or the desires of every parent.

Now that we have had a century of experience with this "one size fits all" approach to designing high schools, it has become obvious that the assumptions it is based on have serious shortcomings in handling the demands for individualization in the new Information Age.

Students and parents are becoming increasingly dissatisfied with the inflexibility of schools. Recent developments such as vouchers, charter schools, virtual schools, magnet schools, home schooling, online learning, and a growing list of nontraditional educational choices are indications that we are not meeting the needs of all of our students in the public system.

To a large degree, this trend toward alternatives to the traditional public high school is a result of a combination of unresponsive schools and the increasing choice to which people are becoming accustomed in the world outside the school system. The Industrial Age notion of comprehensive school design was that all schools were similarly designed, equipped, and operated—stamped out as though they were made with a cookie cutter. But this is not an adequate way to deal with the diversity of students that attend a school. And because there is not just one generic kind of student with uniform interests and life goals, it is foolish to think there is one school design that will meet the needs of all those who attend.

In the Information Age of the 21st century, schools will be customized to meet the specific needs of each community in which they operate. This tailoring of schools to meet specific needs will be part of a much larger trend of mass customization that is already beginning to sweep over the modern world.

In *Free Agent Nation,* Daniel Pink (2001) talks about the astounding level of customization available to us in the technologically infused life we are beginning to experience. There are a multitude of examples of how choice has already become a part of the approach businesses have towards their customers. Here are just a few:

- Technological advances in food cooking mean that you can now go into a fast food restaurant and customize your order.
- Automobile companies will let you go online and customize a vehicle as it is moving down the production line.
- Levi Straus will let you custom order clothes that are made to fit.

- Frank has been getting custom-made shirts from Lands' End for the last few years.
- Websites will allow you to create your own designs for wallpaper, business cards, T-shirts, or kitchen cabinets.
- Apple's iPod allows you to customize your playlists. By going online, you can customize the music content you listen to by downloading the song files for the kind of music you prefer.
- CRAYON.net allows you to **CR**e**A**te **Y**our **O**wn **N**ewspaper with the information customized to match your own specific needs and interests.
- The Expedia Website (and several others) allow people to create their own customized travel itineraries.
- TiVo allows you to customize your television experience.
- Kitchenaide allows customers to order from a wide range of colors for household appliances.

As a result of the rapid move toward customized products, there has been a huge shift toward just-in-time production in manufacturing. This means there has been a drastic reduction in inventories of premade items because premade goods have been manufactured without customer input. In *The Long Tail,* Chris Anderson (2006) discusses these and many more examples from the new era of customer choice.

In the same way, education must be caught up in this trend of tailored goods and services if it is to keep pace with the world of the 21st century. Instead of fitting students into the existing school system, we must shape schools to fit the needs of students. If we hope to create schools that fit into and reflect modern society and adequately prepare students for their life in that society, it is critical that we consider what this trend will mean for education. What will it mean to have tailored schools?

SCHOOLS MUST OFFER MORE CHOICE

The trend toward tailored goods and services in the modern world will mean that schools will have to offer much more choice to parents and students than they currently do because, as we have just outlined, increasing choice will be one of the hallmarks of 21st-century life. Technology is providing an unprecedented level of choice for an ever-increasing range of products and services. The trend toward more choice in life will naturally lead people to demand more choice in the schooling their children or they themselves receive.

Students and parents will increasingly demand that their schools provide educational programs that are customized to the individual aspirations of a single student. Each school and school district will have to make a huge shift in attitude toward students, parents, and the community. Schools will have to become far more client driven than they are today.

Just as businesses continually monitor their customers to keep in sync with their changing demands, schools and school districts will have to treat kids and their parents as customers and continually monitor their preferences for the kind of education that will best meet their needs. Phil Schlechty made this point a number of years ago in *Inventing Better Schools* (1997).

This shift in thinking has already begun in schooling that takes place outside the public school system. Why is there such growth in the range of alternatives to traditional public schools? Why are these alternatives attracting so many students? Why are there long waiting lists for openings in these institutions? It's because these schools are much more client driven than typical public schools.

A recent interview Frank had with the principal of an exceptional magnet school in Houston was quite revealing in terms of the shift in mindset needed to make that school run. The school has an exceptional record of student achievement and has five applicants for every space available. Frank asked the principal what he thought was the secret to the success of the school. The principal responded that kids are forced to attend most high schools, but that he has to attract kids to his school because they are not compelled to come—they must *want* to come. He observed that his school has to be one of the very best high schools in the country if he hopes to get any kids at all.

To do this, the school has to continually reflect on the services it provides students and adjust its approach to ensure that it meets the needs of its students. This represents a colossal shift in thinking from the mindset of the vast majority of school administrators and school district staff. It is critical that school districts come to terms with the idea that the virtual monopoly that public schools have had until now in providing K–12 education is not at all assured in the future.

Once schools are more client driven, they will discover that students and parents will want choice in three major areas. First, they will want options in the focus of instruction. Individual students may want to have their studies focus on a specific area of interest. This may be a science focus for medicine or engineering, or a visual arts focus for drawing and painting or sculpture, or a sports focus on athletic development, or a business focus on accounting or marketing. Students will also demand that they be able to take courses that are not currently offered at the school.

Second, students will want a choice of instructional delivery. Some students will choose a self-paced, self-directed approach to instruction. Others will want a project-based, group-oriented approach. Some students will prefer an approach that incorporates mentors from real-world jobs. Other students will want to do their learning using online resources and tools.

Third, students will want a choice in the time in which their instruction takes place. Life in the 21st century is becoming more complex, and people will increasingly want to fit their schooling around their individual schedules, both daily and over the school year.

So the million-dollar question is, "how can we meet the diverse needs of our clientele in one school or in one district?" To do this, we must abandon the cookie-cutter approach to school design. Many effective alternatives to the comprehensive public high school have emerged, proving that there are options aside from the traditional approach to school design. Therefore, effective schools and districts must offer multiple instructional approaches to students.

For example, regardless of the size of a school district, with creative use of technology, a single high school could offer a variety of learning opportunities including virtual schools, community mentorships, an extended school day and school year, academies, a school within a school, or just about any combination of the models outlined in subsequent chapters. All of these models are intended to address the interests and needs of individuals or specific groups of students. In the following chapters, we outline a number of different ideas for organizing high schools that begin to address the needs of modern students. The question is not which one of those models is the best, but which one is best for a particular community. In fact, the question should be refined even more to be, "which features of two or more of those models can be combined with any new ideas we haven't covered, and altered to create just the right hybrid to meet the needs of a particular community?"

The point is that we must get beyond the idea that all high schools must look and operate the same way, that there is something that could be considered a standard high school and every other variation is something special for kids with unusual needs. This will also mean that school districts will have to embrace the idea of multiple school designs within a single district. This will certainly increase the choice of instructional options for students.

But this strategy will also force school districts to embrace a much more flexible approach toward the way schools operate. No longer can a school be built and be expected to operate in the same basic way for 30 years or more. Even with the best efforts in gauging the instructional needs and desires of their students and creating the various school models to meet those needs, some school designs may prove to be more effective than others.

In addition, changing demographics, new technological developments, and a myriad of other factors may render some school designs less or more effective over time. Just as businesses modify their products and services to meet the changing needs and desires of their customers, school districts will have to monitor the instructional needs and aspirations of their students and change the way schools operate as required. If a model for instruction proves to be less effective, then that school must be recon-figured and realigned to a model that will work.

Abandoning the cookie-cutter approach to school design goes even further than this. Within a school district with multiple high schools, dif-ferent schools could specialize in different instructional approaches. For example, within a single district there might be a virtual school; a com-munity mentorship school; a school with an extended school day and school year; a school with an academy focus on medicine, business, fine arts, or athletics; or just about any combination of the models we describe later in the book. Again, all of these models are intended to address the interests and needs of individuals or specific groups of students.

School districts will also have the responsibility to vary school models according to the learning preferences of their students. A client-driven school district will monitor which school models are most popular and effective with students and parents and adjust school organization to meet demand. This is how successful businesses operate. If there are 1,000 students applying to go to one school with 500 seats and only 250 students applying to go to another school with 500 seats, a strong message is being sent to the school district. Client-driven school districts create schools that are based on how students learn, not where they live.

SCHOOLS MUST DEAL WITH UNPRECEDENTED CHANGE

The previous section dealing with increased choice in schools probably gave many school planners and designers fits as they began to wrestle with the implications of how school districts could possibly embrace those ideas in the everyday details of planning, designing, building, and operat-ing the high schools in their community.

Unfortunately, there's even more to consider. In fact, what we are going to discuss now will have even more far-reaching implications than dealing with the increased choice we just covered. What we must now consider is that the very nature of change is changing in the 21st century.

In the 20th century, especially the mid-20th century, change was pre-dictable. It followed a relatively linear growth pattern as shown in Figure 2.1. Growth in the power of technology, for example, could be predicted from past or current changes. This made change manageable. It was fairly easy to extrapolate into the future and see where things were headed. This kind of change persisted for many years. Planning for schools was straightfor-ward in this environment, and because the rate of change remained quite sta-ble for a long time, planners got used to being able to easily predict where things were going.

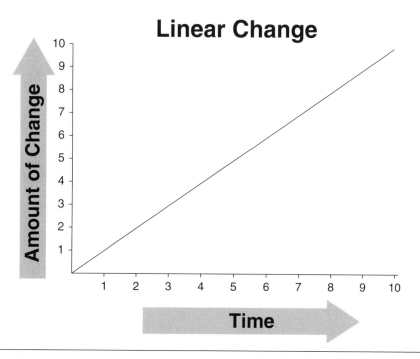

Figure 2.1

However, something dramatic happened in the latter part of the 20th century that made planning for schools much more difficult. Technological development increasingly changed the way the world operated. Sudden developments burst onto the scene with great power. One of the best examples of this is the rapid emergence of the World Wide Web as an integral part of everyday life. It was developed in the early 1990s, and it exploded into everyone's consciousness in the summer of 1995 shortly after a powerful free program called Mosaic was released (re-released as Netscape Navigator in 1995). In the short time since then, the World Wide Web has grown into an essential tool for business, education, and personal use that couldn't even have been imagined in 1995. The world seemed like it had changed overnight. New methods of information access, marketing, and instruction rocketed into action, rendering many old approaches and procedures obsolete.

How could a development with such global impact have exploded onto the scene so rapidly? Even more troubling is how something of this magnitude could happen so quickly without anyone knowing it was about to happen. What was going on? What was going on was a radical shift in the way change takes place. In a very short time, we have gone from the linear and relatively predictable change of the late Industrial Age to the exponential and highly unpredictable change of the Information Age.

So how is exponential change different from linear change? Linear change occurs when development increases by a fixed increment. For example, if the power of a computer is increasing in a linear fashion, then each day you add a fixed increment to the number representing its power. This was shown in Figure 2.1. But if you are experiencing an exponential growth in the power of the computer, then each day the power might double or triple from the previous day. This kind of change based on the daily doubling of power is illustrated in Figure 2.2. Notice that the growth in power in the exponential change graph develops slowly for a while, then makes a dramatic swing upward as the doubling really kicks in. Once this occurs, the power increases each day are astounding. This explains why the development of the World Wide Web exploded into our lives. It was increasing in size and power exponentially.

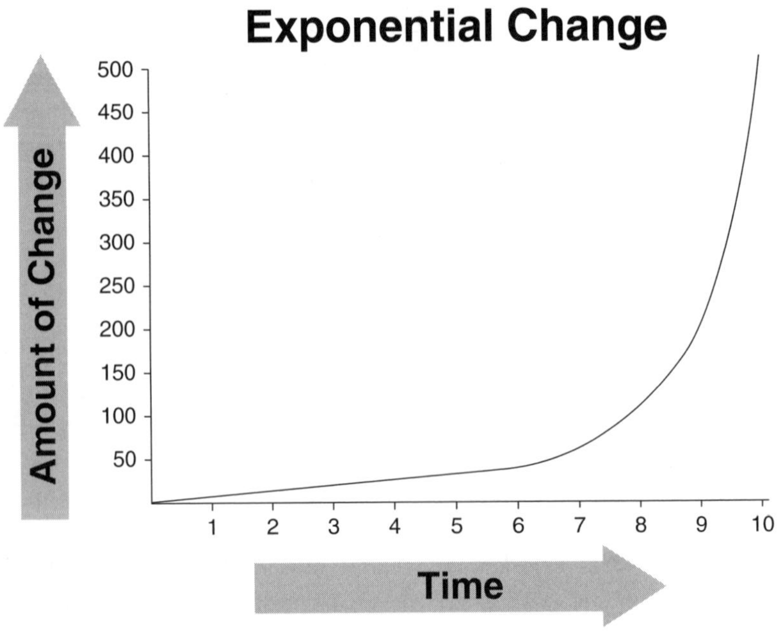

Exponential Change

Amount of Change

500
450
400
350
300
250
200
150
100
50

1 2 3 4 5 6 7 8 9 10

Time

Figure 2.2

In *The Singularity Is Near*, Ray Kurzweil (2005, p. 21) states that there are more than 75 exponential trends occurring in technological development in the world today. Taken individually, these trends are thought provoking. Taken collectively, these trends are absolutely staggering in their implications for life in the future. The exponential nature of the change means that in the 21st century, it will become increasingly commonplace for overwhelming developments of enormous power to appear suddenly.

Further, Kurzweil indicates that not only will change be increasingly exponential in nature, but there will be more of it in many more areas of life than we have seen previously. It will truly be a world unlike anything we have ever experienced before.

What will this mean for school planning and design? It will mean that the old ways of doing things will quickly become obsolete. Those who persist in using the old tried-and-true approaches of the 20th century will encounter more and more difficulties and feel more and more stress as the world experiences more and more exponential change.

Ideas developed for the Industrial Age simply won't work in the Information Age. We must employ new approaches if we want to have any hope of succeeding in designing effective schools in this new era of change. What is needed is nothing short of a radical new mindset for school design.

No longer can we think of schools as static facilities that are built and then essentially left standing with minor renovations for 30, 40, 50 years or more. New school designs will have to be incredibly flexible to accommodate the shifting demands of the 21st-century world as it experiences exponential change.

Some businesses are already using facilities that are designed to function in an environment of change. Just think of the conference facilities at hotels. They have movable walls and other features that make it easy for hotel staff to reconfigure the conference space to meet the needs of their various clients.

For years, shopping centers and office buildings have been designed with customizable interior spaces. Walls are made out of easily removed metal studs, ceilings are made out of easily removed suspended tiles, and the mechanical, electrical, and network systems are constructed in the ceiling so they can be easily accessed and modified. When new clients want different interior spaces, the building owners can reconfigure the structure to meet their needs.

Schools planners will have to adopt a similar mindset when creating new facilities. One thing we can count on in the 21st century is change, so schools must be designed with change in mind. This will radically alter the way we approach the design of school facilities. In the past, we have typically spent more on school buildings to ensure that they last a very long time. Extra money is often spent on the cost of masonry partitions, terrazzo floors, and the like. In the future, however, we will spend less on some materials as we recognize that the interior spaces will be changed multiple times over the life of the building.

This will require a major departure from the current thinking that school districts have toward their school buildings. They must come to see the interior of a school as temporary. Although this is new for school districts, it is exactly what office building developers have done for some time. They plan and budget for the shell of the building. Everything inside that shell is considered temporary and related to the specific needs of the tenants, who will change numerous times over the lifespan of the structure.

The notion of continual change will force school districts to alter their thinking even further. As we have seen, change, especially the exponential change we are seeing in the modern world, will be sudden and not easily predicted. This is the worst nightmare for the traditional mindset of school planning. But dealing with rapid and unpredictable change is not new.

Look at how businesses are dealing with the rapid and unpredictable changes in technological development. Although they do not always know what the changes will be, businesses know that new computers will continue to hit the market and their new power and features will compel their use. To handle the continual turnover of high-tech equipment, many businesses no longer purchase the equipment. Instead, they lease or even treat them as consumables with a very short lifespan, typically two to three years. These businesses do not think of technology as capital goods, but treat it more like office supplies. At the end of the lease, they return the computers. If they have treated them as consumables, then the businesses give the computers to employees to take home. In either case, this allows the business to replace the computers with the latest, most powerful models available. This keeps the businesses up to date with the rapidly changing world of computer technology.

Because the world of the 21st century will be a rapidly changing environment for education, school districts will have to consider this option as well. Knowing that schools will have to change to meet the changing needs of their students, school districts may decide to rent or lease space for schools. This would allow schools to move to more suitable locations when the term of their lease is up or at least put the burden of renovations on the building owner if they want to keep the school as a tenant.

Schools and school districts will take on a radically different look when they embrace these ideas. The bulk of core instructional spaces could be housed in typical office or retail leased facilities. Districts may choose to sign shorter term leases for certain programs so they can move to more suitable facilities as their needs change. School districts may own only highly specialized spaces such as science labs, art studios, theaters, music halls, and specialized spaces for career education programs. Some districts may choose to own physical education and athletic spaces and fields, whereas others may leave these to community groups.

THE REAL ISSUE FACING SCHOOLS

It should be clear that all those involved in creating new learning environments will face some amazing challenges in the 21st century. It should also be clear that schools cannot stay the same if we hope to keep them relevant, effective, viable, and filled with kids. If we want the innovative schooling that will be needed to keep high schools relevant for learners in this new age, then we cannot continue to create them using ideas and approaches that were developed in another age for a world that no longer exists. That means schools must change. And there, as the Bard would tell us, is the rub.

The most important issue facing schools today is not how to incorporate the fantastic new technology we have discussed. It's not adjusting to the new ways digital students think. It's not implementing the new planning approach we outlined. It's not even deciding which of the models for high schools discussed in subsequent chapters to use.

No, the most important issue facing schools today is the reluctance of those in control of education to let go of what they are used to, whatever their role in the system. Teachers must let go of instructional approaches that were designed to work in the Industrial Age schools of the 20th century. Administrators and school district staff must let go of traditional ideas of managing students. School district facilities staff and architects must let go of their preconceived ideas of how schools operate and what schools look like.

It really boils down to an issue of comfort. It took a lot of time and effort for people to acquire the skills necessary to make the school system work the way it does now. Many have invested their entire careers learning how to teach in the Industrial Age schools we have today. Others have invested their professional lives in obtaining the knowledge and skill required to plan and design these 20th-century facilities. And because schools have remained the same for such a long time, people have become very comfortable with the way things are done. The status quo is firmly entrenched in the way schools are financed, and in the laws governing curriculum, student assessment, school accountability, the length of the school year, as well as in labor laws, family habits, community self-images related to sports, and so forth.

Now we come along and say that the world of the 21st century will be radically different from the world that most of us grew up in, that it will require a major shift in the way we think about education. This upsets the apple cart. Making the shift to a 21st-century approach to school design will be a challenge for anyone who is used to doing things the old-fashioned way, and the more time a person has invested in the old way of doing things, the greater the challenge will be. Simply put, making the shift will be uncomfortable. It will force people to start examining what they think about students, learning, instructional strategies, school organization, and school design all over again. It will require time and effort. It will be messy. It will also be easier to cling to and defend the way it's always been done.

One of the metaphors we use in our visioning exercises with school districts is comparing people's minds to rubber bands. Our goal at the beginning of our visioning sessions is to stretch the rubber band by examining what is happening in the digital world and the impact it is having on our kids, the things we discussed in Chapter 1. We ask people to consider the implications these developments should have on the way we teach, the way we assess, the way we plan for new schools, and the way we design new facilities. Without exception, we have found that the teachers, administrators, district staff, board members, businesspeople, students, parents, and community members have seen that we cannot continue to do things the way we do them now. Our initial visioning sessions are very stimulating as the people involved get excited about new ideas for how schooling could take place. By the time we have finished exploring what 21st-century schools could look like, the rubber band has been significantly stretched!

Then something remarkable happens. The people involved in the visioning session, especially those who work in the school system, begin to grasp the significance and the implications of the changes that they've envisioned. To make the vision become a reality will require people to make substantial changes in the way they currently do things. They begin to realize that this will require real effort. They begin to understand that this will be extraordinarily uncomfortable. Consequently, they start to second-guess the wisdom of creating such a wild new vision for their schools. And the rubber band snaps back.

Then those involved in developing the new vision start getting feedback from those who were not directly involved in the visioning exercise. The vision that was developed in the first session is written up for others to see and distributed for feedback. Some will respond positively, but the majority of responses will be negative.

Here is a sample of actual responses we have heard to new visions for 21st-century schools:

"Are you crazy? You can't expect teachers to teach that way."

"Do you have any idea how much this will cost?"

"Yeah, those are great ideas, but they'll never work here."

"What makes you so sure the world is going to be that different in the future anyway?"

"I've been through all this before. This technology thing is just another fad like open classrooms. It will pass and things will return to normal in a little while."

"If schools were like that, I couldn't use all the lesson plans I've developed."

"The Department of Education will never let you do something like this."

"What will happen to test scores?"

"People aren't trained for this kind of school. What were you thinking?"

"What's wrong with the schools we have now? They were good enough for me so they should be good enough for kids today."

We have found that the majority of people respond from their comfort zone. As they begin to grasp the magnitude of the change required to make this new kind of schooling a reality, they begin to see how much time, effort, and struggle it will take. They respond accordingly.

The end result is that the new vision is reeled in so it isn't so challenging. The new learning that was seen as so important when the original vision was created is now questioned and its new features dismissed. People come up with all of the reasons why it can't be done instead of looking for all the ways it could be done. Teachers attack the new kind of instruction because it doesn't look like anything they have ever seen before. Parents don't like the new schools because they don't look like the schools they attended. School district staffs don't like the new ideas because they can't see how to manage students in such a new environment. Everyone sees only problems with the new vision for learning. By the time the facilities people and the architects get through with the planning for the next school, the vision has been seriously watered down or lost altogether.

Why? Because the status quo is so firmly entrenched, it is much easier to keep doing things in schools the way they always have been done than it is to change. You must remember that schools have been the same since before everyone alive today was born. People have literally grown up with schools as they are.

Embracing the kind of change we see that is needed for the 21st century will require rethinking much of what we have taken for granted for so long. When confronted with this kind of change, most people retreat to what is familiar. They deny that the change is needed, they ridicule those who espouse such nonsense, they avoid dealing with the implications of such change, they dismiss the need for considering new ideas, and they point to any problems as reasons for dismissing the change outright. Why? Because it is easier than getting down and doing the hard, messy work of changing the longstanding and ineffective way we have taught our kids and the way we have designed the schools they use.

Here is a powerful reason we know that change is avoided in the school system. Most of the ideas in this book about reorganizing schools are not new. Yes, we have added some of our thoughts to each of the models, and we have extended the idea of school design to include the Cyber School, but most of the models for school organization we cover are just the repackaged ideas of others. And their ideas are not new.

For example, recognizing the need to teach students differently, J. Lloyd Trump wrote *Images of the Future* in 1959. Since then, there have been many who have come to similar conclusions about the state of schools and the need for change. Yet despite the mounting body of work pointing to the need for substantial change in our schools, those responsible for education have steadfastly resisted most of the calls for new forms of instruction.

What is most troubling about this situation is that those responsible for schools have decided to ignore the calls for change and continue with traditional approaches despite the growing evidence that schools are performing very poorly. Here are just a few of the grim statistics regarding the performance of schools in the United States.

- "Almost one third of all public high school students and nearly one half of all blacks, Hispanics, and Native Americans fail to graduate from public high schools with their class" (Bridgeland, DiIulio, & Morison, 2006, p. 1).
- "The United States has one of the lowest high school graduation rates among industrialized nations" (National Governors Association [NGA], 2005, p. 3).
- "On state assessments of English and mathematics, roughly one in three high school students fails to meet standards" (NGA, 2005, p. 3).
- "Nearly a third of high school graduates who go on to college require immediate placement in remedial education courses" (NGA, 2005, p. 3).
- "The percentage of 9th graders that make it through the education process: 68% of them graduate from high school, 40% of them immediately enroll in college, 27% of them are still enrolled in their sophomore year, and 18% graduate from college" (NGA, 2005, p. 3).
- "84% of employers say K–12 schools are not doing sufficient job preparing students for work—in Math, Science, Reading and Comprehension—even in attendance, timeliness, and work ethic" (National Association of Manufacturers, 2005, p. 16).
- "Nearly half of Texas students entering college now must take remedial classes" (*Houston Chronicle*, July 7, 2006, p. B1).

These statistics paint an incredibly damning picture of the performance of schools. But if those in education have resisted any major changes even though the poor performance and need for change have been well documented, it makes us conclude that people in education are choosing, consciously or unconsciously, to hold onto inefficient, underperforming approaches to instruction rather than embrace the change that is desperately needed because that is the most comfortable thing to do.

That illustrates the difficulty of breaking out of the mold of current thinking about education. It also illustrates the power of TTWWADI. We have done things the same way for so long in schools, and people have become so comfortable with the way things are, that change is extremely difficult. Like the width between the rails of train tracks, the way we teach students is accepted without question because it's been that way for so long. Conventional wisdom is that it takes strength to hold on to something. However, the truth is that it takes the greatest amount of strength to let go of something familiar.

WHAT CAN BE DONE?

Is the situation hopeless? Far from it. But it will take real effort if we want to get the school system out of the deeply entrenched ways of doing things that are the status quo.

Where do we begin? The starting point is to embrace the new planning process we outlined earlier. As you begin to ask questions about where the world is heading, the implications of technological development, and the digital world kids are experiencing, a new vision for what learning could and should be will naturally emerge. If you are having trouble getting started, get help. There are people who have been helping school districts develop new visions for 21st-century schools for several years. Seek them out.

Do not rush through the visioning process. It has been our experience that school districts that have not taken the time to create a new vision for learning encounter a great deal of resistance. This invariably occurs because they have not involved everyone associated with the design and operation of new schools in the visioning process.

A key step of the process of effecting change in an organization is the development of a collective vision that comes from real dialogue with all those who will be affected by any departures from established ways of doing things. If those people are not involved in the visioning process, they will not fully understand the reasons for the changes being contemplated. Consequently, they will resist any move away from what they are currently doing.

Although it takes time and money to bring everyone into the visioning process, it is the key to bringing about significant change. Once all the stakeholders have had the opportunity to be involved and have real input, you can then produce a vision document that captures the new direction for your schools. Use this document as a standard to measure any work on new facilities. And be sure you take the time to fully create a comprehensive new vision for schools before spending a dollar on planning or construction.

Developing a new vision for schools is hard work to be sure, but don't be fooled into thinking the work is done once the vision has been created. In fact, the hard part is what comes next. It will take great courage, steadfast commitment, and a lot of just plain hard work to sustain the vision. The rubber band can still snap back.

Make no mistake about this—the process of transferring the new ideas for instruction and learning into actual practice with students is the critical and most difficult part of shifting schools to new approaches to education.

You will have as critics all those who are married to traditional methods for instruction and conventional school design. Their opposition to the new vision will rise as they begin to see that they will have to make personal changes as schools shift away from the familiar 20th-century designs and methods of operation.

To counter the criticism that will inevitably come, those advocating the new vision must understand that changing longstanding approaches to learning will require a concerted, long-term effort. We cannot view transferring vision into practice as a one-shot, short-term thing. Without continual encouragement and assistance, people will slip back to what is familiar and comfortable.

To create new schools for the 21st century, all those involved must receive support and training over a period of years, long after a new building has been constructed. It will be hard. It will be a struggle. Many will complain. You will wonder at times why you ever started with this harebrained idea of creating new schools. It will be incredibly important to remember the number one reason you started looking at new approaches to instruction and learning—our children and their success in the unfamiliar, technologically infused world of the 21st century.

We began the first chapter with the following definition of insanity: *Doing the same thing you've always done, but expecting or wanting or needing completely different results.* We see this insanity being lived out daily in the schools our children attend. We have written this book in an attempt to bring sanity back to the way we design 21st-century schools. We firmly believe that if you embrace the new planning process we have outlined and apply some combination of the school models that follow, you will create the innovative new facility designs the school system desperately needs to engage modern students and to prepare them for their life in the future. We can't wait to see the kinds of schools you create.

Reflect on Your Schools and How They Serve the Diverse and Changing Needs of Your Students

- Assess your own personal comfort level with the way schools are today. Whatever role you play in designing or operating a school, are you resisting new ideas because they will force you out of your zone of comfort and familiarity?
- How do your high schools reflect the diverse needs of the students they serve? How are your instructional methods and offerings different from school to school?
- How do parents and students decide which high school to attend in your district? Do they have choices of schools and instructional methods?
- How are your high school instruction and facilities planned to accommodate the exponential change occurring in the world in which your students live?
- When a new school opens, how do you assure that the vision that shaped the school will be realized in its long-term operation?
- What percentage of your students graduate from high school? How do those who graduate fare in college and at work? Over time, are these acceptable for your community?

3

Strategic Leadership

Encouraging and Assessing Technology Integration

Lynne Schrum and Barbara B. Levin

> For professional development to be effective, it must offer serious intellectual content, take explicit account of the various contexts of teaching and experiences of teachers, offer support for informed dissent, be ongoing and embedded in the purposes and practices of schooling, help teachers to change within an environment that is often hostile to change, and involve teachers in defining the purposes and activities that take place in the name of professional development.
>
> —Shanker, 1996, p. 223

WHAT YOU WILL LEARN IN THIS CHAPTER

♦ Strategies for managing change surrounding the integration of technology.

♦ Two models for understanding and dealing with change and innovation.

♦ Considerations for professional development around technology integration.

♦ Roles of the technology coordinator, technology planning committee, and teacher leaders.

♦ What to look for when evaluating a technology-rich lesson.

KEY WORDS IN THIS CHAPTER	
Concerns-Based Adoption Model (CBAM)	Hall and Hord's process-oriented approach that examines individual reactions to change, particularly in school contexts, is known as the **Concerns-Based Adoption Model**. It examines where individuals' issues are and then focuses support at that level to raise awareness and implementation.
Adoption of Innovation	Everett Rogers' theory of the way organizations and individuals adjust to new programs, projects, or technological implementations is known as the **adoption of innovation** theory.
Professional Development (PD)	**Professional development (PD)** activities are designed to assist individuals in learning skills and knowledge attained for career advancement; it encompasses all types of learning opportunities and is typically situated in practice.
Professional Learning Community (PLC)	A **professional learning community (PLC)** includes attributes that support teachers' professional growth and includes collaborative inquiry, develops a shared body of wisdom, and models shared decision making. Participants together create an environment considered beneficial to significant change and reflection on teaching practice.
Teacher Leaders	**Teacher leaders** are developed by providing specific professional opportunities that encourage and support educators in new roles within a school; these teacher leaders typically do remain in their schools.

INTRODUCTION

This chapter extends school leaders' understanding about how innovations spread, offers exemplars of organizational structures to support those innovations, and provides a rubric for observing and offering feedback to educators. It introduces two frameworks to consider in understanding the nature of individuals' change. Next, the chapter explores the various organizational structures that will assist a school leader in supporting the use of information technology. Finally, school leaders have a need to understand, observe, and provide feedback to educators who use technology-rich lessons, and a structure for doing this is offered.

WHAT CAN BE DONE TO PROMOTE INDIVIDUALS' TECHNOLOGY INTEGRATION?

Looking at what is known about promoting any particular innovation, it is once again worth considering the work of Michael Fullan (2007). He suggests that "The litmus test of all leadership is whether it mobilizes people's commitment to putting their energy into actions designed to improve things. It is individual commitment, but above all it is collective mobilization" (p. 9). Further, Testerman, Flowers, and Algozzine (2002) suggest, "If educational leaders continue to demonstrate developmental lags in their knowledge and technology competence, the expected benefits of innovative technology practices will likely be unrealized" (p. 60). Several successful ideas have been used by school leaders in promoting the effective use of technology in schools.

In terms of technology, a recent study (CDW-G, 2007) may serve to set the context for this chapter and provide a glimpse into teachers' thoughts regarding the use of technology. Respondents to surveys state they are moving from learning how computers work to being able to use technology to change how they teach and believe that this is transforming how students learn. They believe technology is having an impact on how they teach thinking and learning skills, as well as the development of lifelong learners. Teachers articulate that technology is effective as a tool for teaching, but they also see it as useful for administration, communication, and research functions. The numbers of teachers who agree with these statements has grown through the last three years of this study. According to the results, elementary school teachers struggle to find enough time to integrate technology into their curriculum, and middle and high school teachers struggle with access to technology (p. 15). Most relevant to the purposes of this chapter, almost 20% of the teachers responding reported that they had no technology professional development in the last year. And most interestingly, the report concludes, "The more hours of technology professional development that teachers receive, the more likely they are to feel that technology is an important classroom tool" (p. 20).

Given this information, it appears that a school leader must do many things simultaneously to lead and support educators to function in a 21st-century school and to employ technology when appropriate to that end. Bogler (2005) showed that empowering teachers and giving them decision-making opportunities improved their professional commitment. Further, Bartunek, Greenberg, and Davidson's (1999) work suggested that teachers' empowerment affected positive evaluation of change initiatives. It follows that principals' support and empowerment are key factors for teachers' involvement in decisions concerning school change. Additionally, a study by Leithwood, Louis, Anderson, and Wahlstrom (2004) suggests that three types of activities make up the core

> Principals' support and empowerment are key factors for teachers' involvement in decisions concerning school change.

of good leadership: (1) setting direction, (2) developing people, and (3) redesigning the organization to meet changing demands. As this chapter explores the process of change, it is worth keeping this information and possible administrator actions firmly in mind.

ADOPTION OF INNOVATION— UNDERSTANDING THE PROCESS

We can perhaps all agree that each and every change is difficult, whether as an individual or for an organization. Changing the culture of a school is complex and challenging for many reasons. When the infusion of technology is also involved, then change is even more multifaceted. In fact, Marzano, Waters, and McNulty (2005) stated,

> One of the constants within K–12 education is that someone is always trying to change it—someone is always proposing a new program or a new practice. . . . Some of the more visible [programs] that have not endured are programmed instruction, open education, the Platoon System, and flexible scheduling. (p. 65)

Perhaps the most frequently referenced framework that informs and examines the nature of organizational change is the work of Everett Rogers (2003). His work relates the adoption of innovation to the typical bell-shaped curve that we are used to when considering any examination of individual differences. That is, not all of those involved in the change are going to adopt or change at the same rate of speed.

Rogers (2003) identified the following five categories of individual change, presented here with the percentage of individuals who typically fall into that category during an innovation implementation:

Innovators: brave people pulling the change (2.5%)

Early adopters: respectable people, opinion leaders, trying out innovation in careful ways (13.5%)

Early majority: thoughtful people, careful but accepting change more quickly than average (34%)

Late majority: skeptical people, use new ideas once majority is using it (34%)

Laggards: more traditional, critical toward new ideas (16%)

Rogers also described that each adopter's willingness and ability to adopt an innovation depends on his or her interest, the value placed upon the innovation, and the trial or interaction with that innovation. Rogers explained why the adoption of this type of innovation is different from others. He related that a critical mass of adopters is needed to convince the "mainstream" teachers of the technology's efficacy, regular and frequent use is needed to ensure appropriate success, and finally, the use of this set of tools evolves as individuals adopt, use, and share them. There is ample evidence in the organizational literature that participation in decision making is a major motivator of change, and as such enhances organizational effectiveness (Martin & Kragler, 1999; Somech, 2002; Somech & Bogler, 2002).

It is important, of course, to support individuals moving forward as they are ready, and not to punish or threaten those who are unable to adopt the innovation, whatever it may be. Thus, it is worth looking at one other model of change that is directly related to education. Hall and Hord (1987) created the Concerns-Based Adoption Model (CBAM), a process-oriented approach that examines individual reactions to change. For the past 20 years, CBAM has provided information and guidance as one begins to think about introducing change, including technology. This framework, shown in Figure 3.1, provides a context for thinking about change.

Figure 3.1   Stages of Concern (CBAM)

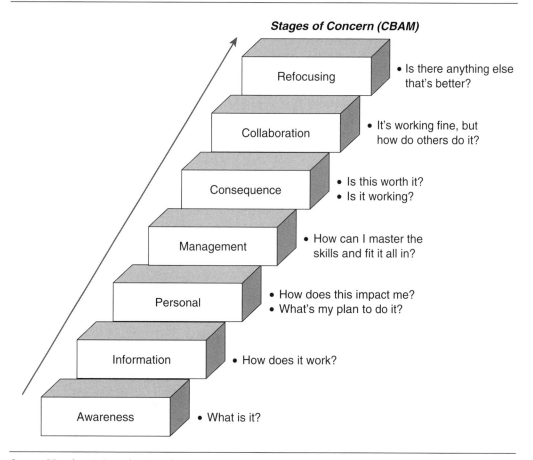

Source: Horsley & Loucks-Horsley, 1998, p. 18.

In particular, this model helps explain the way that the process of change may work for individuals. According to Horsley and Loucks-Horsley (1998), the lower three stages focus on the self, while the middle stage focuses on the mastery of tasks to the point they become routine. Finally, the upper stages of concern are focused on the results and impact of the innovation. It is useful to consider that this model offers insight as to where an individual may be in his or her process by paying attention to the types of questions that person is asking. Early questions may be more about self, while later questions will be more focused on the task. Last, individuals may focus more on impact. Keeping open lines of communication and acknowledging individuals' questions will be an important task of any school leader trying to manage change or promote an innovation, such as moving toward becoming a 21st-century school. This model is also useful in planning and differentiating professional development opportunities, which will be discussed more below.

STEPS TOWARD CHANGING THE CULTURE

A school leader must be able to recognize a well-designed, technology-rich lesson; however, it may be even more important to be able to provide support and encouragement to improve those lessons that are not as well developed. Jonassen (1997) describes several attributes of meaningful and engaging learning environments; in general, they require students to be active learners who are working in complex and intentional activities and doing so in a way that allows them to be collaborative and responsible for their own learning.

It is also worth remembering that teachers, as adults, respond best when we keep in mind two significant factors (Little, 1982). First, adult learning is improved when others demonstrate respect, trust, and concern for the learner. Second, adults, more than anything, wish to be the originators of their own learning; that is, they wish to select their own learning objectives, content, activities, and assessment. Manouchehri and Goodman (2000) found that changes in teachers' practices do not occur by osmosis when innovative materials are placed at their disposal; rather, it is essential that discussions occur that focus on pedagogical understandings. Additionally, one study (Crawford, Chamblee, & Rowlett, 1998) found that nothing happens quickly. They studied a project with seven daylong workshops aimed at introducing teachers to a new curriculum and found that after a year of implementation, teachers were really beginning to change their uses and questions about the new program. Other literature (Nir & Bogler, 2008; Somech & Bogler, 2002) has shown that on-the-job professional development programs are most beneficial when they are long term, focused on students' learning, and linked to the curricula.

In another investigation, elementary teachers were part of a large project that involved preservice teachers and university faculty in collaboration and conversation to develop strong relationships prior to any implementation of the project (Heflich, Dixon, & Davis, 2001). The goal was to assist teachers to "effectively and authentically integrate technology and mathematics into their inquiry-based science instruction" (p. 101). By involving the educators in the project at the development stage, the researchers concluded that the experiences of participation and authentic science activities changed the teachers' views of the purposes and results that might ensue if they changed the ways they taught science and included technology. So, school leaders seeking to change school culture around the use of technology and other 21st-century skills may want to consider allowing their teachers to select ways they want to get involved with the goal of focusing on their students' learning (by selecting their own learning objectives, content, activities, and assessment), provide opportunities for long-term professional development and collaborative conversations with others, and then show them respect, trust, and empower them at each step along the road to implementing change and adopting something new or innovative.

It is also important to recognize that a school leader is not alone in accomplishing these goals. Four organizational structures exist in many schools that will provide support and also work together in ways that will assist in accomplishing steps toward the vision.

Professional Development Continuum and Professional Learning Communities

It is quite clear that no matter how much equipment a school or classroom has, unless the educators are well prepared, confident, and have had the chance to practice, little will change in the classroom (Hernandez-Ramos, 2005; Norris, Sullivan, Poirot, & Solloway, 2003; Sandholtz & Reilly, 2004). Ultimately, the creation of learning experiences that take advantage of the unique affordances of new technologies require educators, as key to any meaningful changes (Bai & Ertmer, 2008), to reconceptualize their new role. It has become clear that without a well-developed, ongoing professional development program, educators will not be able to reconsider how they design learning (Schrum, 1999). Unfortunately, a great deal of professional development that has focused on technology has been ineffective. Researchers report many reasons for this: training on unfamiliar equipment, focus on the hardware and software but not on the integration into their instructional practice, lack of connection to students' and teachers' real needs, and no shared vision (Bauer, 2005; Glassett, 2007; Hernandez-Ramos, 2005).

What does it mean to create a professional development plan to support technology? School leaders have discussed the need to be good listeners

(Tate & Dunklee, 2005), and so perhaps the most important challenge is creating a conversation about the topic. What do people know? What are their concerns? What do they want to know? The development of a shared vision is essential (Reeves, 2006) and leads to the essential growth and development of a professional learning community (PLC) (Louis & Kruse, 1995; Schmoker, 2001). Louis and Kruse identified the characteristics of successful learning communities, and it appears that time to meet and talk (which might be face-to-face or electronically), teaching roles that are interdependent, communication structures, and teacher empowerment are all very important. DuFour (2004) suggests that "To create a professional learning community, focus on learning rather than teaching, work collaboratively, and hold yourself accountable for results" (p. 6).

Through examination of successful professional learning communities, several significant attributes are required to truly sustain and encourage teachers' growth; each of these depends on administrative support and encouragement (Southwest Educational Development Laboratory, 2008). Supportive and shared leadership is needed, and this may take many forms, but in general, the group needs to determine its own plan of action. It is difficult for school leaders to admit that they too can benefit from participating in such joint effort. Through collective creativity and shared visions and values, the PLC determines where it is headed and how it may get there. Louis and Kruse (1995) explain that this is demonstrated by people from all levels of the school working together. This might include a book that everyone reads to support a school or districtwide focus, or it may be demonstrations of members' expertise. The community needs supportive conditions; again, this is where an administrator has the ability to assist. This might include time to meet, with schedules that allow the interaction. Finally, shared personal practice requires that individuals have a chance to talk about, show, and even visit each other's classroom activities.

While establishing viable professional learning communities may not always be possible, it is certainly worth considering ways to create them in small topic, content, or grade-level interest groups. The creation of the culture of learning and studying has the potential for impacting the implementation of technology throughout the entire staff (Adamy & Heinecke, 2005).

Once goals have been established, then the professional development experiences need to be designed. What do individuals need, and what types of activities will be essential for the entire staff? First, it is important to remember that one type of learning does not meet everyone's individual needs. One study (Schrum, Skeele, & Grant, 2002–2003) found that offering a wide variety of ways to learn was effective. Providing a menu of options is often one way to encourage even reluctant educators to participate in professional development activities. For example, one-to-one, small group, just in time, or large group may all be viable ways to provide information and practice to educators. Some teachers may prefer to see demonstration lessons; for example, what does a science lesson that requires technology really look like?

Before teachers begin designing instruction, it is important they become comfortable with using the technology for their own professional activities. Poole (2006) suggests six things that a teacher must be able to do with technology before being able to effectively integrate technology. These include

> Before teachers begin designing instruction, it is important they become comfortable with using the technology for their own professional activities.

- Productivity Tools: Every teacher should be proficient in the use of productivity tools (word processing, presentation software, spreadsheets, etc.).
- Troubleshooting: Every teacher should be able to troubleshoot technology-related problems that commonly crop up in the classroom.
- Technical Assistance: Every teacher should know where to go for technical assistance.
- Internet Resources: Every teacher should be familiar with what's available on the Internet in his or her subject area.
- Search Skills: Every teacher should have well-honed Internet searching skills.
- Interest and Flexibility: Every teacher should be open to new ways of doing things. (Adapted from Poole, 2006)

As discussed in Chapter 2, most new teachers will have all these skills, but it might still be a good idea to ask during an interview. At the very least, this will send the message that technology-savvy teachers are desired at your school.

Technology Coordinators—First Step to Change

Many schools have recognized that it is essential to designate one person, most typically an experienced educator, to become a technology coordinator. This role frequently balances curriculum integration and technical aspects of supporting technology; however, more and more, these individuals are focused on supporting teachers, assisting with curricular activities, offering demonstration lessons, and teaching students directly.

Some of the duties of these individuals include providing teachers with strategies about how technology can be used to achieve learning outcomes, creating an environment encouraging creative and independent use of technology tools, as well as promoting student skills in using these tools. They coordinate and provide professional development to educators and training to school staff in network and software use. These individuals model effective use of current and emerging technology in the classroom and media center for teachers and students. They may also be responsible for teaching appropriate use for legal, ethical, and safety purposes. Doug Prouty (http://www.thesnorkel.org/articles/Top10.pdf) suggests that in addition, they must

1. Be an effective leader;

2. Be an effective communicator;

3. Establish priorities and stick to them;

4. Increase budget and funding sources;

5. Provide and organize staff development;

6. Provide and oversee technical support;

7. Unify levels of infrastructure, hardware, and software;

8. Distribute access;

9. Maintain network reliability and security; and

10. Attend to politics. (Adapted from Prouty, n.d.)

Technology coordinators have banded together through a variety of organizations to support and inform each other. For example, The Snorkel (http://www.thesnorkel.org/) is a support forum for K–12 technology leaders and offers a variety of interactive forums for assistance, resources, and links to materials.

> In the first years of deployment, the largest share of the technology budget is normally devoted to hardware in the form of networks and new computers. As time passes, a greater proportion of the budget should shift to staff development and support. (CoSN, 2001, p. 11)

Some educators divide the use of educational technology within the curriculum into two types of activities. Type I activities utilize technology tools for productivity purposes. For example, Kirschner and Erkens (2006) categorize these as activities where students "carry out a specific task in a learning situation—that is, it is used for learning—more effectively or efficiently one speaks of learning with the tool or application" (p. 199). In essence, student learning is limited to using word processing programs, Internet searches, and presentation programs in order to reduce the amount of instructional time devoted to completing a specific task. Much like an administrative assistant using a word processing program rather than a typewriter, students would interact with a tool simply for utilitarian purposes.

The other way of using these tools, Type II, are designed to change the nature of teaching and learning. Type II activities facilitate collaboration among students and promote dynamic interaction with the breadth of human knowledge (Kirschner & Erkens, 2006; Kongrith & Maddux, 2005). In addition to the collaborative nature of these activities, they also allow the user control over the content, require students to creatively and actively interact with the IT tool, and afford students the opportunity to produce new knowledge as opposed to consume it (Kirschner & Erkens, 2006; Kongrith & Maddux, 2005). Through these activities, IT tools are allowed to complete the lower ends of the Bloom's Cognitive Process Dimension, thus freeing up the students' minds for the more dynamic processes.

The focus of this section has been on the importance of the entire faculty in changing the nature of a school or a district. Educators can assist in all aspects of training and support. It is important to share the leadership, planning, and support for multiple reasons; the educators need to be involved of course, but also it assists the school leader in building consensus and sharing responsibilities. Instructional technology support-staff members are vital in helping design a process and a program for integration of technology, technical assistance, and supply purchasing. These members of the team become essential for vertical and horizontal progress.

A Technology-Planning Committee

Many districts and individual schools garner support through the development of a technology-planning committee for promoting technology skills, knowledge, and use. These committees provide an opportunity to bring together teachers, administrators, parents, community members, and (depending on the age of the learners) students. The National School Boards Association (NSBA) provides a framework with which to examine the roles that various stakeholders take in implementing a school or district technology-planning committee (http://www.nsba.org/sbot/toolkit/ritp.html). They stress the need to begin with determining what students need to learn and then to outline the roles for teachers and others in meeting these goals.

One of the more important aspects is gathering support for the funding stream that is required to maintain and develop a real technology-implementation plan. As the number of computers and other technology has expanded, frequently the number of support personnel has not. Teachers have frequently expressed frustration with printers that do not have ink, laptops that do not have power, and software that is out of date. All of these items take a steady stream of funding and a replacement plan for all technology.

What role do site administrators play in this technology committee? NSBA suggests that principals play an important role in the planning stage (helping determine the change and building support for it), at the implementation stage (being open to feedback and bringing order to possible confusion and processes), and at the institutionalization stage (enhancing and standardizing processes and procedures). It is also worthwhile to examine the way that the technology team interacts and works; tools abound to examine how the process is working (http://www.nsba.org/sbot/toolkit/TeamSur.html)

Teacher Leaders: A Model Worth Considering

Recently teachers have begun to take on more leadership roles throughout the educational community; they have lead reforms, organized curricular activities, and served as educational guides in school systems. Begun in early 2001, the process expanded with the creation of the Teacher Leaders Network (http://www.teacherleaders.org/) in 2003. This project was designed to foster teacher leadership and also to provide a forum for teacher leaders to discuss and share their experiences. The chance to make a difference is a major reason an individual chooses to become a teacher (Sadker & Sadker, 2005), and today many teachers are eager and willing to extend their influence beyond their individual classrooms. Danielson (2006) sees this desire to expand influence as paramount to teacher leadership. Given the flat hierarchy of schools, a teacher's willingness to assume a greater degree of responsibility could prove a vital support system in leading a 21st-century school. It may raise teachers' levels of contribution and multiply their possible impact (Ackerman & Mackenzie, 2006; Fullan, 1993). When teachers recognize that leading increases their overall difference-making ability, they will be more inclined to seize the chance to serve in this capacity. Danielson (2007) reported that "Effective teacher leaders display optimism and enthusiasm, confidence and decisiveness" (p. 17). What does this mean for school leaders who are ready to change the school or district in which they work? Clearly these processes can be used to take steps toward leading in a 21st-century school. Shared vision is a start; however, shared responsibilities, professional development, and rewards for progress are all going to be important as you begin to make changes.

The school administrator plays a crucial role in fostering the conditions that facilitate teacher leadership; however, it is worth examining what school leaders must do to encourage and develop a strong teacher leader network. Sometimes, teachers themselves are reluctant to take a leadership role; Danielson (2007) reports that in Australia this is called the *tall poppy* syndrome: Those who stick their heads up risk being cut down to size. Teachers may be reluctant to let their colleagues know of any efforts to expand their knowledge or recognition (e.g., starting a terminal degree, for instance, or seeking National Board for Professional Teaching Standards recognition). This is where a school leader must step in and develop a culture that promotes teachers' efforts to take leadership roles. In such circumstances, teachers need their school leaders to support them and provide clear expectations and also to provide opportunities that take advantage of their skills and talents as well as make available opportunities for appropriate professional development (Henderson, 2008).

Lieberman and Miller (2004) emphasized three roles of teacher leaders: (1) advocates, (2) innovators, and (3) stewards. They described the differences, that is, that *advocates* speak up for what is best for student learning, *innovators* are creative doers, not just thinkers, and *stewards* are those who positively shape the teaching profession itself. In order to accomplish any of these goals, a school leader needs to encourage teachers to become the type of leader they are comfortable being and provide a safe environment for this level of risk taking. Teachers must be confident that school leaders will support and encourage them. This model of teacher leaders may be particularly useful in the integration of technology because teachers need a supportive and trustworthy environment (Semich & Graham, 2006). Technology has often been the impetus for teachers taking on a leadership role, according to Riel and Becker (2008). They report that through informal networks and conferences, "computer-using teachers gained a sense that they belonged to a community of innovators at the leading edge of change in educational practice" (p. 397).

> In order to accomplish any of these goals, a school leader needs to encourage teachers to become the type of leader they are comfortable being and provide a safe environment for this level of risk taking.

Of course, without support throughout a school, especially from an administrator, a teacher's readiness and willingness to move in the direction of a leadership role may not be realized. However, it is worth approaching the idea of teacher leaders through the lens of these effective strategies; thus, it might be a place to begin by helping individuals self-identify where they are on this continuum and where they would like to see themselves.

A TECHNOLOGY-RICH LESSON: WILL WE KNOW IT IF WE SEE IT?

Once educators are ready to integrate the technology into their curriculum, it will be important for someone to observe, support, and provide feedback to them. How will someone know how to do this; or will an administrator be prepared to observe with a skilled eye and provide that feedback? It may be helpful to use a framework or set of goals for this. No matter what lesson-plan format a teacher uses, an observer could use the list found in Table 3.1 to recognize if the main components are evident and then be ready to discuss with an educator or group of educators ways to enhance or increase the viability of those lessons that include technology.

One way to use Table 3.1 is as a series of questions the observer might ask as the lesson unfolds. It may also be valuable to have a copy of the NETS·T (introduced in Chapter 1) to use alongside these goals as a way to consider what the teacher is doing, how the objectives are being addressed, and in what ways technology is woven into the lesson.

It is also important to think about what the learners are doing and ways they are demonstrating the knowledge and skills of the lesson. These questions may link the observer back to the NETS·S standards and 21st-century skills also introduced in Chapter 1. Are the learners active, creative, and communicating their ideas? An observer may consider this framework as a conversation starter and as a way to raise awareness (rather than as an evaluative tool). Similarly, if the teachers and school leaders watched a typical lesson together, they might then have a conversation about how the lesson might be more in line with the NETS. Or, grade-level or content-level teams might think about a particular unit or lesson together. Just collaboratively going through this process will allow everyone to begin thinking about ways to reconceptualize a lesson.

Table 3.1 Considerations for Evaluating a Technology-Enhanced Lesson

Category	What You Will See
Standards/Objectives	Evidence of connections between standards, student outcomes, and the appropriate uses of technology.
General Purpose of Technology	Technology is used in transformative ways, and students understand the expected outcomes. Familiar and/or new tools are chosen to match the lesson goals. Technology is used to promote 21st-century thinking and skills like collaboration, communication, problem solving, critical thinking, or innovation.
Technology Use Linked	Technology adds specific content, practice, or attributes that are not otherwise available, or it results in unique learning benefits. The technology used extends or expands the learning outcomes that would be impossible otherwise.
Learning Activity	Students are active, engaged, and supported throughout the lesson. Multiple levels of cognition are addressed, including synthesis, evaluation, and knowledge creation. Students are expected to create a representation of their learning rather than restate information.

Category	What You Will See
Professional/Preparation	Supporting materials and handouts are prepared, clear, complete, and appealing to students. Equipment is ready, prescreened, and in working condition.
Implementation Strategy	Clear guidelines are established for managing and using technology and modeled for students. Students are reminded about selecting appropriate resources. Sufficient time is planned.
Assessment Component	Assessment is directly related to objectives and standards and includes an assessment of technology component. Assessment provides opportunities for students with varying learning styles and strengths to excel.

Two School Leaders' Story . . .

Leading the Way by Developing Professional Learning Communities: Executive Director Dr. Enid Silverstein and Coordinator Mary Wegner's Story

As the director of curriculum, I issued a call to action to curriculum-content leaders to propel instructional change to mesh with exponential technology trends, 21st-century learning needs, and creating communities of practice within their spheres of influence. I created a project, *Transforming Instructional Practice through Action Research,* as a professional development initiative mutually designed and supported by the Anchorage School District's Curriculum and Instructional Support and the Educational Technology departments. Action research was selected for its potential to solve local educational issues through continuous monitoring and revision and because of its potential to engender and strengthen membership in a community of practice. The major prongs of this initiative were to have curriculum specialists learn about and then directly infuse the principles of action research along with Web 2.0 tools into their curricular/programmatic responsibilities. Participants in this project included all content-area curriculum coordinators and support teachers along with various curriculum support program heads. Teachers in the Educational Technology Department embarked on an action-research project the previous school year and through a partnering process were available to support the exploration of action research as applied to the use of Web 2.0 tools. Cofacilitation by the Educational Technology Department guaranteed a continuous avenue to best practices in educational technology pedagogy. Additional project activities included common readings and group discussions related to action research, communities of practice, and connectivism. Individualized support was organized via a schedule of face-to-face meetings, videoconferences,

(Continued)

(Continued)

and electronic communication with Dr. Lynne Schrum, who had previously worked on the Educational Technology Action Research project. Using Web 2.0 tools as an alternative to face-to-face training and collaboration in working with teacher groups was emphasized; for example, participants communicated with each other through the Curriculum and Instructional Support Wiki that hosted resources and discussion prompts.

Project activities yielded several benefits: First, they built upon previous departmental initiatives to explore best practices in 21st-century teaching and learning, which includes the exploration of technology-infused learning. Second, collective learning processes and reflective practices centered on modeling the purposeful choice and use of appropriate Web 2.0 tools and resources as 21st-century teaching practices. Third, participants will use the information in the process of doing their job and will publish and present on their specific project and findings as relevant. Here are some sample curriculum department action-research projects:

The World Languages Department identified teachers who were using technology tools to increase students' oral language skills and discover the particular tools that had the most positive results. A survey revealed barriers to effective use of these tools but many teachers were using technology to assess students. Next steps for this project are to encourage teachers to use these tools to assist students to practice language acquisition and to assess in a more organized and consistent fashion. Other goals are to provide a forum for teachers to share activities, make tool implementation more global, overcome perceived barriers to effective use, and more intentionally "map" professional development into a strategic plan.

The Social and Emotional Learning (SEL) and the Health/Physical Education coordinators teamed up to use a Ning to provide professional development to 30 elementary Health and SEL specialists. Survey data revealed differing comfort levels with teaching SEL lessons and with self-perceptions as school SEL leaders and teachers. An online forum was created to assist these teachers to collaborate and share ideas, and it also has videos for teachers to use instructionally or for professional growth. The Ning provides space for teachers to exchange successful lessons and strategies, as well as SEL connections with the health curriculum.

A language arts project goal was to nurture professional and social networking linking English and social studies ninth-grade teachers through shared best practices. Site visits identified key practices and issues of interest that needed to be addressed. With encouragement, individual teachers began hosting lessons that have been effective and also identifying questions that needed investigation, as well as see responses to teacher-posted questions on a Ning.

The middle school math team morphed their original question, "How does the wiki foster collaborative teaching?" to "How does being part of a professional learning community foster collaboration?" Cohort groups, school meetings, and a wiki were used to collect data. One conclusion is that specificity in questioning techniques is the key to being able to compare and record changes in thinking amongst teachers. Project data also led to researching professional learning communities and enhancing relative interactions at specific school sites.

The music action-research project was to enhance interactive communication networks with parents and the community and increase awareness among music staff in all three divisions concerning K–12 music activities and education. Calendaring of all music events by grade level was added to the website, and professional development on use of Google tools and wikis was provided for staff. A survey is in progress to gauge the ability, comfort with using, and professional development needs relative to use of technology tools within the department. Increased use of these tools has been noted through a web-based counter.

As schools retool to meet the learning needs of 21st-century students, all educators can benefit from professional development opportunities like this one that offer avenues to examine solutions through action research, an iterative process that is grounded in the context of the practice of being an educator while using 21st-century tools and resources.

Enid Silverstein, EdD, Executive Director,
Curriculum & Instructional Support
Anchorage School District, Alaska

Mary Wegner, Coordinator,
Educational Technology, Elementary
Anchorage School District, Alaska

This story exemplifies NETS·A Standard 3. Advance Excellence in Digital Age Professional Practice; Standard 4. Ensure Systemic Transformation of the Educational Enterprise.

CONCLUSION

This chapter has focused on the challenge of supporting, encouraging, and promoting the use of technology in curricular applications for all grade levels and in specific content areas. It presented the challenges and complexity of teachers' evolution toward using technology integrated within their teaching of lessons. It also presented ways for school leaders to examine and understand the many ways technology can be used. We also offered criteria for school leaders to use when observing lessons and providing feedback. We hope, through conversation, demonstration, and interaction, you will find ways to acknowledge the work teachers are doing and help them move toward more integration in student-centered learning.

ACTIVITIES TO CONSIDER . . .

- Share the information you read in this chapter about diffusion of innovations (e.g., stages of concern in CBAM) with your faculty and discuss where they are now with technology and what they need next to move ahead with integrating technology into their teaching.
- You might also use Rogers' (2003) types of innovators (innovators, early adopters, early majority, late majority, and laggards) to determine who in your faculty is ready to lead others in implementing some of the Web 2.0 tools in this book.

- Ask one of your tech-savvy teachers to do a demonstration lesson for others at a faculty meeting. Alternatively, either you or your tech coordinator can offer to do a demonstration lesson for a specific grade level or department that is trying to integrate technology.
- Another evaluation tool for a good technology lesson can be found at the Teaching With Technology website http://128.148.108.120/media/bpinter/1163/elements.html.
- Offer incentives to groups of educators who propose new ways to collaborate in redesigning a content curricular unit by including technology in their plans. Schedule an opportunity to showcase and discuss their ideas.
- How well do your teacher evaluation skills work? Read this article, *Making Teacher Evaluations Work,* for ideas and a guide for new directions: http://www.educationworld.com/a_admin/admin/admin224.shtml.
- A resource worth checking out each week is the *Education World: School Administrators Channel*—a place for articles, links, and connections to others who have questions like you: http://www.educationworld.com/a_admin/.
- We also recommend reading:
  - Borthwick, A., & Pierson, M. (2008). *Transforming Classroom Practice: Professional Development Strategies.* Eugene, OR: International Society for Technology in Education.
  - Hall, D. (2008). *The Technology Director's Guide to Leadership.* Eugene, OR: International Society for Technology in Education.
  - Nelson, K. (2007). *Teaching in the Digital Age: Using the Internet to Increase Student Engagement and Understanding* (2nd ed.). Thousand Oaks, CA: Corwin.
  - Schamberg, C. (2007). *English Language Arts Units for Grades 9–12.* Eugene, OR: International Society for Technology in Education.
  - Thombs, M., Gillis, M., & Canestrari, A. (2008). *Using WebQuests in the Social Studies Classroom: A Culturally Responsive Approach.* Thousand Oaks, CA: Corwin.

Emerging Roles Within the Knowledge Community

Alan November

Chapter Map

TEACHERS AS DIGITAL IMMIGRANTS

In immigrant families, the children often learn the ways of the new culture—such as language, music, and slang—before the adults. It is not that the kids are smarter; it is just that they have less to give up. They are more willing and more motivated to learn because they want to fit in with their peers, with whom they are in constant contact at school. In many ways, teachers are like digital immigrants. They are not native born to this world of technology. Our students, especially our elementary students, are similar to second-generation immigrants. They have almost nothing to lose, and they see technology as an easy plaything, while adults might see it as a challenge. I have experienced what it is like to be an immigrant in my own land: school. Immigrants survive.

The real bottleneck to the creative use of technology is staff development. There are too many exciting technologies—web design, digital video editing, presentation tools, probes, content specific tools—and not enough time for teachers to learn them. To be realistic about managing the transition from the isolated to the connected classroom, we may have to let go of our traditional strategies. At the top of my list of letting go is the idea that teachers must learn new skills before the students. It would be folly not to take advantage of how fast students can learn technical skills and how willing they are to be helpful—as the relationship between Yves, whose story was discussed in the Preface, and me illustrates well.

Following his break-in at the computer lab, I asked Yves to teach me what he knew about programming. I can remember feeling overwhelmed with what looked to me like a combination of mathematics and a foreign language, but it was not quite like any math I had ever seen! Fortunately, Yves was patient and enjoyed his role as the teacher. He made programming fun and accessible. He taught me how to develop strategies for testing my own progress. What I thought would be laborious and boring turned into a learning adventure. I could really tame the machine! It was the beginning of what would be many role changes from the traditional teacher-student relationship for me. I was a student again. My student was my teacher.

Reverse Mentoring

Teachers do not need a lot of technical skills. Teachers need an ability to manage the use of many technologies in the classroom without having to know the technical details. Managing student brainpower is one of the most important survival skills for teachers. For example, requiring or expecting every teacher to learn how to design his or her own website is impractical today. But asking students in the class to learn how to design a website is feasible, fast, and inexpensive. How many fifth graders do you think will raise their hands when their teacher asks for help with building a world-class website? Teachers should maintain the role of publisher and editor in chief of the material on the class website. The essential skill is to know what to publish, when to publish, and how to help students make meaning of the feedback from people around the world. Of course, asking students for help is a skill that some teachers will have to polish or learn from scratch.

Building a Class Website

The teacher should act as publisher and editor in chief.
The teacher should practice reverse mentoring.
The essential skills to know include

- What to publish
- When to publish
- How to help students make meaning of feedback

The teacher should allow students to manage their own learning—up to a point.

To put reverse mentoring into practice, find two or three students who can serve as your mentors. Ask your students to teach you what they have been doing on the Internet, especially from home. If students have a favorite digital skill, such as video editing, web design, or working in Adobe Photoshop, ask them to give you an introductory lesson. Students often pick up skills outside of school that can add value to a teacher's understanding of the impact of technology on student motivation. Do not worry about actually learning the skill. It is more important to learn what students can do with the skill that might add value to their class work. For example, once you learn how easy it is for a student to do video editing, you might provide the student with the option of producing a video documentary instead of handing in a paper.

As more technology finds its way into the classroom, teachers are faced with the challenge and opportunity of giving up control of the traditional teaching/learning dynamic. I found that the more control I gave to the students to manage their own learning (up to a point), the more students excelled. Technology is not necessary for teachers to practice reverse mentoring, but it is a powerful catalyst for reshaping the prevailing dynamic with a dynamic that is better suited to today's environment.

HELP AND SUPPORT IN YOUR OWN BACKYARD

In the traditional classroom setting, teachers often find themselves iso-lated from their colleagues and the community during the school day. In many ways, teaching is a solitary job. While there is a tremendous amount of knowledge and wisdom within the profession, it can sometimes be very hard to access. Quite often, teachers in the same building are not aware of the unique skills and insights of one another.

The circumstances that have enforced this isolation are beginning to change because of the pressures and potential brought about by the digital world. Beyond school, the newly connected knowledge society increasingly requires a more flexible role for workers across many professions. Having knowledge is not enough anymore. Collaboration and sharing knowledge are the highly prized skills. This expectation of collaboration will eventually reach the teaching profession. Teachers will be valued for their ability to share their knowledge and solve problems about teaching and learning that an individual teacher could not solve alone. For example, as band-width increases and live video is installed, teachers will be able to share best practices as exemplified in their own classrooms with other educators.

Collegiality

As online learning explodes, more teachers build websites to support learning, and families gain more access to information about the progress of their children, collegiality will become more practical and necessary. Every teacher's best ideas can now be published so that other teachers and, in turn, their students, can benefit from them. If we expect students to be able to publish to a global audience, it is essential for teachers to model this same skill.

For reasons that once made sense, the organization of schools was designed in the mold of a highly controlled and departmentalized Industrial Age model. School organizations are filled with boundaries, such as departments and grades, that can impede the exchange of ideas and the development of innovation. The school leader's role is to make sure that these boundaries become permeable.

C. Edwards Deming, a leading proponent of the quality movement, taught that one of the very first things leaders can do to help colleagues adapt innovation is to honor them in their current paradigm (Rinehart, 1993). We need to honor the knowledge and wisdom of teachers. You will not find a more humble profession than teaching. It is time to celebrate the best practices of all teachers. Each school can use the web to share the powerful stories that represent teachers' experiences. On a wonderful site by the Advanced Learning Technologies in Education Consortia, at www.4teachers.org, teachers can share ideas they have that work and find ideas for "powering learning with technology."

Additionally, in many school districts across the United States and around the world, teachers are being given access to laptop computers and hand-held devices for their use both at school and at home. This gives teachers a chance to share with colleagues their ideas that work—through e-mail, blogs, wikis, and videoconferencing.

The Anonymous Reviewer

One of the most powerful and helpful online collegial relationships is that of the anonymous distant reviewer. Kathie English and Nancy Hoatson, from Aurora High School in Nebraska, connected their students to editors across the Internet. They learned that expanding student relationships with distant anonymous reviewers can be a powerful motivator for students to improve their writing. English and Hoatson explain on www.4teachers.org:

> The [online] forum encourages students to produce more text and their reviewers to comment more honestly. Each piece of writing is considered for its own merit with no regard to author status: economic, social, or academic. Due to this anonymity, authors [students] cannot blame criticism on outside factors; therefore, they tend to heed the suggestions made by reviewers and, as a result, improve their writing. Reviewers enjoy the distance as well and tend to give more honest responses than they might in face-to-face peer editing.

While English and Hoatson found editors and writers to provide assessment services, any two teachers can create an assessment partnership. When a teacher assesses student work from another's classroom, there can be a very positive impact on student motivation and quality. The role of the face-to-face teacher can switch from judge to student advocate, helping students to understand how to interpret the outside review. When students no longer worry about personal judgments from their own teacher, students are more willing to make mistakes and to accept criticism.

In addition, the concept of teachers who share the review of student work has enormous implications for professional growth. If teachers are trading assessment services, the comments of each partner teacher are bound to add depth to the knowledge base of the team. Staff development becomes a normal part of the ongoing team relationship.

An international teaming of a teacher in England with a teacher in Japan illustrates how teachers can share knowledge as part of the ongoing process of sharing student assessment. In this case, a British teacher needed help with assessing her students' haiku. The teacher in England searched the Internet for a teacher in Japan who was also teaching haiku. When the assessment came back from Japan, the teacher in England was surprised and enlightened. "Haiku has a philosophy of life-giving forms," the Japanese teacher commented. "Imagery in the poem is very important and must be consistent with the philosophy. Some images that your students are using are not appropriate for the haiku form." The British teacher had been teaching haiku for many years in a very prestigious high school, but the exchange of student work allowed her to deepen her own understanding of the subject.

Collaboration With Parents

An obvious resource for teacher support is a parent or guardian. The role of the family in the learning process is well researched. One of the most powerful technologies to promote collaboration between the home and school is video. Many schools are utilizing video production as a means of sharing student work with parents at home. Contrary to popular thought, a video camera is a more developmentally appropriate device for a primary student to show expression and communicate than a pencil. Many parents will watch videos of their kids in the comfort of their own homes. It would not be unusual for tapes or DVDs to be shared with grandparents and be reviewed again and again. This technology can give teachers a powerful tool for sharing and celebrating student projects and providing parents with insights into how their students learn. In some cases, parents will send in videos of their comments. This media can add a level of communication and understanding that paper does not provide. The home VCR or DVD player and the color TV are "sleeper" technologies. They are readily available, easy to use, inexpensive, and possibly the fastest and easiest way to improve learning. It is just that there is very little tradition of building strong collaborations between the home and school.

E-VENTURE: Dino Documentary

Purpose: to allow for creativity, expression, and connection among and between students in the primary grades and beyond

Investigation

1. Using the Internet, interviews with experts, print materials, and observation during field trips, students create a simple script for a dino documentary.

---

2. Kindergartners, first graders, and second graders will need assistance from adults to construct the script, which should be written out on cue cards for nonreaders using a mix of symbols, pictures, and words.

3. Students film the project, or projects, using a digital video camera. Students should be able to function as cinematographers with supervision and appropriate respect for the value and function of the equipment.

Presentation

1. The film can be played at open houses or curriculum nights and can be made available on a JPEG file on the class, school, or district website.

2. Teachers can coordinate an online film festival where films are viewed and critiqued by students from other parts of the state or country, or from another country.

Variation

1. While this technology is easy for younger students to employ, it works equally well for older students. They can create their own documentaries related to stream monitoring or other ecological projects, homelessness, education, volunteerism, "a day in the life of . . .," or any other appropriate topic.

2. Students may adapt fiction books to film production.

3. Older students studying foreign languages can serve as translators for the primary grade film projects by writing subtitles for the films that will be shown to non-English language audiences.

4. Students may be asked to dramatize an original piece of fiction that one or all of them has created.

BENCHMARKING EDUCATIONAL PRACTICE TO THE KNOWLEDGE COMMUNITY

In a recent conversation with high school students, they expressed a clear desire that their teachers understand the world outside of school. Knowing this, teachers may want to consider reading about topics outside of education to track developments in the knowledge society. An indirect way to look into the world outside of education is to read material written for that audience. Magazines such as *Fast Company* and *Red Herring* are filled with stories of real people building the digital economy and the trends that are reshaping the structure of many organizations.

> ### Business Technology Sources
>
> - Fast Company
>   www.fastcompany.com
>
> - Red Herring
>   www.redherring.com

Another way to benchmark against other industries that can be even more eye opening is to spend time with someone who works in a business that depends upon technology for its survival, such as banking, medicine, printing, or farming. Observing a friend or a parent of one of your students on the job gives you a direct link to information. See Figure 4.1 for a list of observation questions to ask during your visit.

Figure 4.1　On-the-Job Observation Questions

- What technologies are used?
- Could the business function without the technology?
- What sources of information are needed to manage the business?
- Does the business depend on the web for any part of its work?
- How do people work together?
- How is the quality of work measured?
- What are the essential skills in the business?
- Does the technology create opportunities for new relationships, services, or markets?
- Are there skills that we could be teaching in school to prepare students for this kind of work?
- Are there leadership skills that can be adopted by the school organization to improve the quality of work?
- Are there any specific problems that students can try to solve?

SHIFTING CONTROL

Armed with new knowledge from my benchmarking, I designed a course that would not teach any programming—heresy at the time—and instead would focus on new tools and problem solving. On the first day of the new course, I boldly announced to my students that they would be the ones who would come up with the problems for the course. My role would be to teach them how to use the technical tools and to help them define and develop solutions for their problems. When I was finished with my introductory remarks, I cheerfully invited the students to share examples of problems in the world that they would like to solve. No one moved, no hand was raised; it was as if I had asked them to be absolutely silent and still. Finally, there was movement. A female student sitting in the front row explained the appropriate roles to me. "Mr. November, you are the teacher and we are the students. You are supposed to give us the problems. It does not work the other way around." There it was, simple and clearly stated: the definition of the high school teacher-student relationship in three sentences. The teacher teaches and then the students are taught.

My request was counter to the culture of schooling. In retrospect, it was naïve. While students must be given the opportunity to solve real problems that have meaning to them, they cannot be left adrift without guidance in how to define problems and how to progress. If schools have conditioned students to see teachers as people who assume control for managing learning, then it is unfair to expect students to take the initiative with problem solving. The responsibility for learning must shift to the students if we expect them to solve real problems in and out of the classroom. While it is a struggle to redefine and unteach the traditional roles for both the students and teachers, the process of shifting control of who owns the problems can result in some of the most motivated and focused student work possible. It just takes a while to get started and a willingness to shift control of who manages learning from the teacher to the students.

This shift in control was realized by Mrs. Taylor, a middle school social studies teacher in Deerfield, Illinois, who wanted her students to deeply understand the issues involved in globalization. In the past, her students would have read articles and written reports (some found with a search engine on the Internet) to get all of the information they needed and to relay what they had learned. This year, her students used Skype to contact a worker in Chicago who lost his job to outsourcing. She then arranged a live conversation with a worker in China who gained a job that was lost in the United States. Her students' understanding of the issues extended beyond the story portrayed in words. Her students were more engaged to frame the questions and to debrief the meaning of globalization in terms of what happens to real people on opposite sides of the planet. An added bonus of the project is that these conversations were recorded and published on the class blog. Students and teachers studying globalization in England listened to these conversations and benefited from the work of the students in Chicago.

By allowing students to work with global partners in this way, teachers can empower students by teaching them how to seek answers to their own questions. As students grow older, teachers can teach them to do high-quality research for real clients. At the same time, we can link these authentic experiences to make learning standards real and exciting.

Real Problems

The teacher's emerging role in a classroom centered on solving real problems is to facilitate student discovery, to offer resources, and to ask timely questions that refine and extend student thinking. The teacher needs to identify, with student input, an ill-structured problem, and then establish guideposts to help students address and define that problem. Technology in its various forms and degrees cannot solve a problem absent human input. Technology can provide a means for several functions (see Figure 4.2).

Figure 4.2 What Technology Can Do

Technology can provide a means for

- Simplifying calculation—calculators and spreadsheets
- Accessing information—the Internet and e-mail correspondence with experts
- Producing data logs—probes and personal digital assistants (PDAs)
- Displaying findings—presentation software and websites
- Making long-distance people-to-people connections—telephone, fax, e-mail, videoconferencing, voice over IP

When technological tools used in the real world are put in the hands of students, those students can better see themselves as problem solvers and can better and more fully communicate their capacity to solve problems to the larger world community. By giving students access to powerful machines, a wide range of problems that would ordinarily be beyond the reach of students to solve can become achievable. The number of student projects adding value to the world is extensive and growing, from extending the longevity of blood plasma supplies by a New York city biology student, to applying systems thinking and calculus to design shopping malls by a San Francisco student, to the digital recordings of American Indian chants of the Southwest by a Red Rock, Oklahoma student. Technology does not replace the importance of the teacher, but rather extends the teacher's role to challenge students to exceed their own expectations. One of the highest forms of validating the importance of teachers is to have students apply what is learned in class in order to add value to the world.

Real problems exist in every subject taught. Each year, find one real problem that your students can help solve. The people who will benefit from student action and investigation into the real problem can be called *clients*. One of the most important skills to teach students is how to conduct the initial client interview. Many students expect that the adult will know exactly what they want to see in a project. This is usually not the case. Students must be prepared to lead the client interview with a set of core questions for a discussion that can generate a clear understanding of the scope of the project with realistic expectations (see Figure 4.3). It may be helpful to invite potential clients to come in to class and to have students conduct their interviews there.

Figure 4.3	Questions for the Client Interview

- What is the current project or problem to be solved?
- Who is involved, and what are their roles?
- Who can help contribute to the solution?
- What information sources are available for the project?
- Has anyone else tried to solve this problem?
- Is there a desired format for the final project (database, website, presentation)?
- How will the project be evaluated for success?

Teachers can use parent conferences as a time to ask parents to offer real problems that are aligned with curriculum and state standards. For example, a parent who is a police officer provided sample police reports of real accidents to the Algebra 1 class. The students measured skid marks on the road and used algebraic equations to calculate the speed of the car. The class took raw data from an accident scene and wrote a police report and submitted it via e-mail to the lieutenant for review. How motivated do you think high school freshmen are when their assignment is going to be reviewed by the police department?

RAISING EXPECTATIONS: STUDENTS AS KNOWLEDGE PRODUCERS

While students have to learn to take responsibility for inventing and managing their own work, teachers need to raise their expectations of what students can accomplish. Emerging technologies can fundamentally challenge the current (low) expectations that exist for many students. For example, the power of probes or computer-based labs (CBLs) generates real-time feedback in the form of graphs as real events happen. This demonstrates that technology can help raise the level of what students can learn. Educators such as Carolyn Staudt at the Concord Consortium, at http://www.concord.org, now realize that we can teach middle school students to apply concepts from calculus to everyday life, fourth- and fifth-grade students to examine rates of change, and second-grade students to explore models of heat transfer using data loggers. One of the major barriers to using technology well is that many of the expectations for student success were set when the dominant media was paper and chalk. Paper is a very powerful medium, but it is not dynamic and it does not provide the sound, animation, real-time feedback, and capacity for continuous expansion of global relationships. Powerful machines allow for more dynamic teaching, and best of all, perhaps, they allow students to show what they know in nontraditional and nonlinear ways that more closely approximate the skills they will need to be successful in the adult world.

To illustrate, a student named Colleen taught me to expand my expectations of what young adults are willing to do in order to solve a real problem—especially if the solution adds value to the community. The clients are a social service agency and individual disabled persons.

Colleen's Story

Colleen's Health Care Database Project

By the time Colleen was enrolled in a course I was teaching, she was a veteran at avoiding schoolwork. In her, I saw a student slipping through the cracks. Somewhere along the line, I learned that someone in her family was physically disabled, and I knew that a local social service agency needed some help with organizing services for the community's disabled population. I invited one of the social workers to come to class to present that organization's real problem. The problem was providing the handicapped community with access to information. While there were a number of services available for the area's disabled population, potential clients' awareness of the services was limited. Sure enough, this problem touched Colleen and inspired her to work harder than she had ever worked before. With the guidance of a local agency, Colleen decided to create a database to list all of the recreational services available for the handicapped population in the greater Boston area.

Colleen's project grew so large that she had to enroll the volunteer help of her friends. Now there were students coming into the computer lab after school who were not taking the course, and they were willing to learn how to use a database to produce this knowledge product. The final project included the services of nearly 100 agencies in eastern Massachusetts.

Colleen deserved to be proud of her accomplishments. Ultimately, her work was recognized by a team of professional health care providers who asked if they could pay her to continue to expand her work. She was asked to train adults to expand her database. She refused to accept the payment. Her work was important to her, and she politely explained that this was her project and that she did not start it to earn money. She volunteered to come to school during that summer to continue her work. There is no way that I would have predicted at the beginning of the year that she would show that kind of personal commitment to solving a problem. I had to learn to recalibrate my understanding of student motivation. When the control of managing work shifts to the student, expectations need to be raised.

Colleen also taught me that students who are labeled as failures can have the integrity to define, manage, and persist at solving a complex problem—even when the design parameters are constantly shifting. Although Colleen never did well on the written tests that I gave in class, she had thrown herself into the practical and important work of creating a database. Through this experience, Colleen became a different person; she was motivated and actually glad to come to school.

Promoting Student Responsibility for Learning

As Colleen's story shows, it is important for students to share in identifying the problem. Students must have a sense of owning the problem rather than seeing it as an assignment from the teacher. Teachers can certainly help students shape a problem and identify resources and tools. Figure 4.4 shows how teachers can facilitate student acquisition of the skills necessary to deal with the rigors of real-world problems.

| **Figure 4.4** | Skills to Solve Real Problems |

Skill Needed	Teacher Facilitation
Communication	Role playing on video to allow for self- and peer-evaluation. Practice with written communication for inquiry and analysis.
Confidence	Access to feedback from outside reviewers (students, teachers, clients) to allow students to broaden their self-perceptions by seeing how their work is received by a potentially global audience.
Critical thinking	Teach students the grammar of the Internet and the critical thinking strategies necessary to evaluate information they encounter through their exploration and inquiry (see Chapter 1).
Interpreting data	Facilitate interactions and activities that allow students to collect their own data, evaluate, present, and draw conclusions from PDAs, probes, and large-scale student-conducted surveys.
Collaboration	Teach the project management skill of organizing and assigning work to different members of a team. Collaboration is an essential skill for our emerging

(Continued)

| **Figure 4.4** | (Continued) |

Skill Needed	Teacher Facilitation
	knowledge society. Big projects, such as Colleen's database, require many different skills, from graphic design to communications with clients to database programming.
Organization	Provide guidance with establishing realistic expectations of project management, including a clear description of the project, timelines, job descriptions, and communication between team members. New and evolving project management can help with this.

Drawing on areas of student interest promotes fully engaged learning, as Colleen's story demonstrates. She was passionate about issues related to people with disabilities because of her personal experience. Likewise, using media that students are interested in adds another compelling dimension. Video recording is a good example. It is amazing what students are able to do when given a video camera or a tape recorder and allowed to use these tools in their research. When students create a video of an environmental problem they are studying or record interviews with those affected by the problem, it can create great excitement in a project and add to the real-world skills they learn in the process.

Colleen's experience creating the database not only helped her become a better student, it also helped her contribute to society. Students, young and old, have an unlimited capacity to add value to their communities when given the opportunity. One of the most powerful uses of communications technologies is to connect students to real clients who have real problems to solve. In Madison, Wisconsin, and in St. Louis Park Schools in Minnesota, children in the fourth grade use the Internet to explore their communities and to compile research updates for their own state legislators. These students are doing more than taking part in the educational standard of learning how state government works. They are also directly participating as citizens in state government. Within Colleen's story is the blueprint for a learning environment that promotes student assumption of responsibility for learning (see Figure 4.5).

| **Figure 4.5** | Promoting Responsibility |

- Encourage and expect students to construct their own knowledge.
- Allow students to work with their preferred media.
- Choose real problems that are ill-structured with more than one answer.

- Have students add value to their community and the world.
- Ask students to develop a team approach.
- The teacher takes on the role of collaborator.
- Publish results of student inquiries.
- Link problem-solving skills to standards.

E-VENTURE: Connecting With Congress

Purpose: to facilitate student connections to the real world by allowing for access to real problems and avenues for addressing those problems

Investigation

Using the Thomas Legislative Information on http://thomas.loc.gov (a service of the Library of Congress), or simply by reading the newspaper, the teacher and/or the students can identify current pending legislation that has the potential to affect them.

In small groups, students create a letter to send to their Representatives and Senators asking about their position on the pending bill.

The following are good sites to begin researching legislative contacts:

- U.S. House of Representatives, at www.house.gov
- U.S. Senate, at www.senate.gov
- Open Congress, at www.opencongress.org

The letters should include offers to help with any "on the ground" research and an invitation to visit the class either in person or via videoconference.

The students should track the progress of the bill frequently. The Congressional Record can be accessed from 1994 through the present at http://www.gpoaccess.gov/crecord/index.html.

Presentation

The students can post legislative updates on their class website with links to the House and Senate sites.

Variation

The above can be done on a more local level as well. The local mayor, school board president, city or town council members, or state representatives can be contacted for local matters.

Linking With Legislators

Read the Linking with Legislators page at http://alpha.musenet.org:81/community/call_stories/story_madison.html (created by the Madison Metropolitan School District in Madison, Wisconsin) to read about the report that the students in Mrs. Walser's fourth-grade class researched and authored for their state senator, Fred Risser.

Senator Fred Risser of Wisconsin needed basic research for his pending bill about regulating the sale of cigarettes in vending machines.

The list of skills for this one project is impressive: writing, Internet research, community interviews, and mapping.

Best of all, these students learned that they can directly participate in the real work of their communities.

The provided content supports a unit on drugs and tobacco.

As it turns out, the bill did not pass through the senate. However, any lobbyist will tell you that failure on the first attempt is an important lesson in how state government works.

MANAGING FEAR

As is happening in the broader world of business, information and communication technologies will enable a massive shift of control from the organization to the customer. In the case of education, the shift in control will be from the organization (the school or district) to the client (the learner and the learner's family). It is only natural that a shift of control creates fear and anxiety. Trepidation and fear attend any change, good or bad. The change that comes with the increased and more pervasive use of technology is not what elicits the most fear, although many might think so. The real fear lies in people's hesitancy about the changing roles necessitated by the meaningful use of the technology. It is essential that the fears and anxiety felt by those who are affected by the change not be ignored, but instead be confronted, so that the potential inherent in the change can also be fully explored and realized.

A wonderful activity called *Worst Fears/Best Hopes* can help all teachers face fears and articulate hope at the same time. An individual or group can complete a list of worst fears and then a list of best hopes. See Figure 4.6 for an example of a Worst Fears/Best Hopes list. When in a group, discuss the fears first. Leaders should support and validate every fear and talk about strategies that can be used to minimize realization of the fears. When possible, make the connection between a fear, such as "the loss of social skills," to a hope, such as "we can now connect more students to people around the world." In this way, a map of moving from fear to hope can be generated. The connected lists can become an important document that can be revisited every year to make sure that the fears of the faculty are not coming true. Research suggests that adults will attend a workshop and listen for confirmation of their fears. If fears are articulated, validated, and discussed, adults are in a better position to learn new skills.

Figure 4.6	Worst Fears/Best Hopes

Worst Fears

- o Less physical activity
- o Demand for increased instant gratification
- o E-mail pressures for quick responses that may lack careful contemplation
- o Blurring the lines between professional and private life
- o Rising costs for uses of technology
- o PC use increases the expectation for perfection
- o Addiction to use of technology
- o Increased accentuation between haves and have-nots
- o Increase in destructive hacking
- o Dealing with stress and mental breakdowns as a result of information overload
- o Increased feeling of being less socially active and more isolated
- o Danger in the abundance of inappropriate material available
- o No privacy and a loss of personal identity
- o Loss of the capacity to judge information and an increase in deferring to the computer
- o A loss of caring and sense of community
- o PC use may create a loss of reality
- o A decrease in interpersonal relationships
- o A loss of enjoyment in the simple pleasures
- o A loss of family values and a dehumanization of one's world
- o Computers could control humans
- o Not being able to keep up with information and people
- o Alienation of our youth
- o Others may be in a position to control our future
- o Becoming dependent on technology
- o Colleges may become obsolete

Best Hopes

- o All will learn better, faster, and more
- o Technology will be the equalizer regardless of social status and income
- o People will work more efficiently and have more leisure time
- o Increased exploration of micro and macro worlds
- o Increased opportunities to celebrate our students' work with their communities
- o Teachers will share ideas and knowledge

(Continued)

Figure 4.6	(Continued)

o Families will be more connected to their children's learning
o Students will develop more sensitivity to people around the world
o Expensive educational material will become available to all learners
o Students will be able to access courses beyond their own communities
o Better travel opportunities to more countries for our children
o Supportive society
o Increase in adaptive technologies resulting in no disabilities
o Expedite tasks with minimal errors
o Greater productivity
o Time savings
o More comprehensive learning opportunities
o Increased communications
o No more drudge work

PROFESSIONAL GROWTH OPPORTUNITY

Relate and Reflect on Chapter 4

The following questions are intended to further promote discussion about learning in planning boards, department meetings, school board meetings, and inservice preparation. They do not require any technological skill or expertise to answer. Space is provided after each question so that you may begin to answer them here. Remember that there is no right or wrong answer.

• Which collegial relationships add value to student work or to the knowledge and skill of the teacher?

• Can teachers within the district form new partnerships based on sharing work?

• Are there potential partnerships that can be nurtured beyond the school district?

• What are the new roles of teachers and students?

• How much control can be shifted from teachers to students to manage learning?

• What are the emerging collaborative relationships for teachers?

Part II

Technology-Powered Classrooms

Understanding Youth and Digital Media

Jessica K. Parker

Today's student is likely to engage daily in numerous literate practices, from print to film to multimodal forms such as websites and video games. She lives in a media saturated world and averages nearly six and a half hours a day with media.[1] She is a media multitasker, watching television as she instant messages and completes her homework. When she plays video games, she usually works as a member of a team and with intense concentration even on these long, time-consuming projects. She searches for information on the Internet, displays herself on myspace.com, and takes pictures on her cell phone, then chooses between a number of media sharing sites in which to upload them. She can simultaneously be an actor, director, editor, and publisher with the movie software that came with her computer. She expects her teachers to guide her through this information era, not dictate "correct" answers to rote questions that Google can provide in seconds through multimodal means, e.g., text, video, and digital images.

For educators, this student is a symbol of ongoing change in which new media technologies offer emergent modes of communication, learning, and play. *Teaching Tech-Savvy Kids: Bringing Digital Media Into the*

---

1. I created this student based on research from A Kaiser Family Foundation Study (2005) titled, *Generation M: Media in the Lives of 8–18 Year-Olds.* Download the study at http://www.kff.org/entmedia/7251.cfm.

Classroom, Grades 5–12 addresses how new media technologies are alter-ing and expanding literate practices among our everyday acts of commu-nication, our informal learning environments and our leisure activities. We are living in both an exciting and nerve-wracking time as notions such as space and time shift, issues such as portability and interconnect-edness become widespread and standardized, and long-standing divisions between private and public spheres are blurred (Burbules & Callister, 2000). These issues, as well as the experiences of the student described above, push educators to question how to think about the changes hap-pening beyond school walls and how these changes affect school-based learning. The answers to these questions cannot be to ignore these changes or to be satisfied with superficial solutions such as wired class-rooms or additional hardware. When educators discuss and analyze emer-gent modes of communication, learning, and play, we are forced to rethink long-standing practices and relations within schools.

TOUGH QUESTIONS EDUCATORS MUST ADDRESS

One of our goals as educators in understanding youth and digital media should be to frame our discussion around learning, literacy and knowl-edge rather than merely concentrating on the integration of and access to technological tools. For this reason I believe educators need to ask them-selves and discuss collectively some tough questions:

1. What does learning look like in the 21st century?

2. What does literacy look like in the 21st century?

3. What is knowledge in the 21st century? (Or what does it mean to *know* something in our mediated culture?)

These are three questions we must ponder, rethink, and explore within ourselves, with colleagues and parents, and with students. Pedagogy, curriculum, and assessments are important philosophical issues and determining factors within education, but the most basic issues we as teachers need to address are our core assumptions around learning, literacy, and knowledge and the relationship between the three. The tech-nological changes that are currently taking place—and will continue to do as they have throughout human history—are reshaping everyday practices and relations. As teachers we must try to understand this phe-nomenon in order to grow professionally, to continue to have influence over our teaching environments, and to support student learning. This book will assist you in understanding these changes, help you adopt some of these new media practices as your own, and present tangible ways for you to incorporate these issues into your teaching. Additionally, the book can help stimulate your thinking around learning, literacy, and knowledge in the 21st century.

Addressing these three questions will test our ability as educators to see past our training, to see past our own experiences with technology and to see past the fear and uncertainty of institutional change in order to create learning environments and interventions based on the most recent and the most informed research on youth. It is pertinent to discuss education and schooling in the 21st century, for our schools are neither situated in a vacuum nor immune to changes and conditions impacting the rest of our lives. Historically the educational system in the United States has not been prone to change, and for administrators and teachers to offer competitive, engaging classrooms, we need to account for the massive technological changes currently taking place. This is not meant to scare but to motivate us. The chapters in this book bring together the latest research on youth and digital media and offer educators opportunities to understand and explore this relationship both personally and professionally. If we are working and teaching in an institution still wedded to a dated vision of schooling, we have the ability to learn from research, ask ourselves tough questions, and strive to create learning environments in which a 21st century student is entitled.

I realize these questions do not have easy *answers* and one of the arguments of this book is to move away from an outdated school-based view that there is "one right answer" or one "right" way to learn. We must shift our understanding of learning and literacy as:

- *Broadly* conceived and not easily defined or standardized
- *Complex* and not based on effortless transmission
- *Socially and ideologically constructed* and not merely neutral entities (Street, 1995)
- *Inclusive* of the intellectual funds students gain at home and from youth culture (Moll, Amanti, Neff, & Gonzalez, 1992)
- *Changing* over time and not limited to static definitions

When we shift our understandings of learning and literacy to encompass these characteristics, educators can come to view new media through a relational lens and avoid discussions in which new media technologies are presented as an either-or proposition.

Unfortunately the current discourse around youth and new media technologies is based on extreme views. One extreme suggests that kids' use of digital media is dumbing down an entire generation, while the other side suggests that school is now irrelevant and should be replaced with kids directing their own learning online. Educators cannot continue to get caught in a polarized debate only to judge if school-based learning is better or worse than informal learning. This dichotomy will not allow us to initiate a dialogue regarding new media; it will only condone or condemn such learning experiences. Starting with three tough questions about the state and nature of learning, literacy, and knowledge in the 21st century can open up new spaces for discussion, queries, insights, and change.

WHAT IS NEW MEDIA?

What is new media or digital media? *New media* is an umbrella term used to describe technologies of the late 20th century and that are *new*. This currently includes but is not limited to the Internet, cellular phones, interactive television, computer games, and virtual worlds. New media is relative though; radio was considered new in the early 1900s, although it was not considered new in the early 2000s. As new technologies are integrated into our daily lives, they become part of our everyday experiences and, as the years go by, are viewed as commonplace and unoriginal—almost invisible as a technology, e.g., writing, pencils, paper, and chalkboards.

Adding the term *digital* to the phrase digital media signals a form of content that is created and distributed electronically based on binary codes. Digital media is currently the predominant form of new media. Due to its digital code, content such as a digital video or e-mail can be edited, shared, and even in some cases—such as in virtual world—interactive. Social networks and websites in which people can read and generate content are possible due to digital computers. But I do not want to simply focus on a laundry list of digital media nor do I want to focus on technical definitions. For teachers it is important to concentrate on how new media technologies are being integrated into our daily lives. This includes how our cell phones, our laptops, our iPods, our video game players, and even our digital video cameras get woven into the ways we develop and maintain our relationships, negotiate our social status and our ability to communicate. From this **relational perspective** (Burbules, & Callister, 2000) we can discuss students' participation with digital media including how they produce and distribute media and engage in appropriating, recirculating, archiving, and annotating media content in powerful new ways (Jenkins, 2006). By discussing how new media influences our lives, teachers can come to appreciate how learning, literacy, and knowledge in new media environments differ from traditional school-based experiences.

But the terms *new media* and *digital media* should not imply that all forms of mediation are new. For instance, students seem to be addicted to text messaging with their cell phones, but writing is not a new medium. What's new is the fact that we can write to each other on our cell phones, since the telephone was previously limited to verbal communication. When I was growing up in the 1980s, the phone was something I used while at home. I was delighted when my parents finally bought a cordless phone so I could talk to friends in the comfort of my own room. Yet the cordless phone created tension and often times disagreements between my parents and me: when I was in my room with the door locked, my parents were less likely to monitor my conversations with peers and evaluate my overall time on the phone and ostensibly away from my homework. So new media can affect communicative practices and relations. Currently the age of kids who have their own cell phones keeps getting younger and younger and they often carry them at all times (and seem to be texting all the time) even though they are still using language and words to communicate.

And don't think these text messages are unsophisticated. In fact, they are just the opposite. Christo Sims, a doctoral candidate at University of California, Berkeley's School of Information, studies how kids use technologies such as cell phones and instant messenger as part of their everyday lives and that using lower and upper case letters, misspellings, and the casual appearance of a text message can often be quite purposeful (personal communication, December 12, 2007). From a teacher's perspective, text messages can appear sloppy and rushed. It might seem as if the student may not know how to spell or rarely puts energy into composing a legitimate sentence. Here is our (adult) mistake. We want to judge our students' text messages based upon standards for written English. In fact, we should take the perspective that our students are communicating much more about themselves than just their mastery of English (Baron, 2008).

Christo Sims (personal communication, December 12, 2007) argues that the casual, even sloppy, appearance can be seen as an attempt to explore social connections without exposing, too quickly, the degree to which they are emotionally invested in the outcome. He draws a comparison between such writing practices and that of youth fashion. In both cases the display is highly crafted and yet done in a way that hopes to suggest casualness and ease; as many youth say to suggest "no big deal." For youth it can be scary to put oneself out there when trying to develop friendships and, as such, youth often appear casual as a way to hide the degree to which they are invested in their friendships. Thus they slowly feel out the other person. They get to know each other by writing short messages, ones where what is said can be carefully controlled. Remember when we were teenagers and there were high stakes involved with making new friendships, being accepted by peers, publicly humiliated, or scrutinized? Those days were potentially horrible, and today's youth use text messaging to allow conversations to develop more slowly and allow rejection to be carried out more silently. Essentially sloppy text messages may be a way for youth to protect themselves.

> **MYTH:** Today's high school students should be called the "look at me" generation. They are self-absorbed, superficial, narcissistic teens who are always online for no apparent reason. Their behavior is baffling.
>
> **REALITY:** Our students' forms of expression have changed from when we were kids. Once we come to understand how our students are using digital media, then their behavior becomes incredibly familiar. They may be online and texting all the time, but they are actively working to promote a social identity and, of course, maintain their friendships.
>   For a video interpretation of this "reality," go to YouTube and watch "Are Kids Different Because of Digital Media?" from the MacArthur Foundation: (http://tiny.cc/teachtech_1_1).

At the most basic level, today's students' ability to communicate and hang out with one another looks different from our educational vantage point and may even appear like a waste of time or unproductive and does not equate with *real* learning. The questions and concerns around their communication practices are understandable. Hopefully after reading this book, today's teenagers will look less like *failures* and more like typical teenagers who are interesting in dating, flirting, having fun, and creating and reinforcing their own creative youth culture. As today's students develop a sense of self and identity, they become heavily invested in establishing and preserving relationships with peers; however, the way they go about maintaining their relationships just looks different from previous generations. Although these communication patterns may feel foreign and off-putting, the main thing to remember is that their forms of communication are often based on how they want to present themselves to other teenagers.

KEY CHARACTERISTICS OF NEW MEDIA

I was fortunate enough to be a collaborator on a research project titled, "Kids' Informal Learning with Digital Media: An Ethnographic Investigation of Innovative Knowledge Cultures." This project was funded by a grant from the John D. and Catherine T. MacArthur Foundation and jointly carried out by researchers from U. C. Berkeley and the University of Southern California. One of the goals of the project was to put current academic research on the learning and new media practices of youth into the hands of classroom teachers and educators. As such, this book draws extensively from the three-year ethnography of the "Kids' Informal Learning with Digital Media" project and represents the most current instantiation of research on youth new media practices. I also drew from other research projects from the MacArthur Foundation and educational leaders in the field of new media and learning. Thus, each chapter includes stories and quotes from interviews and written materials from various sources.

From this broad research corpus, it becomes apparent that new media environments foster and support a *community of learners*, a shared culture of participation in which youth contribute their knowledge of the world and simultaneously demonstrate a keen sense of creativity within these mediated experiences. In these new media environments, youth are usually invested in *friendship-driven* and *interest-driven practices* where peer-based learning is the norm (Ito et al., 2008). According to Ito et al., friendship-driven practices of youth are based on the "day-to-day negotiations with friends and peers" (p. 9). These negotiations take place between age-based friends and peers from school, religious groups, sports, and other local activity groups. Ito et al. argue that these local friendship groups, from which youth navigate affiliations, friendships, and romantic partners, reflect their lives online. So a student's friend and peer group at school (or other local activity groups) is most likely to be the primary source for the student's friends' list on social network sites such as MySpace and Facebook.

Interest-driven practices, according to the authors, place "specialized activities, interests, or niche and marginalized identities first" (Ito et al., 2008, p.10). Hence, *friendship* is not necessarily the driving force behind the formation of these peer networks rather the specific interest is foremost. For instance, digital video (Chapter 3) production and online role playing are popular interests in which youth can pursue self-directed learning, develop online friendships and affiliations, and gain recognition. These specialized interests are the impetus for an online social group to come together (Ito et al., 2008).

CHARACTERISTICS OF NEW MEDIA ENVIRONMENTS

A community of learners usually includes:

- Peer-based learning (Ito et al., 2008; Jenkins et al., 2006)
- Collaboration
- Creativity
- Interest-driven practices (Ito et al., 2008)
- Friendship-driven practices (Ito et al., 2008)

Peer-based learning is a common characteristic of new media environments. In these mediated settings, peer feedback and critique are highly prized. Although these environments are usually informal and less structured than school-based settings, a culture of shared participation helps to nurture a sense of membership and identity; thus youth can become heavily invested and committed to sharing their creative efforts and resources and providing feedback and critique to peers. Specifically in interest-driven settings, self-motivated learners can observe and communicate with people engaged in the same interests (Ito et al., 2008). As a result, youth can learn skills, receive recognition for their work, gain status as experts, and promote an ongoing identity based on a shared interest. In friendship-driven settings, youth can learn cultural norms of online interaction and gain valuable and sometimes painful lessons in growing up (Ito et al., 2008).

The characteristics of new media environments are ripe for integrating into the classroom as they foster engaging, student-centered learning experiences. Although I have intentionally separated each chapter into a discussion about a specific medium or media, these characteristics are the threads that weave the chapters of this book together to create a snapshot of youth and their new media practices: In Chapter 2, Christo Sims highlights Lynn—a young girl who is home-schooled—and her friendship-driven practices on a social network site that allow her to stay connected to her current group of friends from church and the local area; in Chapter 3, Patricia G. Lange details the story of Wendy who uses her interest in documentary video to engage in the civic issue of maintaining and enjoying local facilities such as parks; in another chapter, C. J. Pascoe chronicles the story of Clarissa, an avid writer and reader who finds an online writing community in which to create fabulous fictional stories and receive insightful feedback from peers. These examples and the other research-based Stories from the Field demonstrate that teenagers, when given the opportunity to pursue their interests in a communal space and receive support and feedback from peers, are hungry for chances to express themselves in creative ways.

Educators have an opportunity to tap into this hunger in the form of a community of learners, peer collaboration and feedback and interest-based subject matter. Our classrooms can be sites in which collaboration is demonstrated through sharing knowledge, creativity is demonstrated through production and publication, and students are asked to respond to peers with authentic feedback and critique. Teachers do not necessarily need to rely on the latest and most expensive technology to incorporate the key characteristics of digital media into their classrooms. It is feasible to foster a classroom environment based on a community of learners, peer collaboration and feedback, and creativity without the help of the latest and most expensive technology. Educators do not have to get weighed down by a need to adopt technology at a record pace. Instead, start with the assumption that youth culture and its new media practices are a point for learning, discovery, and interest-based pursuits in which youth are agents in their own education. From this vantage point, it can become much easier to find a balance between integrating characteristics of new media environments into the curriculum and incorporating technology into classrooms.

WHAT TEACHERS CAN GET OUT OF THIS BOOK

Although Christo Sims's insights into youth and their text messaging exchanges are interesting, how can teachers benefit from this book? What can teachers get out of a book that focuses on digital media practices? There are several answers to these questions. First and unfortunately, there remains a gap between our students' participation with new media in school and outside of school. If many of our students are engaging in new forms of play, new online communities, and new types of communication, these technological distinctions are important for teachers to understand. This book will assist you in adopting and converting these new relationships with new media into your personal and professional lives and help you bridge this gap and discuss with your students the digital era and its impacts on the ways in which we live.

Second, our jobs as teachers are drastically improved if we can come from a perspective that understands the behaviors of our students. If all we see from our students are behaviors that appear foreign or are prohibited by the school, e.g., cell phones and texting, then we are missing out on myriad ways to connect with our students and their youth culture. I am not suggesting that teachers adopt youth culture as their own. Rather, I am suggesting that making a conscious effort to empathize with life for today's teenagers is a prerequisite for good teaching.

Third, we are currently living in a digital age and there is new affiliation for, and new meaning associated with, geek status. It's now extremely cool to be a geek. To "geek out" is to "dive into a topic or talent" as Ito et al. (2008, p. 2) describe it. For youth, to engage interest-driven practices is to throw themselves into open-ended projects that are time consuming and focused on gaining deep knowledge and expertise within a specific area. While providing a social space with access to peer support and feedback, these interest-based practices also promote self-directed learning (Ito et al., 2008). Interest-driven engagements provide educators with examples of how youth geek out, and for educators looking for ways to motivate students, these insights are invaluable.

Fourth, Henry Jenkins (2006), a media educator, suggests that we need adults to help mentor and guide teens with their media-laden experiences. He is not advocating for a surveillance culture. Rather, Jenkins suggests that there are ethical concerns when chatting online or posting a video of one's self and adults, such as teachers, can assist teenagers in this uncharted territory. Additionally, youth can assist adults in their quest to understand new media and participatory culture. Thus, there is a need for cross-generational perspectives when discussing new media environments.

By focusing on new media practices, teachers can harness the communicative practices of youth within the classroom. Read how Maryanne Berry uses ***instant messaging***, or ***IMing*** in her twelfth-grade English class.

A TEACHER'S PERSPECTIVE

Online Conversations Support Student Engagement With Literature

By Maryanne Berry, English Teacher

As educators, we generally assume that the incessant texting, messaging, and e-mailing that students conduct distracts from learning. But what if this fast paced style of communication could be used to foster conversations that supported learning? About five years ago, I decided to experiment by assigning online conversations in response to an independent reading project on contemporary novels. For years I had assigned my Advanced Placement Literature and Composition students reader response journals as a way of following students' progress through their books. While reading their chosen novels, twelfth graders would periodically jot down questions, predictions, observations and insights. They would copy powerful passages from the text and analyze them. Some of the journals had a kind of "canned" quality; the predictions were safe, the interpretations bland. Sometimes I suspected that students used supplementary sources in order to fake their way through the process. Though students exchanged journals in class with peers who had read the same book, the conversations generated by these exchanges lacked the liveliness one experiences when reading a book with someone equally engaged. A student whose journal was weak might learn something by reading stronger writing but when she went back to the book after class would she have been given the support she needed to engage more confidently with the novel? Could the interest of the struggling reader be sustained?

I told the students that they were welcome to form their own groups (of two to four people) but that I wanted all groups to be coed. I'd read a little research about the differences in the way boys and girls interacted in online settings that suggested that all male groups might be less successful than mixed or female groups and I also wanted students to extend a bit beyond their single gender friendships to include students with whom they had not previously worked. Once the groups were formed, each member was responsible for researching book reviews in order to propose a novel to the group. This part of the project, though time consuming, allowed students to discuss the kinds of books they enjoyed and to acquaint them with the process of researching various media in order to discover acclaimed contemporary fiction. Students ultimately selected novels and set reading schedules that would allow them to meet the goal of completing their reading within the time frame of the quarter semester.

After reading a designated number of pages, they chose either to e-mail journal responses to one another or to meet online to discuss their reading using an IM or chat room program. All groups were required to respond to their books a minimum of four times and to submit the transcripts to me. I read the transcripts and asked questions and made comments that I hoped would provoke further thought and analysis. A few class periods were devoted to discussing the critiques I provided and pursuing discussions generated in the online sessions.

Seven of the 10 groups chose instant messaging as their chief mode of response. The dialogue texts that they produced were generally longer than those who contributed e-mailed journal responses. In a few cases, students who instant messaged were able to code their responses by the minute of each exchange and I was surprised to find that several groups would meet as long as an hour at a time. Transcripts of those students who opted to instant message revealed lively exchanges and while there were digressions—mostly about homework—students stayed largely on track.

With those who instant messaged, it was easy to see how one student's ideas influenced another's; the exchanges were lively, sometimes antagonistic or erratic, punctuated with "lol" the term for "laughing out loud." The e-mailed journal (e-journal) responses were more deliberative. Students often responded to each other's points specifically, giving the exchanges a dialogic quality. One drawback, however, was that the first sender's responses seemed to prompt his peers to respond only to the issues he generated. Though the writers of e-journals made reference to specific aspects of the novels they read, the structured nature of the "paragraph response" demanded that students develop a "take" on a character, event, or description, so that the journals did little to reveal questions or misunderstandings. Instant messaged dialogic texts created a different structure, the screen became a space where students could talk/write in a free flowing negotiation their interpretations of text. The e-mailed journal responses resembled short written letters between readers, while the instant messaging resembled spoken conversations.

(Continued)

(Continued)

While e-journal accounts read much like other assignments submitted for a grade, transcripts of the instant messaged dialogue offer greater insight into reading as a social process as it unfolds over time. I noticed a number of interesting features of students' digitally mediated experience. First, it is interesting to note that the students, while not close friends, seemed very natural in their exchange; the transcript suggests that the exchange was lively and convivial. Second, students used the process of creating a dialogue to reveal both their understanding and their questions about the book they read. Finally, they moved from character analysis of the protagonist, a low level of interpretation, through empathetic and personal responses, until they arrived at more abstract and complex understanding of the novel's central questions.

In all online conversations students complemented one another's understanding and took turns leading each other. Together they constructed a process of shared questioning, similar in style to the one we practiced in our English class, a kind of spiraling activity mediated by the novel they read and their written responses to each other's thoughts. Both the affordances and constraints of instant messaging shaped the ways that they responded to each other. The intimacy of the virtual "space" in which instant messaging is conducted created an opportunity for my students to demonstrate aspects of their learning rarely witnessed in classroom settings. The transcripts revealed both students as actively engaged in making meaning of the shared experiences of reading and writing.

Teachers need to investigate the possible uses of online communication rather than dismiss them out of hand. I have facilitated this project over the last five years, sometimes modifying it, in order to discover how it can be most effective with a particular group. The instant message program was not devised with literary analysis in mind. In order to be successful using instant messaging to discuss a text, students need to bend the rules of the program; they need to slow down the rate of exchange and allow each other to complete their thoughts. The results offer us an unusual and telling look at a process of communication that clearly supports learning. We owe it to ourselves and our students to encourage them to think with the tools they love to use.

Issues to Consider:

- Though this project focuses on works of literature, any work of length might be an apt substitute for novels in an online conversation project. Students appreciated the support of the members of their group in meeting reading deadlines. One student told me, "I kept up with the reading because I didn't want to let my group down."
- Students can often suggest methods for convening in an online setting. Both Google (googlegroups.com) and Facebook (facebook.com) offer free tools for forming collaborative groups.
- Teachers can rely on instant messaging to foster both free-form and directed (the teacher offers guiding questions) discussions. In this manner, virtual spaces are created for collaborative learning that can continue outside the classroom.

This book is designed to give teachers access to the latest research about what kids are doing in their everyday lives with digital media, discuss potential implications for how it can connect to classroom practices and also give teachers a space to begin what can only be considered a long and engaging discussion about bringing new media into the secondary classroom. The point of the book is not to prescribe "cut-n-paste" activities for teachers to integrate into their classrooms but to really grapple with serious technological and communicative changes that deeply affect how and what students learn in school. This book is first and foremost a philosophical discussion regarding education in the 21st century.

There is a tendency among classroom teachers to argue, "Just tell me how to weave these technologies into my curriculum. I don't have the time to analyze and understand technological and communicative change." Here is the problem. We are acting as if these technologies are neutral, somehow just inconsequential tools to be used to further instruction when in fact these technologies are used as socio-cultural forms and connected to larger cultural contexts (Buckingham, 2007). Buckingham argues digital media

> provide new ways of mediating and representing the world and of communicating. . . . The problem with most educational uses of such media is that they continue to be regarded as merely instrumental means of delivering information—in effect, as neutral tools or "teaching aides." (p. 145)

Thus, it is expected that readers of this book are not solely looking for activities to insert into their curriculum or new *tools* to assist instruction. It isn't as easy as *insert technology, out comes student learning.* Instead, my hope is that teachers will commit themselves to understanding the numerous ways youth are participating and learning with new media and, at the same time, how new media are essentially altering our understanding of learning, literacy, and knowledge.

6

"Short"

Social Networking in a Low–Tech Environment

William Kist

> Some teachers work in schools with very little technology. And some teachers work in schools that have lots of technology but choose not to use that technology, whether because they are too busy to learn something new or are just fearful. This chapter describes some activities that I adapted that can be done in a very "low-tech" environment. These activities help students explore some foundational questions that are timely for any classroom but have particular relevance to the social networking skills of our students, whether on- or off-screen.

I have a confession to make. As I was writing my first book, which was a profile of new literacies teachers, I realized I was not "walking the walk." In my scholarly life, I was attempting to be a proponent of multiliteracy reading and writing (Kist, 2000, 2003, 2005). But when it came time for me to teach actual students myself after years of being in an administrative position, now that I was teaching again at the college level, I was far from being a new literacies teacher.

What's more, I was now teaching future teachers—people who will be teaching for many years into the 21st century. I was potentially influencing

---

Portions of this chapter originally appeared in Kist, W. (2005). Walking the walk: New literacies in my own classroom. *Ohio Journal of English Language Arts*, 46(1), 49–57.

---

pedagogical practices that would impact thousands of children as my students graduated and taught hundreds of young people over the courses of their careers. Not only did I need to "walk the walk," I needed to pick up the pace.

Beginning in late 2002 and throughout 2003, I visited classrooms throughout the United States and Canada—from Los Angeles to Snow Lake, from Chicago to Montreal and beyond—watching some of the most visionary teachers who were immersed not only in the technology but also in the implications of using these new media in their classrooms. During my travels, I began to be quite conscious of my own less-than-current uses of technology and new educational practices; I was embarrassed that I didn't even have my own web page. When people asked me for the URL for my web page, I tried to cover and say that it was on my department's website at Kent State, and that the URL was so long I couldn't remember what it was (which was actually true). I never told people that I didn't own a computer in my home until 1996 or a cell phone until 2003.

Originally, I had become interested in this line of research because of my interest in film, not because of any particular interest in computer technology. Now, however, film was rapidly becoming an "old" medium (although very much integrated into new media), and as I was spending time chronicling the practices of the pioneers of this movement just like the silent-film stars chronicled by Brownlow (1969/1976), the parade was passing me by.

Mindful of the need to teach my lessons in the context of lessons that the preservice teachers could emulate, I reviewed all the outstanding new literacies assignments I had found and then created some myself. What follows in this chapter are descriptions of some of the assignments I have used with my students at Kent State University. Over the years of using them, I have found that they group themselves according to questions that get at some characteristics of new literacies classrooms, starting with the notion that these kinds of new literacies classrooms feature daily work in multiple forms of representation, not just occasionally, and that "reading" and "writing" these new media takes some practice and reflection.

How Have We Been Shaped by Media Experiences?

For years, I had started my courses by having students complete a "Literacy Autobiography" on paper. This assignment requires students to look back over their past reading and writing. As I became immersed in new literacies myself, I decided to broaden the assignment and get students thinking about how we have all been shaped by many kinds of texts that surround us. To model the activity for these preservice teachers, I have loaded many pictures into a PowerPoint presentation that demonstrates how my own life has been shaped by such diverse texts as sitcoms—*All in the Family,* for example—and "high art" (jazz performances by Bill Evans and works of art hanging at the Cleveland Museum of Art). As the images flash by on the screen, music starts to play, and I see moments of recognition as students witness that they and I have been influenced by some common texts even across a generation.

SELECTED ITEMS IN WILLIAM KIST'S POWERPOINT MULTIGENRE AUTOBIOGRAPHY

A *Peanuts* cartoon

Picture of Woody Allen and Mariel Hemingway in *Manhattan*

Music playing: "Watermelon Man" by Herbie Hancock

Book cover: Willa Cather's *My Ántonia*

Picture of Adam West in *Batman*

Painting: *Stag at Sharkey's* (1909) by George Bellows

TV Guide cover with Jackie Gleason

Picture of Bill Evans playing the piano

Book cover: *David Copperfield* by Charles Dickens

Picture of plastic figurine of the cartoon character *Pogo*

Picture of Stan Laurel and Oliver Hardy

Picture of Cleveland Kiddie Show TV Host "Barnaby"

Picture of Derek Jacobi in *I, Claudius*

Picture of the four main characters in *Seinfeld*

After my life has finished flashing before their eyes, I ask the students to immediately jot down texts that have been influential in their own lives—pieces of music, poetry, films, and even fashion and architecture. We share these texts with each other in a kind of freewheeling brainstorm that is equal parts nostalgia and recognition of how we are all immeasurably shaped by the various forms of communication around us. Then, I send them home to create their multigenre autobiographies. These may be turned in using multiple forms—PowerPoint, for example, or MovieMaker or iMovie. The criteria for the project's success is whether the students can demonstrate a clear link between the various texts and how their lives have been influenced by those texts. The actual assignment I give them is adapted from a couple of sources and includes suggested questions they might use to spark their thinking about different kinds of texts.

MULTIGENRE LITERACY AUTOBIOGRAPHY: THE ASSIGNMENT

This assignment encourages you to think about all the various texts of your life. Your own history as a reader and writer of various texts has a significant impact on how you "read" and "write" today. Thinking about the following questions and creating a multimodal artifact should help you reflect on your own multigenre literacy of today.

Below are some prompts to help you get started writing your multigenre literacy autobiography:

1. What are your earliest recollections of reading and writing?

2. What are your earliest recollections of watching television?

3. What are your earliest recollections of going to see a film?

4. What are your earliest recollections of music?

5. What are your earliest recollections of using a computer?

6. Were you read to as a child?

7. Before you were able to read, did you pretend to read books? Can you remember the first time you read a book?

8. What pleasures or problems do you associate with early memories of reading and writing?

9. What kinds of texts have you preferred over your life?

10. Was a newspaper delivered to your home? Do you recall seeing others read the newspaper? Did you read the newspaper?

11. How did pop culture (movies, TV, music, Internet) impact your literacy and vice versa?

12. How did your gender, race, social class, and/or ethnicity impact your reading ability, what you read, and/or your attitude toward reading?

13. Did you subscribe to children's magazines? Did your parents or siblings have magazine subscriptions?

14. Did your parents belong to a book club? Did they maintain a personal library? Did they read for pleasure?

15. Can you recall seeing family members making lists and receiving and sending mail?

16. Did you receive and send mail (such as birthday cards, thank-you notes, letters) when you were a child?

17. Can you remember any other indications that reading and writing were valued in the environment in which you grew up?

18. Can you detail your first memories of reading and writing instruction? Materials used? Methods of teaching? Content?

19. Can you remember how alternative (nonprint) texts were used at school, if at all?

20. How were computers used (or not used) during your educational journey?

21. Can you recall reading for pleasure in elementary school?

22. Can you remember writing for pleasure in elementary school?

23. Can you recall the first book you chose to read in elementary school?

24. Can you recall your first writing assignment in elementary school?

25. Did you have a library card when you were in elementary school? Did you use it then? What predominantly did you check out from the library? In later school years?

26. Can you recall the first book you loved (couldn't put down)?

27. Can you recall the first film or television show you loved and watched over and over again?

28. Do you feel that you've ever read a book that has made a difference in your life?

29. Has a nonprint text made a difference in your life?

30. Have you ever read a book that you knew had been challenged or censored? How did you feel about reading it?

31. Have you ever encountered a text online that you thought adults would be upset to know that you encountered? How did you feel about encountering that text?

32. Were you a reader in your intermediate and/or junior high or middle school years?

33. How did your reading and writing habits change when you went to school and over the years?

(Continued)

(Continued)

34. Are there any social, cultural, and/or religious organizations associated with writing or reading that you recall?

35. Can you pleasurably recall sharing books with friends?

36. Can you pleasurably recall talking about nonprint texts with friends?

37. Did you read a certain type of book (such as mysteries or biographies) at a particular age? Why do you think you made such choices?

38. Were you required to read certain novels in middle school or high school? How did you feel about that?

39. What is your all-time favorite children's book? What is your favorite book that you've read as an adult?

40. Have you ever seen a book you've read turned into a film?

41. Have there been times in your life when you have viewed reading as a pleasurable activity?

42. Have there been times in your life when you have viewed writing as a pleasurable activity?

43. Is there a specific teacher (or several) who stands out in your memory as someone who had an impact on your reading and/or writing?

44. What contributions have your reading and writing abilities made to your life?

45. Are you a reader now?

46. Are you a writer now?

47. What alternative media do you peruse most often now?

48. Do you feel comfortable modeling reading and writing for your students?

49. What are you currently reading? Writing?

Source: Adapted by William Kist from McLaughlin & Vogt (1996) and Brown (1999).

Because this assignment is given very early in the course, I don't suggest much of a structure or even medium for turning in their literacy autobiographies. I tell them they can turn in the assignment in whichever medium they prefer—from writing an essay, to shooting a video, to doing a PowerPoint presentation. Because nervous students always want to know how they're being graded (and because they deserve to know), I do present them with a very simple list of criteria.

> ## MULTIGENRE LITERACY AUTOBIOGRAPHY: EVALUATION CRITERIA
>
> For this assignment, you will be evaluated on the following criteria:
>
> - *Thoughtfulness of your response:* Does your autobiography appear to have been just thrown together at the last minute or has some real thought gone into it?
> - *Thoroughness of your examination of your literacy past:* Have you used a variety of texts to represent different eras of your life?
> - *Insights into the influences of your literacy history on your life:* Have you drawn conclusions as to how the various media texts have influenced your life?
>
> You will not be evaluated on mechanics issues or technical proficiency in whatever medium you are using.

As we debrief the assignment, students enjoy the reminiscing but also begin to realize how deeply all these texts are embedded in their memories and how much the media, both print and nonprint, are tied to their life experiences. Many students talk about the first film they attended or how excited they were to check a book out of the library for the first time or how excited they were to meet Bert and Ernie in person when they were taken to see *Sesame Street: Live!*

As we talk about these important texts in our lives, both print and nonprint, we start writing recurring themes on the board—themes of establishing identity; the power of autobiography; how certain texts, such as books, seem privileged; and the evident increasing influence of a screen-based literacy (Kress, 2003; Schofield & Rogers, 2004). We talk about the broad spectrum of literary practices—everything from getting a library card to creating a password—that make up our literacy lives (Barton & Hamilton, 1998).

Beyond the issues revolving around new literacies that this activity brings out, there are also qualities of the assignment itself that students begin to notice. This early in the course, students already are talking about how addicting these kinds of assignments are. Many students admit to sitting at their computers working for hours assembling their multigenre autobiographies. After we exhibit them, many students go back to add more content to their own autobiographies because their memories have been stimulated by what their peers have done.

How Do New Forms Shape Reading and Writing?

For many years, I did the first of the next activities as a fun way of helping kids to sequence—put the events of a story in order. The

Garmston and Wellman (1992) activity is a silent game in which students attempt to line up in order of their birthdays, finding their correct places in line without talking, communicating only in sign language. Once this task has been accomplished, it can be used to teach sequencing by having students put the events of a story on note cards or sticky notes that they affix to their shirts and then place themselves in the order that the events follow in the story. At the end of the activity, the class has formed itself in a straight line that traces the events of the story.

ACTIVITY ONE: HOW DO WE READ IN A "NONLINEAR" WAY?

Ask students to line up in a straight line facing the teacher.

1. At the signal, students are to reassemble in the order of their birthdays, starting with January birthdays all the way to the December birthdays at the end of the line. Students aren't to give their years of birth—this isn't an exercise in age!

2. As students are doing this, they are not to talk. They may communicate using hand signals.

3. Once students have lined up in order of their birthdays, have a discussion about what linearity means.

4. Next, place the events of a story on note cards and give one to each student. The students must arrange themselves in order of the events, again without talking.

5. Walk down the line from left to right and demonstrate how we usually read a book from beginning to end.

6. Go back to the beginning of the line and demonstrate how we read in a nonlinear fashion. Walk down the line until you get to the fourth or fifth person, then jump to the 10th person and walk down the line for a little while until you get to the 16th person, then jump back to the first person, then back to person the 20th, and so on. Explain to the students that this is the way people read in a nonlinear fashion.

Source: Adapted from Garmston & Wellman, 1992.

After the activity, I walk down the line from left to right, demonstrating how we traditionally read a book from beginning to end. Then, I go back to the beginning of the line and start bopping around in random fashion, walking down the line for a while, then jumping to the end, then back to the beginning, then to the middle, thus signifying nonlinear reading. We then brainstorm about how nonlinear reading is different than linear reading. What does it mean to the author of a screen-based (web-based) text when there is no ability to predict how the reader will read that text?

Of course, it could be argued that we have always had the ability to read texts in a nonlinear fashion by reading the last page first, for example. Many students mention how they read the final chapter of the final Harry Potter book first because they wanted to find out if he lived. Or the plot of a book may also be organized in a nonlinear way, with flashbacks and flash-forwards. Sometimes when students are still lined up, I demonstrate how some works deliberately place the last chronological event first in the story, such as *Citizen Kane* with the opening scene of the protagonist on his deathbed. This opens up a discussion of flashbacks, made so popular now by the television series *Lost* and *Heroes*. So it has probably always been appropriate to talk about the nonlinearity of "reading" texts, but with more texts now being screen-based and embedded with hyperlinks, this distinction between nonlinear and linear reading is more appropriate for discussion than ever.

QUESTIONS TO CONSIDER

1. Think about how you normally read a book. Do you normally read it from beginning to end, or do you sometimes skip to the end?

2. How do you think it changes the writer's task when the text being written will be read in random order—for example, a website?

3. How is reading on the web different than reading a book?

4. Do you prefer one style of reading?

5. Does it confuse you or entertain you to read a text that seems to proceed in random order? What might the author's purpose be for writing something in a nonlinear fashion (such as in films such as *Citizen Kane* and *Crash*)?

I have used the next assignment to get students to think about how to create hybrid texts. Since so many new media texts contain elements of different forms of representation, it is worth exploring with students how hybrid texts become more than the sum of their parts. This simple assignment can be adapted to many different texts—it obviously isn't confined to *Julius Caesar*!

ACTIVITY TWO: JULIUS CAESAR, THE MUSICAL

The objective of this assignment is to provide the students with a reason to go back and look over the play *Julius Caesar* by William Shakespeare, which they have just finished reading. This helps them see it as a unified entity, as a theatrical work that Shakespeare wrote with playgoers in mind, as a story that progresses from ideas to action to results, as a literary work that explores both internal and external conflict. Students must select five musical works, one for each act of the play. Each musical selection should reflect an event, incident, character, or mood in that particular act. Musical selections must be school appropriate, but they may represent any musical genre. For example, "The King's March" by Jeremiah Clarke could be used for Caesar's triumphal march into Rome in Act I, Buddy Miller's "Worry Too Much" could convey Brutus's internal conflict at the beginning of Act II, and "Belle Watling" from the *Gone With the Wind* soundtrack could represent the sadness of Portia's death as Brutus reveals it as the source of his emotional outburst in Act IV. Students should be prepared to share their selections with the class.

Source: From Karen Barta, Black River High School.

"It allowed me to take a risk. I am not usually an artistic person."
—Diane

Tom Romano's multigenre paper project is another similar way of getting kids to think across genres as they are writing on a defined topic (Romano, 1995, 2000). In a multigenre paper, students must write in several different genres—such as an obituary, a journal entry, a painting, a song—as they explore a certain topic, such as "Injustice in the American West" or "Growing Up in China." Having students create a hybrid text, such as "Julius Caesar, the Musical," or a multigenre paper gets them thinking about how works of art in different media still get at some of the same themes and that, in a new media age, many texts we encounter contain multiple forms of representation (music, print, image) within the same text. Sometimes, after students are given the freedom to create these kinds of hybrid texts, they continue to ask if they can add music that they themselves create or some visual art they have made in reaction to a page-based text. Other students report being challenged by the experience of working in hybrid forms.

"I got the opportunity to play with art, which is something I don't usually do." —Ariel

QUESTIONS TO CONSIDER

1. How did it change your opinion of *Julius Caesar* (or whatever text you used) when you added music to it?

2. What can "hybrid" texts get across that a text written in a single genre cannot? What can single-genre texts do that hybrid texts cannot?

3. Would you prefer to create a hybrid text rather than a single-genre piece? If so, why?

4. What are some examples of texts that could be considered hybrid?

When we talk about "hybrid texts," that often leads to pulling the components of that hybrid apart and focusing on the different forms of representation that make up the whole. This can lead to a discussion of the affordances with each medium. I often start this discussion with the form that brought me into the new literacies research in the first place: film, an inherently hybrid text that includes speech, music, and images.

How Do We Respond to Film Texts?

Helping kids learn to respond to texts is probably one of the most crucial tasks we need to accomplish with them. With print texts, many students, sadly, are stuck at the decoding stage, just struggling to make sense of whatever text they are reading. But for those students who get past the decoding stage, there is the question, "Now what?" This response process gets more complicated when we are now responding to both page-based and screen-based texts and when our response itself can be formed using both page-based and screen-based texts.

My interest in new literacies really was generated when I started showing short silent films to my high school English students. As a new teacher, I struggled with how to make the literary canon that I was expected to teach relatable to the urban teenagers I was working with. Because of my own love of film, I stumbled upon using silent films in my language arts classroom. One of the most memorable moments I had as a teacher was showing my students Charlie Chaplin's *The Kid*, a silent film that was made in 1921. This silent film traces the ups and downs of Chaplin's attempts to help an orphan child of about six or seven, played by child star Jackie Coogan. I showed it to my students one day because film as a genre was tangentially mentioned in my curriculum but mainly because I loved it and wanted to show it off to an audience that had never seen a silent film. I was soon amazed to see how my students loved it too. They were transfixed by the story, especially at the part in the film when the child welfare authorities come to take the child away from Chaplin. I saw my tough urban kids melt as the orphan boy is thrown in the police wagon and taken away, leaving Chaplin desolate. The kids were truly engrossed in the film. This classroom experience with a Chaplin film was one of those moments that teachers have when we know we are onto something big. That one teaching moment is one of the key events in my career that has led to the book that you are reading at this very moment.

I knew that my students were responding to this film, and I knew that they could also respond to Shakespeare and Dickens, and I knew that they could respond to Miles Davis and Jackson Pollock and all the other great artists who create texts. In my classroom, I began to break down the hierarchy of texts, so that we discussed Poe's "The Cask of Amontillado" at the same time we discussed *The Addams Family*. Before I even went to graduate school to learn what I was doing, I was creating a postmodern classroom with the result that, to this day, I run into former students who comment on how they still remember some of the things we did. I ran into one of my former students recently who wondered if I still had a copy of the video adaptation they had done—an urban street video version of "The Knight's Tale" from Chaucer's *Canterbury Tales*. Fortunately, I did still have a copy of their video, and I burned a copy for him. He and his group of friends now have careers in business and law enforcement, but he later told me they regressed to their teen years when they got together to watch their old video—work they had not seen in 10 years. I always think of this story when I hear people suggesting that the new media are "dumbing down" the curriculum—I challenge any British literature teacher to name a project that would have the students still talking about Chaucer 10 years later.

But I betray my print-centric background as an English teacher, as I talk about returning to Chaucer. A breaking down of this kind of hierarchy of symbol systems probably begins by helping kids to respond to texts, both print and nonprint—and not necessarily tied to print texts—in a thoughtful manner. To launch such a discussion, I use an activity I took from noted media educator Frank Baker of the Media Literacy Clearinghouse (http://www.frankwbaker.com/default1.htm).

ACTIVITY ONE: ANALYZING FILMS ELEMENT BY ELEMENT

Show the students the first seven minutes of Steven Spielberg's *E.T.: The Extra-Terrestrial* with no introduction. All they have to do is watch the clip. After the clip is done, break them into small groups, and give each group a "Film Analysis Card" with printed directions that ask them to watch the clip again but to concentrate on one element of the film production.

Lighting

What time of day is it?

What are the clues?

What effect does lighting have?

Use two or three adjectives to describe the lighting.

Sound Effects

Close your eyes.

You are only to listen to the scene, after which you will be asked to make a list of everything you heard and then share.

Music

Describe the music at the beginning, middle, and end of the scene.

What happens and why?

How does the music contribute to the mood or feel?

Is the music effective?

What might happen if there were no music in this scene? How would that impact your impressions?

Camera: Movement

Document when the director or cinematographer uses the following:

Pan (left or right move)

Tilt (up or down move)

A crane shot (high above)

What is the purpose of these actions?

Editing

Count the number of edits in this scene. What impact does editing have?

Camera: Lens

Document when the director or cinematographer uses the following:

Wide shot

Medium shot

Close up

Zoom in or out

Why does he or she use these shots when he or she does?

Mood

What mood does this scene put you in?

How do you feel?

Why do you feel this way?

What has the director done to push your emotional buttons? (Be specific.)

Just by asking students to concentrate on one element of a film, it opens their eyes to see how many formal elements go into the production of the film and that a film can indeed be looked at as formally as can a sonnet or a painting. Students report that it is difficult to go back to watching films casually after looking at scenes in a very focused way after doing this exercise. Sometimes students confess that they didn't realize that watching movies "counts" as participating in a serious art form. Frank reports, "It is my experience that students are most anxious to share what they now see, hear, and feel" after doing this activity. "It is empowering to hear their newly discovered understandings of what the director of the film was attempting to do."

Similarly, Heidi Whitus, communications teacher at Communications Arts High School in San Antonio, uses specific prompts to help her students think about different aspects of a film's message and appeal. She uses the following prompts to get her students thinking and writing analytically about film as a medium worthy of thoughtful response.

ACTIVITY TWO: FILM PROMPTS

- We watched several films in class in which the main characters are not exactly "good guys." Unlike George, the quintessential "good guy" in It's a Wonderful Life, they violate basic societal rules on a daily basis. Think of another film you have seen (not one we have watched in class) in which the protagonist is a bad person in the eyes of traditional society yet is still a likeable character. Describe how you felt about the character; what made that character "bad," and how did the film resolve the issue (think about what happened to the main characters in The Public Enemy and Bonnie and Clyde).
- Westerns are easily identifiable by their location: typically the American West, usually in the 19th century. However, some of the markers that identify a Western can be found in films with different settings. Describe a film you have seen that has the markers of a Western but takes place elsewhere. Explain the markers that make this film a "Western."
- Compare and contrast a remake of a horror classic with its original (e.g., Psycho, The Haunting, The Fog, and many more). Write 200 words in which you explain which version you thought was a more interesting and effective film. Consider such factors as the following:

  o how the film was changed to satisfy a different audience,

  o technological developments since the original, and

  o our society's evolving standards for how much gore and violence is acceptable (or required) in a horror film.

  Alternate question for those who have not seen any horror film remakes:

- We are viewing four black-and-white films in a row in class (The Cabinet of Dr. Caligari, Bride of Frankenstein, Psycho, and The Haunting). Many people say they hate black-and-white films; others love them. Describe how you feel about black-and-white films compared to color films and whether your opinion is changing as you get older. Use specific films you have seen as examples.

- *The Abominable Dr. Phibes* is considered a cult classic, a film that has a small but devoted body of fans. Describe the elements of this film that you believe make it beloved by some fans but at the same time prevent it from achieving wider popularity.
- Also, if you have any favorite "cult classic" films, talk about them here.
- *New requirement*: In addition to your initial response of *at least 150 words*, you must also *respond* to at least one of your classmates. This means that you must have at least two entries for this week.

Source: From Heidi Whitus, Communications Arts High School, San Antonio, Texas.

What Does It Mean to Represent an Idea Visually?

Once we have looked at the moving image, we begin to look at the static image. Many English teachers (and other subject matter teachers) may believe that this kind of activity is more fitting for art class. In English class, we have traditionally focused on the printed word as our communication medium. Both the reading and writing of print have been the focus of this field since it began around the beginning of the 20th century (Eagleton, 1983). Now, we face an age in which we are shifting to a screen-based society (Kress, 2003) in which much of our reading will be from a screen, and therefore, reading will not only encompass print but also images, sound, and motion as well. Visual literacy skills should be included if we truly want to prepare students for this new kind of reading. I think many teachers approach this by looking at paintings and visual art, and I have done this also. But I have also used a very old parlor game that has been suggested by Jeffrey Wilhelm (1997) to get kids visually representing what they read.

SNAPSHOT OR TABLEAUX DRAMAS

1. Form students into groups of three to five and assign each of them a scene from a book, a historical event, or a scientific process.

2. Explain that each group is going to have to visually represent this event somehow using their bodies. That is to say, they will not be permitted to draw a picture or use sign language. They must somehow reenact the event in such a way that it is somewhat recognizable.

3. Groups should be given time to "rehearse."

(Continued)

(Continued)

4. Once they are ready to perform, each group will take the stage and freeze in a tableaux representing the event they are supposed to be depicting.

5. A variation on the activity allows audience members, if they can't guess what the event being depicted is, to ask one or more of the actors "yes or no" questions about what is being represented.

Source: Adapted from Wilhelm, 1997.

One of the main reactions I get when doing this activity is from the shy students—they just feel uncomfortable standing up before the class and representing some scene with their bodies. Of course, there are many outgoing students who may even have some theatrical experience who love such an activity. So this opens up a discussion (after the students are done presenting their tableaux) about what we can do as teachers to make our classrooms places in which all students can thrive no matter what their modality of choice is for expressing themselves. What is the point of trying to represent an idea or an event visually?

QUESTIONS TO CONSIDER

1. Discuss the challenges of this activity. Are there some things that are more difficult to represent visually?

2. Why would someone decide to represent something visually?

3. Is a picture *really* worth a thousand words?

4. Think about a time in your life when you have appreciated having a picture of something more than you might have appreciated having words to describe it.

5. Think about a time in your life when you were glad to have words. What are the commonalities between the things we tend to represent verbally and the things we represent visually? What are the differences?

6. What were your feelings about getting up and presenting your tableaux in front of the class?

WHAT DOES "GENRE" MEAN, PARTICULARLY WHEN WE ARE WORKING ACROSS TEXTS?

Genre study has been a mainstay of the English classroom for many years. Whether creating entire courses or units around genres such as science fiction or mysteries or grouping literature circles around genres, language arts teachers often have stressed the features of various genres—both from the standpoint of the reader's needing to recognize certain conventions that are identified with certain genres and from the standpoint of the writer's need to compose within certain genre principles. Reading teachers also have focused on genre as a way of organizing and aiding the process of independent reading. Learning how to judge what a book will be about just from its cover comes back to a genre study of book covers.

But what happens to genres in a multimodal world? Are there characteristics of a genre such as horror, for example, that cut across forms of representation? Are there, on the other hand, certain elements of the horror film that don't translate to the horror novel? In a new media world, the genres and forms of communication keep multiplying so quickly that one could be discussing a new form practically every week, so perhaps it's worth having a discussion of certain elements of certain genres that seem to stand up no matter the time period and no matter the form of representation.

TEXT COMPARISONS ACROSS GENRES

1. Bring in examples of any two forms of communication—anything from a poem to an advertisement to the main page of a website. Try to use texts that both come from the same genre—horror, for example—but that are in different text forms (a Stephen King novel and the film *Psycho*, for example).

   1a. Expand the activity to a third form of communication and so on.

2. Brainstorm with students as to the similarities and/or differences between forms of communication: What can be done with digital communication that can't be done with print (page-based) communication? What can be done with page-based communication that can't be done with digital media?

3. Begin an ongoing list of characteristics of various genres and forms of communication.

These discussions sometimes lead to huge bulletin boards that stay up the entire semester in which students begin to list all of the texts that fit with a certain genre. Students can add to the genre lists over a period of time as they encounter new texts that fit within any of the genres. Informal discussions that compare and contrast the different texts within any genre may lead to a more formalized response or may stay at the level of conversation. An interesting next step is to talk about whether there are certain genres that have less fluid elements—elements that stay intact no matter the text.

QUESTIONS TO CONSIDER

1. What are the common elements of the horror genre or any genre, and how do they translate into the different forms of communication?

2. Are there certain genre-specific elements that don't translate well across forms—that are more form specific? If so, why?

3. Speculate as to how an artist makes a decision on which form to use to express himself or herself.

WHAT IS THE POWER BEHIND LISTING AND CLASSIFYING TEXTS?

The pleasure that students have with the previous assignment can lead to a discussion of two key elements of new media activities: assembly and categorization. We are increasingly using new media as digital scrapbooks of our lives, whether sharing our favorite pictures on Flickr or creating a list of our favorite screwball comedies on Amazon's Listmania. Over the years, I have always set up my students with some kind of reading and writing portfolio and have generally followed the model Nancie Atwell (1998) describes. One of the first minilessons Atwell advocates teaching is her "Reading and Writing Territories" activity, in which the entire class, including the teacher, starts keeping lists of all the reading they do and all of the writing. I assign a similar activity, but I broaden it to include categories that Atwell did not, categories that take into account new media.

TEXT CATEGORIES ACTIVITY

1. Give students a list of categories, such as the following:

   Favorite Authors of Fiction

   Favorite Poets

   Favorite Authors for Adolescents

   Favorite Filmmakers

   Favorite Musicians

   Favorite Visual Artists

   Favorite Dancers

   Favorite Websites

   Favorite Video Game

Favorite Blog

Favorite Graphic Novel

2. Model how you would respond to some of the categories above.

3. Ask students to create a document that has these categories (and any others they want to add) and then keep the document open and add to it throughout the year.

4. Give students another list of categories, this time related to writing:

Topics

Genres

Audiences

5. Model how you would respond to some of the categories above, making sure to emphasize under "Genres" that all writing "counts," such as texting, IMing, and even writing sticky notes.

6. Ask students to create a document that has these categories (and any others they want to add) and then keep the document open and add to it throughout the year.

Source: Adapted from Atwell, 1998.

QUESTIONS TO CONSIDER

1. What is your reaction after having seen a list of your reading territories?

2. What is your reaction after having seen a list of your writing territories?

3. Do you see any trends in your reading? What types of books do you prefer? What kinds of texts to you prefer?

4. Do you see any trends in your writing? What kinds of things do you tend to like to write about? How does the genre impact your writing?

5. What is the point of this kind of listing? Is it a waste of time?

One interesting outcome came about as a result of doing this activity. Several students wondered if they could put their lists and then their entire reading and writing portfolios online. One day, I had finished with the Listmania activity described above, and one of my students asked, "Why don't we put our reading portfolios online?" I hesitated for a moment. Why did I hesitate? I suppose the first thing that popped into my head was the security issue—would students' work be safe? I knew that over the years many of the students had written very personal things that they included in their writing portfolios. Would they still continue to write in an unguarded manner if they knew their work was going to be online somewhere? I knew also that some students occasionally read books that contained offensive words even in the titles. Since they are adults in college, this hasn't been a problem, but would it be a problem when their reading logs were online for everyone to see? Or would everyone have to see them? Could I set them up as password protected, and if so, who would get the password?

In short, in about 30 seconds many negative thoughts went through my head. I was stumped, and my student sat before me looking at me with an expression on her face that implied she was thinking, *So what's the big deal?* But of course, I punted and made the "teacherish" comment, "Let me think about it."

Fortunately, as I began to think about the implications of her request, I began to see some positive reasons for keeping the reading and writing portfolios online, especially in this more socially connected Web 2.0 world. These portfolios would be more public than they ever had been. I thought of the benefits to the students' reading and writing that could accrue if these documents were opened up to a wider audience—and not a passive audience but one that could potentially interact with the texts and even shape them. This publication of what had previously been private documents, only for the eyes of the teacher, would now be opened up potentially to the entire world. Perhaps students in other classes, in other schools, all over the globe could comment on both writing pieces and on books listed in the reading logs. Perhaps this would impact the writing severely, making students censor themselves before writing. But perhaps also this is good practice for them in making public some (or all) aspects of their personal lives.

What does "literacy" mean when it is increasingly public and collaborative?

This next group of activities supports questions that center around just that mix of individual and collaborative activities that comprise one characteristic of new literacies classrooms.

How Do We Form Communities?

After talking about our own individual identities and how they are shaped by the texts around us, we then start talking about building community with others and how these communities shape and mediate us whether we are participating in them face-to-face or virtually. I start by using two older activities that were originally designed to promote cooperative learning but can be expanded to point out elements of social networking in a Web 2.0 world. First, we do the activity called "Finding Famous Fictional Friends and Families."

COMMUNITY BUILDING

Activity One: Finding Famous Fictional Friends and Families

1. Put students in groups of three to four.

2. Give each person a 3x5 index card.

3. Ask each group to come up with three or four names that go together. The names don't have to be fictional if you don't want them to be.

   Examples: John, Paul, George, and Ringo

   Harry, Hermione, and Ron

   Barack, George, and Bill

   Marcia, Greg, Jan, and Bobby

4. Once each group has decided on a group of names, direct each person to write one of the fictional names on his or her card. For instance, in the Beatles group above, one person would write "John" on his or her card; one person would write "Paul"; one person would write "George"; and one person would write "Ringo."

5. Collect everyone's card.

6. Check to make sure you don't have two "Beatles" groups, for example, or two Harry Potter groups. For this activity to work, each group has to be a unique combination.

7. Redistribute the cards randomly.

8. Direct each student to get out of his or her seat and stand with the people whose cards "fit" with the one in his or her possession.

Adapted from Silberman, 1996.

Activity Two: Four Corners

1. Come up with 5 to 10 opinion statements.

2. Write the following code on the board:

   1 = Strongly Agree

   2 = Agree

   3 = Disagree

   4 = Strongly Disagree

   0 = Neutral

(Continued)

(Continued)

3. Direct students to number a piece of paper from one to however many statements you have.

4. Read aloud the statements and have students write the number that corresponds with how they feel.

   Example: One of the opinion statements could be, "McDonald's is a better restaurant than Burger King." If you agree with that statement, you should mark 2.

5. Once you get through reading all the statements, go around the room and mark the four corners of the room with the following labels: Strongly Agree, Agree, Disagree, and Strongly Disagree.

6. Direct students to stand up.

7. Read aloud the opinion statements again and direct students to stand in the corner that corresponds with their opinions. The students will thus group and regroup multiple times, forming different combinations with each statement read aloud.

Source: Adapted from Garmston, R. J., & Wellman, B. M. (1999). *The adaptive school: A sourcebook for developing collaborative groups.* Norwood, MA: Christopher-Gordon Publishers.

I usually start by asking students to brainstorm about what was different about the two activities, mainly focusing on how it was to form groups in these two different ways. In Activity One, students found themselves standing in a group that was completely randomly formed (based on whatever name happened to be on the card). In Activity Two, students found themselves in groups that ebbed and flowed based on the opinion statement under consideration. Students like the first activity in that it provides a purely random way of forming groups (something that may be useful to them in their future classes). But most of the conversation tends to be about the second activity as students are amazed at the commonalities and differences between the groups that form and dissipate throughout the activity. "I didn't know you like McDonald's better than Burger King," or "I didn't know you believe in capital punishment." Students like the fact that they must declare their preferences by themselves first so they are not swayed by peer pressure in any way. We explore how affinity groups form online based around common interests and how the people you meet in these groups may surprise you. This leads to a discussion of identity formation. What does it mean when you can declare your likes and dislikes in a relatively anonymous space? Does it lead to more individualism or less? Do we tend to shape our identities purposefully online in a different way than we do when communicating in person?

QUESTIONS TO CONSIDER

1. Which activity was more satisfying?

2. Which activity simulates social networking on the Internet more accurately?

3. Which activity simulates face-to-face social networking more accurately?

4. What patterns do we tend to follow when we socialize with people whether it is online or face-to-face?

5. What patterns break down when groups form truly based on common likes or dislikes, not based on demographic closeness?

6. Is there more or less freedom to be oneself online?

How Can We Work Together?

The ability to collaborate seems to be generally acknowledged as an essential in a new media environment. To approximate the collaborative spirit that needs to be present in order to be an effective communicator in these digital times, I have relied upon some old theater games that are usually played to help actors become better at improvising and coping with whatever may happen on the stage before a live audience. The actors in a play must work together as an ensemble, or the piece breaks down. The "Count to Ten" activity is one that forces a group of people to listen to each other and collaborate toward a goal.

COUNT TO TEN!

1. Direct students to form a circle. The teacher should stand outside the circle.

2. The group is directed to attempt to count to 10 (or whatever number) with members of the group randomly shouting out one number at a time.

3. Any time two members of the group shout out a number at the same time, the group must start over.

4. Group members can't use any signals or patterns to indicate when a number is going to be shouted out.

5. The group wins when they successfully count to whatever number is desired.

Source: Adapted from Loomans & Kolberg, 1993.

The most noticeable classroom element with the Count to Ten activity is the almost instant concentration it engenders in the class. Students really want to accomplish this task. There is noticeable amusement, but also frustration, when they almost get to 10 only to have to start over again when two people say the number "9," for example, simultaneously. When the group reaches its goal, there is a huge, spontaneous, loud cheer. They are truly happy to have reached the goal.

listserv

A listserv is fairly primitive (yet still powerful) social networking tool. It is essentially a collection of e-mail addresses linked to one listserv e-mail address. For example, I could create a listserv of all the readers of this book by asking you to send me your e-mail address. (Please feel free to do this, by the way. You can reach me at wkist @kent.edu.)

I could then go through a link on my university's web page that allows me to create a listserv and name it. Let's say I name the listserv KISTREADERS@LISTSERV .KENT.EDU. Then, as I am the listserv creator, I would go through another link once my listserv is set up and add each person's e-mail address. Any time I want to communicate with these people, I send one e-mail to KISTREADERS@LISTSERV .KENT.EDU, and my message will be received by all the people on my listserv. Listservs can be set up in several configurations with all the people able to send messages to the listserv or with only a few select people allowed to communicate with the group.

Nings

The name "Ning" comes from the website Ning.com that provides free networking space for any group of people who want to form an online community. It takes only moments to set up, and then those who want to join the Ning are able to communicate with the other people who have joined that Ning. The Ning looks like a social network environment such as Facebook in that participants create a profile and then post comments and questions to the group. Many educators are using Ning as a safe way of using social networking in the classroom in that it can be set up to be completely private and so that each post to the Ning generates an e-mail to the teacher. Setting up a Ning is free. For a small fee, the Ning creator does have the option of eliminating advertising. There is also an age requirement—children under 13 cannot participate. Please check out the Ning created for readers of this book at: http://sociallynetworkedclassroom.ning.com.

Almost immediately after having done these kinds of community-building activities, I find there is a change in the classroom community. This is most often evident in the comments on the class listserv. Before the advent of Ning.com and other social networking platforms for classrooms, I set up simple listservs in which everyone in the class is a member and all can send messages to each other. The listserv is hosted on my school's server and only requires me to type in the e-mail addresses of each student once, and they are subscribed to the listserv. It is usually after some of these community-building activities that more animated, humorous conversations start on the listserv. After the class was over, Michelle commented on the use of the listserv saying, "The listserv keeps everyone from the class connected through continuously building and maintaining relationships." Ambrosia wrote, "With the listserv, I get several responses to the question (I ask)," and Riley wrote, "It is a very quick and convenient way to contact many people at once, which ultimately saves time." Cindy wrote, "The listserv was great because you knew that there was someone else who was feeling the same anxiety as you just an e-mail away!"

Beyond the listserv, the students begin to share inside jokes in class as well. They begin to circulate sign-up sheets to bring food to class. I've even had two classes design T-shirts commemorating funny lines and events from the class. One student said, "We were always in classes together but never really were a community until now."

QUESTIONS TO CONSIDER

1. What did you have to do successfully as a group member in this activity for the goal to be achieved?

2. What obstacles did you face individually and as a group?

3. How did you overcome these obstacles?

4. What parallels can you draw between this activity and behavior in an online world? What differences are there?

But what does this have to do with literacy? A lot, I would answer, especially in a new media age. Most of us probably still think of writing as a solitary activity. We tend to imagine a lonely writer holed up in an artist's garret, lost in reverie. The reverie part may still be present, but increasingly, writers are collaborating with other writers on texts—writers who may live thousands of miles away.

wikis

Coming from the Hawaiian word for "quick," wikis have become essential for collaborative writing done in an online environment. Anyone can set up his or her own wiki focusing on any topic of choice. There are many platforms available to host wikis such as Wikispaces.com or PBwiki.com. The person who sets up the wiki determines who is allowed to contribute to the wiki. Once those people click on a link on the wiki, they are able to contribute to whatever text is being cocreated there. Some famous examples of wikis are Wikipedia.org and Lostpedia.org.

(Continued)

(Continued)

There are also platforms that simply store a group's commonly used documents, in Word or Excel, for example. GoogleDocs allows for this kind of storage of documents so that colleagues and friends can collaborate on these shared documents from anywhere and at any time.

While in schools we most often still assign writing to be done individually, outside school writing often is done in a collaborative environment such as GoogleDocs or Wikispaces. Texts are shaped collaboratively, drafted by more than one person, and then revised and edited by others—sometimes by hundreds or thousands more people. Wikipedia.org is an example of this; thousands of people across the world actively participate in suggesting and then writing the entries that are never completely finalized. We need to give students practice in working collaboratively to produce these kinds of texts. For several years, I have used a very old reading strategy activity to get at what it means to create a text with a group.

WRITING COLLABORATIVELY

List Group Label With Found Poetry

1. Put students into groups of three or four. Give each group a large piece of chart paper.

2. Tell students that you are going to be giving them a category, such as "birds" or "spiders." Each group member is then going to have a certain amount of time to write down whatever words or phrases come into his or her head related to the category. Each student is to write on one corner or side of the large chart paper.

3. After time is up, each group is to count the total number of words on each chart paper.

4. (Optional) The rest of the original activity suggests that each group then come up with categories in which to group all the words.

5. Direct students to select their "favorite" 10 to 12 words and write them in the center of the chart paper.

6. Students are then directed to take those 10 words and form them into a poem. The teacher may give students the option of adding a certain number of verbs or other modifiers, if so desired.

Source: Adapted from Taba, 1967.

This combined activity takes up to 40 minutes, and for the entire time, students are invariably on task and collaborating with each other. The first part of the activity gets students to compete against other groups in generating words and phrases. The second part of the activity gets students to collaborate in taking some of these words and forming them into a poem. There are occasionally some students who don't do well with this kind of collaborative writing, but there is something about being grouped around a big piece of chart paper that leads to a true collaborative experience as students debate which words should be used to form their poems and then struggle to form these somewhat random words together into a poem. These found poems often stay posted for weeks and are referred to as common reference points for certain groups long after the groups themselves have faded away.

This is an activity that causes the proverbial "light bulb" to go on over the heads of many of my students when we begin to discuss how much writing is done collaboratively today. While students always want to be able to compose individually, they see the advantage to being able to collaborate and how this activity using chart paper can simulate the online writing experience with all its compromise, negotiation, and serendipity.

QUESTIONS TO CONSIDER

1. How do you feel about the poem you collaborated on?

2. Would you have preferred to write a poem individually that used the words?

3. Did it help the poetry writing to have the group brainstorming (listing) activity? Why or why not?

4. List some "rules" or etiquette that needs to apply when writing collaboratively.

WHO IS THE AUDIENCE FOR OUR WRITING IN A NEW MEDIA AGE?

Not only do we barely know the people we collaboratively write with in this new media age, we may only have a dim notion of who our audience is. This becomes even more complicated when, in a blogging situation, anonymous readers may post comments that run the gamut from cheers to jeers.

AUDIENCE

Snowball Activity

Distribute sheets of standard white copy paper to each student in the room.

1. Direct each student to write his or her name at the top of his or her paper.

(Continued)

(Continued)

2. Direct students to react to a prompt. (It could be anything. The topic of the prompt is irrelevant to the activity.)

3. Have students stand up and, on a signal, wad up their papers into snowballs and throw them across the room.

4. Students should retrieve one snowball from the ground and return to their seats, uncrumple the paper, and react in a sentence or two to what the first person has written.

5. Students should crumple the paper again and then, on a signal, throw the snowball across the room again.

6. Repeat this any number of times.

7. After the last time, ask the student to return the snowball to the original writer (whose name is at the top of the page).

Source: Adapted from Burke, 2000.

blogs and blogging

Blogs are basically online journals or "logs." Over the years, the earlier name (web log) has been shortened to "blog." There are several free platforms for hosting a blog, giving anyone who wants it a potential instant worldwide audience. A blog can be set up in any number of ways, but the essential components are the entries themselves, which are very similar to page-based diary entries with all of the range of length, style, and content that one would get in any personal journal. What makes blogging a key part of Web 2.0 is their interactive nature. There is usually a link following each entry of a blog for readers to leave comments about the entry. In the past, the only respondent to one's diary entries might be found in the history books. Now, the response could be instantaneous, public, and from a mixture of friends, colleagues, and even strangers.

For years, I've been doing the activity above with students as a kind of story-starter activity and just as an example of an activity that gets kids up and out of their seats and engaging with each other. A few years ago, I was doing this activity and realized that its purposes could broaden to include fostering a dialogue about a principle of literacy in the age of Web 2.0 and, in particular, blogging: How do we think about "audience" in the age of Web 2.0?

Of course, a key objective of writing instruction over the years has been getting kids to think about audience before beginning to write. Audience has implication for everything from language to tone and even to length. We've taught kids to think about audience during every stage of the writing process, even during the prewriting stage when they are brainstorming about what it is they want to say. But what happens during the writing process when the writing we're doing is for an unknown and potentially worldwide audience and a rowdy audience at that, capable of making random comments about what we write?

The breakthrough moment for me was when some students reacted strongly to the comments that had been written on their "snowballs." After the "snowball" has been thrown around the room a few times and commented on by various class members, I ask each student to return his or her snowball to the original writer (whose name is at the top of the page). It was always interesting to see how students voraciously read the comments that others had written on their papers or snowballs. But when the snowball was returned to its original owner, sometimes there were outraged comments, such as "Who wrote this?" or "That's not what I meant. I've been misunderstood!" These comments got me thinking about parallels between the comments on the snowballs and comments that are left on blogs in response to the original entries. I asked the students, "How did it make you feel to get a comment that blatantly disagreed and perhaps even misunderstood what you were saying with your original statement? Would it shape how you wrote your original comment if you knew that you were going to get these comments on what you had written?" This opened up a dialogue around some of the following questions.

QUESTIONS TO CONSIDER

1. How did it make you feel to read comments on your snowball? Did you generally agree with what was written, or was there a comment that you felt was totally "off the wall"? How did that make you feel?

2. How does it change your writing when you don't know who's going to be reading it?

3. Pretend your snowball could fall into the hands of anyone in the world and potentially years later. How would that change what you wrote? How would it change your writing when your audience could be anyone in the world?

4. Does it make you feel any different when you don't know who the commenter is (when the names of the commenter are not required on the snowballs)?

5. In the random reading and writing environment that is Web 2.0, what are some guidelines we should follow when blogging or leaving comments on others' blogs?

6. What are some safeguards that can be built into the blog to prevent malicious or hurtful comments?

How Do We Multitask or Do Things Simultaneously and/or Synchronously?

Being able to perform more than one task simultaneously seems to be a key feature of the new media consumer experience. This is a mixed blessing: people (understandably) rant about drivers who text message behind the wheel, for example. But whether this kind of media multitasking is generally "good" or "bad"—leading to shortened attention spans, perhaps—it seems to be here to stay; people are simultaneously performing tasks that used to be considered mutually exclusive. I have noticed during the writing of this book that I am much more of a multitasker than I have been in the past. During the time I've been writing this paragraph, I've been loading tunes into my iTunes, responding to an e-mail message, and checking my Twitter stream (see Chapter 5). Maybe the paragraph would have been better written if I had been attending to it as a solitary task, but I seem to have fallen into a pattern in which I am more productive if I am multitasking in my digital world. The following activity is an old "outdoor education" game that I have used to simulate what happens when we multitask, perhaps beyond our capacity to perform all tasks effectively.

"THIS IS AN APPLE" ACTIVITY

1. Form a circle with students standing and include yourself (the teacher) in the circle.

2. The teacher is the leader of this game and should be holding two objects that are passable—anything from a couple of key chains to some tennis balls or even some very small stuffed animals.

3. The leader takes one of the objects and passes it to the person on his right and says, "This is an apple." The person must say, "A what?" The leader then responds, "An apple."

4. The person then hands the object to the person on his or her right and says, "This is an apple." The second person must answer, "A what?" The first person turns back to the leader and says, "A what?" The leader says, "An apple." The first person turns to the second person and says, "An apple."

5. The second person turns to the person on his or her right and says, "This is an apple," and the process repeats with the "A what" response coming back down the line to the leader, who responds, "An apple," sending that response all the way back down the line to the person who currently holds the "apple" object.

6. After the "apple" has progressed around the circle about a third of the way, the leader initiates the same pattern to his or her left, turning to the person on his or her left and handing the object, and saying, "This is a banana."

7. The challenge occurs at the point in the circle, usually opposite the leader, when the "apple" and "banana" are passing each other. Participants have to really concentrate to say the correct words and multitask, as they may need to say two different actions and perform two separate tasks at the same time.

This game often leads to quite a range of emotions on the part of the players. Some students can't stop laughing at the way their classmates freeze or mess up when trying to perform tasks simultaneously. Some students genuinely dislike this game for the pressure it puts on them. People either love the challenge of the game, or they have the "deer in the headlights" look as they are forced to concentrate and make sure they are performing the task they need to do in order to keep the objects moving.

If the game breaks down, some students are adamant that we keep playing the game until we get it "right." I've even had groups request to play the game once each class time until they can get the objects going all the way around the circle with no breakdown.

When discussing the issue of multitasking, there are many anecdotes told of roommates who could multitask and roommates who couldn't—of people who can write with music in the background and of people who need absolute silence. We discuss multitasking as a feature of both reading and writing in a new media age. What does it mean when one must attend to different tasks within the overall task of reading? Are people really attending to multiple tasks at the same time or just switching back and forth rapidly? Does this multitasking make a difference to the reader or writer of new media texts?

QUESTIONS TO CONSIDER

1. How did this game make you feel?

2. How is this similar to or different from the kinds of multitasking that people do when working with media tasks?

3. Will people who are not adept at multitasking be able to process media tasks as efficiently as those who can't?

4. There are those who claim that when we multitask, we really aren't attending to more than one task at a time but simply switching rapidly back and forth between different tasks. Do you agree or disagree with this point of view?

How Do New Formats Transform Writing?

People now may be glimpsed writing everywhere, from the baseball game to the food court at the mall, from the jogging trail to the Laundromat. Writing and reading messages from our social networks are permeating almost every moment of our waking lives. While some see this as a positive way to stay connected to friends and family, others see it as intrusive and potentially corrupting to the English language. At the very least, the situation is ripe for discussion, and I have used a well-known poetry-writing activity to focus on the advantages and limitations of such forms as texting and Twitter that demand extremely concise, almost coded writing.

RANDOM PHRASE POEM

1. Give each student a 3 × 5 index card.

2. Direct each student to write a random phrase on the card. The phrase cannot have more than 140 characters.

3. Collect all the students' cards.

4. Read them aloud in random order.

5. Tell the students they have just written a "Random Phrase Poem."

   (Note, a variation on this activity is asking students to comment on something they are doing at the moment—as in Twitter—but the drawback to this is that each card then has a variation of "I'm writing on this 3 × 5 card.")

Source: Adapted from Koch, 1970.

QUESTIONS TO CONSIDER

1. Were there any trends or themes in the random phrase poem?

2. How did you feel about the limit of 140 letters?

3. Did you alter something you were going to say based on the length?

4. Apply this experience to the way you communicate outside of school. Has texting altered the way you use the language? If so, how?

5. Has texting made an impact on your writing?

---

texting

The word *texting* is a shortened way of saying "text messaging"—that is, those very brief messages that are typed into one's cell phone (mobile phone) to communicate with friends and colleagues. Because it is somewhat difficult to type full words using such a small keyboard, many people use abbreviated forms of English words and also emoticons or symbols to communicate their thoughts and ideas.

After doing this activity, students are amused by how funny the random phrase poems are and how amazingly well they hang together, given that they were composed completely randomly. We soon transition into a discussion of what writing affordances such short-form media as Twitter, texting, and social networking allow. At about this time, we read about the novels that are being composed across the world, but mainly in Japan, entirely on cell phones. What is so appealing about this format that causes people to Twitter throughout their own weddings and other major life events? Students seem to be fairly evenly spread across a continuum of those who send thousands of texts a month to those rare students who don't own a cell phone. Our discussion gets quite spirited when we start debating whether text message speak should actually be taught in the English classroom as a form of communication worth being studied.

PAUSING TO REFLECT

After doing many of the activities described above, we take a break and pause to reflect on them. Over several years of getting reactions from my students about these new literacies activities, I've noticed some trends in their comments.

New Spaces for Teaching and Learning

Students like to reflect on the experience of what it's like being a learner in a multiliteracy classroom, especially since my students are going into careers in teaching. Students have said things such as, "These activities allowed more free expression than a typical typed assignment," and "It was a great change of pace from normal classwork, although it was difficult at first to actually figure out what you wanted for us to do." Another student stated, "The important thing to remember is that people love to have choices. These activities are perfect for a person who wants 'choices.'"

These assignments seem to create new spaces for teaching and learning for my students.

One of the key elements of these activities is their engaging nature, bearing out one of the characteristics of new literacies classrooms, that new literacies classrooms are places of student engagement in which students report achieving a "flow" state.

Mindy said, "These activities help keep students interested and having fun learning even in college. We can carry these experiences to our own classrooms."

"I will definitely use activities like this in my classroom someday," Diane predicted. "They allow students to use a more creative outlet of expression that I believe they would enjoy. These lessons give students more variety and keep students thoroughly engaged all of the time."

Sharon made the comment, "New literacy experiences allow students to interact with reading and writing in new ways." Nadine also reflected on the meaning of "literacy": "With the extensive ways to look at what literacy is and how to incorporate it into the classroom, we need to be able to expand our thinking beyond traditional print." I don't know if Nadine and Sharon would have made such comments before taking my class. One can only hope, now that they can "talk the talk," that when they get their own middle school classrooms in less than a year, they will "walk the walk."

The experience of teaching these activities has followed a pattern that has followed me since I was a high school English teacher and was surprised by how the kids reacted to an old silent film. The kids taught me what was important both then and now, and I've tried to follow them (and lead them at the same time). The teaching experiences described in this chapter have taught me that it's not about the technology; there were new literacies when there was no Internet, when there was not even an Apple 2E!

I know that I need to keep on trying to "walk the walk" even as this walk continues to take me places I never anticipated. I also know that I need to be part of a Personal Learning Network (PLN) and get back out there to see what new things visionary teachers are doing. Even if I could not travel physically to Snow Lake as I did in 2003, I could go there again virtually. This time around, as I began to become more active in Web 2.0 myself and to interact via Twitter and various Nings with great educators all over the world, my visits could be ongoing and dialogical and part of the everyday conversations of my life. In the next chapters, we will encounter some of the brave teachers in my PLN as they stare back at their students (and colleagues) and say, "Let's try it!"

A Blog Post From the Field

The biggest drawback is the time and effort it takes to use some of this technology. As a first year teacher, pretty much all of my lesson plans are new lesson plans—it's not like I'm a veteran teacher who is just revamping lessons to put on the web, so along with trying to find good online resources, I am also trying to plan my units and lessons, period. So obviously technology will take a back burner this year when it comes to planning time. On the flip side, a few of my lessons have been structured around things like podcasts or a wiki web quest, which has led to some more interesting and active learning lessons. Also, I think using technology helps to validate me as a teacher—it gives me a little bit of street cred, both with the students who are really in tune to the online world and with older teachers, who seem at least mildly impressed that technology can actually work—some of them see it as a weapon that is just going to replace the teacher, but I know I've shown at least one teacher so far that doesn't have to be the case.

—Cassie Neumann
English, Theater, and Media Teacher
Brunswick High School
Brunswick, Ohio

7

Why Use Web 2.0 Tools With ELLs?

Lori Langer de Ramirez

INTRODUCTION

Web 2.0 tools are becoming more and more commonplace in schools. With the change of a "read" web to a "read/write" web, teachers are discovering new ways in which to engage technologically savvy students in computer-based educational activities. Publishing student work to the World Wide Web is a means of providing an authentic global audience for classroom productions. When students write or speak for a broader and more international audience, they pay more attention to polishing their work, think more deeply about the content they produce, and consider cultural norms more thoughtfully. These benefits serve to strengthen all students' skills, but they are particularly relevant to the English language learner (ELL) who is beginning to acquire or continuing to develop his or her proficiency in English in the school setting.

ELLS IN SCHOOLS: SOME CHALLENGES TO CONSIDER

According to the National Clearinghouse for English Language Acquisition and Language Instruction Educational Programs (n.d.):

> Based on state-reported data, it is estimated that 5,119,561 ELL students were enrolled in public schools (pre–K through Grade 12) for the 2004–2005 school year. This number represents approximately

10.5% of total public school student enrollment, and a 56.2% increase over the reported 1994–95 total public school ELL enrollment. Among the states, California enrolled the largest number of public school ELL students, with 1,591,525, followed by Texas (684,007), Florida (299,346), New York (203,583), Illinois (192,764), and Arizona (155,789).

Whether you are an ESL teacher or a teacher of any other subject area, you have almost definitely worked with English language learners in your classrooms. These eager students are faced with the challenge of learning a new language and culture while also studying subjects like science, math, English language arts, art, music, physical education, and health. This can be an incredibly daunting task—even for the strongest of students who have consistent schooling and can demonstrate good literacy in their first language.

According to educational researcher Jim Cummins (1979), English language learners acquire basic interpersonal communicative skills (BICS)—also known as *social language*—within the first two years of exposure to English. This is the language of personal conversations, expressing opinions, requests for information, and expressions of need. However, it takes between five and seven years to develop their cognitive academic language proficiency (CALP)—also known as *academic language.* CALP is the language of textbooks, class lectures, essays, and educational videos. It is the language that students need to succeed in their academic life in an English language medium school (Cummins, 1979).

When thinking about BICS and CALP, it can be enlightening to consider a hypothetical situation in which you were a teenager and somehow relocated to the Philippines to attend a public school there. You will likely learn key words and phrases in Tagalog fairly quickly. It will take a lot longer to be able to write a cohesive essay on the history of the Philippine rainforest—*in Tagalog* (note: for a more challenging scenario, replace the Philippines with Thailand, where not only the language is different, but so is the script).

So, time is of the essence, and yet our ELLs can't afford to wait on either front. They must learn English alongside their other subjects. They don't have the luxury of acquiring CALP first and then entering classes involving the other disciplines. The challenge to learn English and succeed in school—not successively but rather simultaneously—is a daunting one, but it is quite common in most schools across the United States.

WHY WEB 2.0 WITH ELLS?

The gift of time is the greatest gift that an ELL could possibly receive in school. But since the gift of time is one that we simply cannot give, we must look for ways to extend English language acquisition beyond the school day and means of maximizing learning for our students. Web 2.0

tools can provide students with extra opportunities to do meaningful language-learning tasks from the comforts of their own homes or local libraries. On a receptive level, they can sign on to a podcast for extra listening practice or view an instructive video on YouTube. However, Web 2.0 tools work best when students are asked to develop, create, and share their work online. It is in this way that they are active learners, negotiating meaning and creating media for a worldwide audience. For example, students can "meet" virtually with classmates via the web and work on collaborative projects on a wiki. They can also create blog entries, videos, or comment on a classmate's work—all after the school building has closed down for the day.

For beginning English language learners in particular, web-based platforms can also provide a safer, more anonymous space in which to practice English. Beginners can be reticent and uncomfortable speaking in class, sharing their writing with peers in a face-to-face situation, or presenting work to large groups. Part of the reluctance comes from insecurity and fear of making errors and often coincides with the "silent period" in which students are taking in the new language but not yet ready to start producing it on their own. Web 2.0 tools are particularly helpful during these early stages of acquisition as they allow ELLs to be in control by giving them the opportunity to produce work in a controlled setting. If they are creating videos or audio files, they can practice, record, and rerecord until they are satisfied with their work. If using a wiki, they can cocreate work with the help of a stronger peer in a comfortable, nonthreatening online environment. Virtual worlds like Teen Second Life offer students an anonymous place in which to meet others, have conversations, and make mistakes—without need to do so in person. Web 2.0 tools are forgiving of errors and provide students with ways to save face as they practice their new language in cyberspace.

Web 2.0 tools are also beneficial in that they support and even entice students to become creators and not merely recipients of knowledge. According to the Partnership for 21st Century Skills, it is crucial that our students come away from their K–12 educational experience with the ability to not just consume information but also create it. This creation of information has gone from a one-person endeavor to a collaboration with people from many different cultures and from all parts of the world.

Using Web 2.0 tools in the classroom involves students in activities that expand their problem-solving skills as they are required not just to find information but also to judge its worth and accuracy. With the inception of the read-write web, anyone is capable of authoring material. This democratization of the web has lead to a proliferation of information—not all of it trustworthy. Media literacy—in the past mainly focused on television and print media—now includes the web and its explosion of information and material. And since ELLs are only just acquiring more challenging language, such as idiomatic expressions, they are especially vulnerable to advertisements and other media that often use this type of language as a means of persuading audiences. Now more than ever, it is imperative that our students become critical consumers of the material that is available to them at the click of a computer key.

While there are many reasons why Web 2.0 tools are beneficial for ELLs, perhaps the most convincing reason is the one that we teachers often underestimate: The World Wide Web is fun! There is a solid base of research available on the link between the use of technology with English language learners and motivation and/or improvement in certain skill areas. A study by Johns and Tórrez in 2001 found that "the new technologies offer many possibilities to the second language learner" (p. 11). Svedkauskaite, Reza-Hernandez, and Clifford (2003) have also found that

> technology has evolved from its support function to play a role in initiating learning processes. It can provide a flexible learning environment where students can really explore and be engaged. Hypermedia, for example, individually addresses levels of fluency, content knowledge, student motivation, and interest, allowing inclusion of LEP [limited English proficient] students, who can thus monitor their comprehension, language production, and behavior. ("Frameworks for Successful LEP Learners" section, para. 4)

More recently, research about the use of Web 2.0 tools in the language classroom has shown that the use of technology is appreciated by students (Stanley, 2006), linked to greater motivation (Goodwin-Jones, 2005), and tools like blogs have been responsible for improvements in students' writing (Thorne & Payne, 2005).

Students come to us with preestablished positive relationships to these technologies. They own and view MySpace and Facebook accounts, write and read blogs, create and view videos on YouTube, and record and listen to podcasts. The exciting aspect of their familiarity with these platforms is that they not only access and consume but also develop, edit, and share their work with classmates and others via the web—and they are not being asked to do it! What better way to motivate, excite, and connect to our students than to dive into the media that they already know and love?

PREPARING ELLS FOR THE 21ST CENTURY

English language learners in K–12 schools are charged with the task not only of acquiring a new language and increasingly challenging subject area content (i.e., science, math, social studies) but also to be a successful citizen of 21st-century global society; students are also required to be fluent in the use of the most important technologies. While it is still important to have basic core knowledge and skills in a variety of subject areas as in the past, it is no longer enough. According to theorists such as Daniel Pink (2006) and organizations like the Partnership for 21st Century Skills, students need to develop additional skills like crosscultural communication, critical thinking, and creativity and innovation skills as well. The Partnership for

21st Century Skills (www.21stcenturyskills.org) is the leading advocacy organization focused on infusing these newly important skills into education. The organization brings together the business community, education leaders, and policy makers to define a powerful vision for 21st-century education to ensure every child's success as citizens and workers in the 21st century by providing tools and resources to help facilitate and drive change. The Partnership for 21st Century Skills represents these skills through a rainbow image with the important skills listed in the rainbow and the support systems represented as pools below:

Figure 7.1

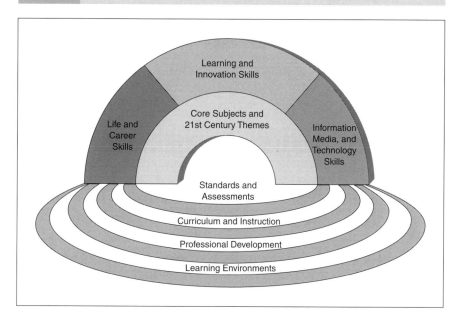

Source: Used with permission from the Partnership for 21st Century Skills.

The skills that make up that rainbow portion of the image are

1. Core Subjects and 21st-Century Themes

2. Learning and Innovation Skills:
   - Creativity and Innovation Skills
   - Critical Thinking and Problem-Solving Skills
   - Communication and Collaboration Skills

3. Information, Media, and Technology Skills:
   - Information Literacy
   - Media Literacy
   - ICT Literacy

4. Life and Career Skills:
- Flexibility and Adaptability
- Initiative and Self-Direction
- Social and Cross-Cultural Skills
- Productivity and Accountability
- Leadership and Responsibility

Source: Used with permission from the Partnership for 21st Century Skills.

Aside from the obvious connections to information, media, and technology skills, Web 2.0 tools provide students with real opportunities to *communicate and collaborate* (Skill 2) in unique ways. Wikis, for example, foster student *creativity and innovation* (Skill 3) by allowing students to make meaning in a multimedia format. Students not only use the written word but also audio, video, and images in their own creative ways. Wikis also offer students a platform through which to coauthor articles or essays, do peer editing of projects and reports, and communicate their ideas to a wider audience. They certainly help students to show *initiative and self-direction* (Skill 4) as they design, edit, and build their wiki to best reflect their own spin on any given topic.

WEB 2.0 AND THE TESOL STANDARDS

Web 2.0 tools can also connect directly and deeply to the TESOL (Teachers of English to Speakers of Other Languages) national standards. Below is a list of the national TESOL standards, followed by examples of Web 2.0 tools and activities that correspond to each one.

Goal 1, Standard 1   To use English to communicate in social settings: Students will use English to participate in social interactions.

Example: *Blogging to share information about favorite music, families, interests*

Goal 1, Standard 2   To use English to communicate in social settings: Students will interact in, through, and with spoken and written English for personal expression and enjoyment.

Example: *Posting information about themselves in Facebook or MySpace accounts*

Goal 1, Standard 3   To use English to communicate in social settings: Students will use learning strategies to extend their communicative competence.

Example: *Commenting on friends' photos on VoiceThread or on blogs*

Goal 2, Standard 1   To use English to achieve academically in all content areas: Students will use English to interact in the classroom.

Example: *Creating a class/group podcast on a particular content area topic*

Goal 2, Standard 2	To use English to achieve academically in all content areas: Students will use English to obtain, process, construct, and provide subject matter information in spoken and written form.
	Example: *Researching a topic and sharing relevant websites on a social bookmarking site*
Goal 2, Standard 3	To use English to achieve academically in all content areas: Students will use appropriate learning strategies to construct and apply academic knowledge.
	Example: *Cocreating a group wiki on a particular content area topic*
Goal 3, Standard 1	To use English in socially and culturally appropriate ways: Students will use the appropriate language variety, register, and genre according to audience, purpose, and setting.
	Example: *Creating a podcast to be broadcast on school radio or posted to the school website*
Goal 3, Standard 2	To use English in socially and culturally appropriate ways: Students will use nonverbal communication appropriate to audience, purpose, and setting.
	Example: *Filming a video for posting to YouTube or to show in school*
Goal 3, Standard 3	To use English in socially and culturally appropriate ways: Students will use appropriate learning strategies to extend their sociolinguistic and sociocultural competence.
	Example: *Sharing comments on a blog or wiki, adding comments to a photo on VoiceThread*

Source: Adapted from Teachers of English to Speakers of Other Languages (2006).

TESOL has also developed technology standards—both for students and for teachers. The technology standards for students are listed below, along with examples of student work or projects that connect to each one.

Goal 1: Language learners demonstrate foundational knowledge and skills in technology for a multilingual world

Standard 1	Language learners demonstrate basic operational skills in using various technological tools and Internet browsers.
	Example: *Using Microsoft Word to write essays, Microsoft Publisher to create a brochure or book, Microsoft Excel to organize and analyze data, or Google to find information*
Standard 2	Language learners are able to use available input and output devices (e.g., keyboard, mouse, printer, headset, microphone, media player, electronic whiteboard).

Example: *Using headsets and microphones to record newscasts and to create podcasts, printing work, creating student presentations on interactive electronic whiteboards*

Standard 3   Language learners exercise appropriate caution when using online sources and when engaging in electronic communication.

Example: *Brainstorming and developing classroom guidelines for safe use of Web 2.0 tools, keeping personal information safe while sending e-mails*

Standard 4   Language learners demonstrate basic competence as users of technology.

Example: *Knowing how to find information on Google or answers to questions on WikiHow*

Goal 2: Language learners use technology in socially and culturally appropriate, legal, and ethical ways

Standard 1   Language learners understand that communication conventions differ across cultures, communities, and contexts.

Example: *Comparing and contrasting texting language from different parts of the world, using Skype to understand different cultural gestures and greetings*

Standard 2   Language learners demonstrate respect for others in their use of private and public information.

Example: *Developing Voki avatars to serve as virtual identities, not revealing addresses or other sensitive private information in e-mails or on Facebook*

Goal 3: Language learners effectively use and critically evaluate technology-based tools as aids in the development of their language-learning competence as part of formal instruction and for further learning

Standard 1   Language learners effectively use and evaluate available technology-based productivity tools.

Example: *Using Microsoft Word to write prose or poetry, using Excel for spreadsheets, posting files to GoogleDocs, finding and saving bookmarks on Diigo*

Standard 2   Language learners appropriately use and evaluate available technology-based language skill-building tools.

Example: *Using podcasts like EnglishPod to practice pronunciation, watching videos on YouTube to observe nonverbal communication*

Standard 3	Language learners appropriately use and evaluate available technology-based tools for communication and collaboration.

Example: *Using wikis to do group projects, posting comments on blogs, Skyping with classmates to practice for a class presentation*

Standard 4	Language learners use and evaluate available technology-based research tools appropriately.

Example: *Using Wikipedia to find intial information on a topic, vetting websites to determine validity*

Standard 5	Language learners recognize the value of technology to support autonomy, lifelong learning, creativity, metacognition, collaboration, personal pursuits, and productivity.

Example: *Using a variety of Web 2.0 tools to create and share school and personal information*

Source: Adapted from Teachers of English to Speakers of Other Languages (1996–2007).

The integration of Web 2.0 tools into ESL and mainstream curricula will create natural connections to these TESOL technology standards both for the students and for ESL teachers. Web 2.0 tools can help teachers develop and maintain technological skills while also learning ways to enhance student learning. These tools also allow teachers to provide more frequent and meaningful feedback and assessments while facilitating record keeping and communication with students.

SAFETY CONCERNS AND THE WEB

Before completing our discussion of the reasons for using Web 2.0 tools with our English language learners, we should address one of the biggest challenges to incorporating them into the school curriculum: safety concerns. There are legitimate fears regarding the sharing of students' identities and the posting of personal information online. However, fears based on sensationalized media reports of cyber stalkers and other relatively rare incidents can cause a school to close itself off to the powerful potential of Web 2.0 tools. According to the website ConnectSafely.org, some of the negative effects of "technopanics" are damaging because they

- Cause schools to fear and block digital media when they need to be teaching constructive use, employing social-technology devices, and teaching new media literacy and citizenship throughout the curriculum.
- Turn schools into barriers rather than contributors to young people's constructive use of technology.

- Increase the irrelevancy of school to active young social-technology users via the sequestering or banning of educational technology and hamstringing some of the most spirited and innovative educators.
- Reduce the competitiveness of U.S. education among developed countries already effectively employing educational technology and social media in schools.
- Reduce the competitiveness of U.S. technology and media businesses practicing good corporate citizenship where youth online safety is concerned.
- Widen the participation gap for youth—technopanics are barriers, for children and teens, to full, constructive participation in participatory culture and democracy. (Adapted from Collier, n.d.)

Every school district must come to some consensus regarding students' (and teachers') use of the Internet relating to schoolwork. Most school districts, for example, have a policy that details what can be uploaded to the school website, what student information can be shared online, and how students can use the Internet during the school day and for homework. Check with your school's technology specialist for information about your school's policies.

Whatever your school's rules and regulations regarding the appropriate use of Web 2.0 tools, there are ways to make the experience safe and enjoyable for your students. For example, some schools choose to allow students to post only their first names and first initial of their last names on their blogs or wikis. Other schools post video and photos of students with no names listed at all. Many schools block sites like YouTube, since students can come across inappropriate videos very easily, while others opt for allowing YouTube and teaching students how to navigate the site safely. Different rules work for different contexts. Before working with Web 2.0 tools with your students, it is important to understand your school's policies. If your school doesn't have a policy in place, volunteer to be on a committee to establish them. (Check out discussions on the topic of "Acceptable Use Policies" on the Classroom 2.0 website at http://www.classroom20.com/forum/topic/listForTag?tag=aup.) To help start the discussion, each chapter of this book contains a section including guidelines for safe use of a variety of Web 2.0 tools.

As the use of these technologies grows in the K–12 school setting, it is imperative that schools establish a clear and comprehensive set of rules that allow teachers and students to feel comfortable and supported in the work they do on the World Wide Web. For more detailed information, download and read the excellent publication: "Enhancing Child Safety and Online Technologies," the final report of the Internet Safety Technical Task Force to the Multi-State Working Group on Social Networking of State Attorneys General of the United States (available online at: http://cyber.law.harvard.edu/pubrelease/isttf/).

8

Assessment in the Partnership Pedagogy

Marc Prensky

Guiding Questions

1. What are the roles of assessment, in general and in partnering?
2. What types of assessment are most useful for partnering students?
3. How can we assess the progress of all participants in the educational process?

As we look to assess our partnering students, let's begin by stepping back and thinking for a minute about what assessment is for. Most of the assessment we do these days is for sorting and comparing. That is, tests allow us to rank individuals, schools, and even countries by who is "ahead" and who is "behind." Almost all of it is based on average scores, across a class, social group, city, and so on.

This comparison is great for managers and politicians. They want to see averages rise. They want to see schools that had ranked lower rank higher. They want to see adequate yearly progress. It is also great for admissions officers, whether we are talking about admission to college, the military, or jobs. In fact, standardized testing started in the military in World War I.

But does any of this really help individual students? In my judgment it does not—at least not directly. What an individual student is (or should be) interested in is not whether his or her class is improving, or even whether he or she has moved up or down in relation to the rest of the class. An individual student should be interested in the answers to these questions: Am I improving? Am I learning? Are my skills getting better? Am I well prepared to face my future? What should I be working on?

USEFUL ASSESSMENT

Beyond Just Summative and Formative

The usual types of assessment we talk about are summative and formative. Summative is the single mark or score on a test, with no other feedback. This is what is used for ranking and comparison. Although perhaps useful for some purposes, it is of little use to a student other than as either an ego booster (or, too often, an ego deflator).

A more useful type of assessment is formative. This is assessment with feedback, the purpose of which is to help a student improve. Formative assessment includes papers and tests marked with comments. The trouble with most formative assessment in our schools is that the feedback comes too late and is too far removed from the creation of the work and the decisions students made to be useful. So despite teachers' often herculean efforts to mark and return homework or tests, the feedback does little to actually help students improve. Because assessment is only truly formative if feedback is actually read, thought about, and acted upon.

Ipsative Assessment

There are, however, other types of useful assessment. One is ipsative, which refers to beating your personal best.[25] Ipsative is the kind of assessment used, for example, in sports. No one gives you a number or letter grade (except in a few types of competition); it is your results that matter. Improvement is just that: doing better—going faster, scoring more points, or whatever the sport requires. Increments are carefully measured. People work hard to shave a tenth or even a hundredth of a second off their best time. Careful statistics and records are kept on individual performances (such as the baseball batting average, or the pitcher's earned run average.)

We do have some ipsative assessments in our schools; they go by the phrases "raising your grade" and "doing better on the next test." Unfortunately, we rarely break performance down into individual skills, although some teachers, schools, and report cards have taken to doing this. It would be useful for partnering teachers to do even more of this, in the same way a complex video game shows players all the different skills they need to get better at, and lets them know exactly where they stand on each one as they strive to move up through the levels of the game.

Peer Assessment

Another kind of useful assessment is peer assessment, which involves having students' work assessed by a group of their classmates or peers in other places. The value of peer assessment is twofold. On the one hand, if done well it can give students a feeling that their work truly has an audience and that that audience (i.e., their peers) cares about their work. And it can also give students some appreciation of the work of their peers and classmates, and where their own work stands in relation.

Peer assessment is easily facilitated by digital technology. For today's students, peer assessment works particularly well with work posted online and online portfolios. Students can see the work of their classmates (or peers in other places) and give feedback. By posting their work online—on blogs, YouTube, or other sharing sites—it becomes easy for students to invite comments from other students. Since comments can be made public, this extends the value of peer evaluation far beyond the traditional "exchange papers with your neighbor."

> **Check It Out!**
>
> Here are some resources for peer assessment:
>
> www.tnellen.com/cybereng/38.html
>
> www.tnellen.com/cybereng/peer.html

Real-World Assessment

Feedback and assessment become "real world" as we extend the meaning of *peer* around the globe, and as students in different schools, cities, and countries give feedback on our partnering classes' online work. Students often welcome this world feedback and seek it out on their own. Blog posts can often be commented on by people anywhere, and students can see the number of comments each post gets. When a student makes a how-to video and then posts it online, getting feedback is a great assessment of their learning. And equally important, doing so adds to the pool of videos available to others. Many students offer up their budding language skills on YouTube for public feedback.

> **Check It Out!**
>
> Here are some language students who have put themselves online in order to get feedback:
>
> www.youtube.com/watch?v=G8RCVg E1CjQ
>
> www.youtube.com/watch?v=VYbUjg bjzCE

A type of real-world assessment often used in business is "360-degree" assessment, whereby a person's work is assessed not only by his or her bosses and peers but also by the people who work for him or her. An equivalent for teachers would be if you were assessed each year not only by your administrators, but also by your fellow teachers and your students.

Two fields that have long used real-world peer evaluation with great success are studio art and architecture. Education programs in these fields typically hold regular critiques (sometimes known as charettes) during which everyone, students and teachers alike, gets to give an opinion of each student's work, with the emphasis on constructive feedback. By doing such critiquing on a regular basis (and having it done to their work), students learn to be better critics of others, as well as to accept criticism of their own efforts offered in the spirit of mutual respect and making work better. It would benefit both students and teachers to use this type of assessment more in all classrooms.

Check It Out!

Guidelines for student critiques can be found at http://artsedge.kennedy-center.org/content/3338/.

Many teachers have found that just knowing they are writing or creating for a real audience (and will receive real feedback and assessment) motivates students to increase the quality of their work.

Self-Assessment

The final kind of useful assessment I will discuss—self-assessment—is by far, I think, the most important. Unfortunately, it is the least used in our classrooms. Self-assessment is critical because it is what today's students will need and use for the rest of their lives in order to control their actions. While in the future they may get some assessments annually at work, most of what they need will be to say to themselves (just as we do, or should), "This is an area where I'm weak. How can I get better?" The more we help our students understand when and how to do this self-assessment on their own, the better off they will be. If they rely only on their teachers, or others, as outside arbiters of their progress, they will be at a loss for how to assess themselves and improve for the rest of their lives.

Assessing Students With Their Tools

There is one more thing that needs to be mentioned in any discussion of assessment in partnering. More and more, partnering students should be evaluated with their tools. This means that they should be evaluated while using the same tools that they carry with them and, hopefully, use daily in their work: calculators, computers, and cell phones. In the 21st century, when students have increasing access to these digital tools and are increasingly integrating those tools into the learning process, it makes little sense, when evaluating students, to take those tools away. Can you imagine a doctor being asked to make a heart evaluation but being told not to use his or her stethoscope?

Most math educators have finally realized that calculators and computers—once students have learned to use them properly—actually enhance students' mathematical capabilities. What is positive about allowing these tools in assessment is that it forces both students and teachers to focus on the true fundamentals of why and how we calculate, rather than on just memorization and mechanical algorithms. Although there are still some tests in which these tools are not allowed, the direction of change is clear.

Similar attitude changes with regard to tools are happening in all other subjects. Teachers are increasingly allowing students to use their computers and/or cell phones during tests and exams. Although this may seem odd or make little sense if the tests are about facts students can easily look up (unless everyone has equal access, and the test is about speed or efficiency), if the tests involve gathering facts and evidence from the web and drawing and supporting conclusions, digital tools should enhance students' ability to demonstrate their understanding (which is, hopefully, what we are testing).

Obviously, as such changes take place, current definitions of "cheating" will need to be changed to accommodate these tools and define their acceptable use. But that is not a bad thing, or even a new phenomenon. In many colleges and universities, and some high schools, the use of tools during certain exams has been going on for years—giving so-called open-book tests is standard operating procedure. So why not give "open-phone tests," as some schools are already doing?

PARTNERING TIP

Think about the situations in which evaluating students with their tools might be a good idea. Ask your students about this. Are they in favor of it? How would they deal with the various issues that might arise?

What do you and your students think of open-phone tests? (Remember the student mentioned on page 105? During one of my presentations, the high school senior told me, "Most of our tests already are open-phone tests—you guys just don't know it!") Think of experiments you and your partnering students might do in this area. Try creating and giving an open-phone test in each of your classes. Discuss the results with your students, and then iterate to make it more effective.

ASSESSING STUDENTS' PROGRESS

In partnering, therefore, the best ways to assess students are to

- give students necessary and helpful feedback (formative),
- encourage them to do better and better (ipsative),
- provide them with feedback from fellow students (peer),
- include evaluations from a global audience (real-world),
- get them to understand their own progress (self-assessment),
- allow them to use their tools (21st century), and
- because we have to, satisfy the outside world by using standardized tests (summative).

Addressing Assessment Fears

The number-one fear that teachers and administrators (as well as parents) often express about partnering and assessment is that students learning in this new way will not do as well on current standardized exams. The second, related fear is that all the new and different things that students are doing, and the skills (verbs) they are learning through partnering will somehow not count, because they are not tested.

The first of these fears is unjustified; the second is at least partially real, and is a concern that we can and should do something about.

The reason I say that the fear that students will not do as well is unjustified is that everyone I have talked to who is in a position to know says the opposite. I have heard a great many teachers and principals (mostly from charter schools, where partnering is more widely practiced) express that partnering students in fact do better on exams, because they are more engaged in their learning. I don't know that anyone has collected data on this in a systematic, quantitative way as yet, but it is something that should be attempted (with the caveat—usually ignored—that quantitative data are easily manipulable to support one's point).

The fear that important skills go unmeasured is, however, justified, because they do. We need to upgrade and expand almost all our assessments to include more skills-based learning around all the partnering verbs. Organizations such as the Partnership for 21st Century Skills (www.21stcenturyskills.org) are working on ways to measure and assess a variety of these skills, and partnering teachers should be aware of their, and others', efforts.

ASSESSING TEACHERS' PROGRESS

I have already referred to teachers self-assessing their own partnering skills, that is, figuring out where they are along the partnering continuum (or progress line) and setting goals to move ahead. Believing as I do that self-assessment is the best and most important kind of assessment, we could just leave it there: every partnering teacher can and should self-assess, at least annually, on the partnering criteria. But it is also important to make that self-assessment known, certainly to administrators and probably to students and parents as well, and to see if it jibes with the assessments of others, particularly of the partnering students.

One could conceivably do this sharing of where people stand through a system of colors (preferably noncontroversial ones with no other meanings) or other symbols. So one might call the six partnering levels Red, Orange, Yellow, Green, Blue, and Indigo, where teachers and students are striving "across the rainbow" toward the "unattainable violet." Both teachers and students could somehow display the colors and be recognized when they move up to another level.

Another function of the colors, and the public knowledge, would be that those who are further along down the road to partnering could more easily find and help those who aren't as far along to help them move forward. Such a buddy system is best if voluntary, but it could also be imposed if progress is unacceptably slow.

It is, of course, important that progress along the partnering scale not be wholly conflated with being a "good" teacher. There are many qualities that make a teacher good, and the ability to partner—important as it is—is only one of them. There are many other key qualities, including empathy for students (i.e., liking kids); knowledge of, enthusiasm for, and being up-to-date in one's subject area; and ability to relate to and deal with all the interested parties (including colleagues, administrators, and parents). A teacher may have many of these qualities, but to have them all requires dedication and effort. It's a lot like golf—for a professional golfer to win even a couple of major tournaments requires many different skills (driving, chipping, putting, concentrating, decision making under pressure, etc.). Most professional teachers are, like most professional golfers, "journeymen" or "journeywomen" (in golf terms), that is, far better than any nonprofessional, but always striving to do what they do better.

Because the skills of partnering are enormously important to students, all teachers should be motivated to get better at them. It has been suggested by some that progress along the partnering continuum be made part of teachers' annual assessment, with expectations for progress set and actual progress reviewed. Whether this is done formally or not depends on each individual school and district, but it is certainly something that is worth thinking about.

ASSESSING ADMINISTRATORS' PROGRESS

Given the way the U.S. education system works, school administrators are, as I write, all over the board in their support of partnering as a pedagogical goal. I speak often to groups of "converted" administrators—those who listen to kids, see the future, and are willing and even eager to move toward it. But I also hear often from teachers trying to accomplish many of the things outlined in this book that they feel unsupported, or held back by their administrators, as they try to move forward on their own toward partnering.

Thus it is worth having some form of assessment for administrators as supporters of the partnering pedagogy. One could certainly ask the following questions:

- Do administrators (in a school or district) believe partnering is the way to go?
- Is there consensus? If not, where is the discord?
- Do administrators know where each of their teachers stands on the partnering continuum?
- In what ways do administrators support partnering?
- In what ways do administrators support teachers who are looking to partner more?
- In what ways do administrators help recalcitrant teachers change?
- In what ways do administrators support partnering students and their parents?

Based on the answers to these questions, one could certainly rate administrators on their propensity toward, and support of, partnering. But who would do this? It needs to be done throughout the administrative hierarchy, from the school board on down.

ASSESSING PARENTS' PROGRESS

Parents, as everyone knows, are crucial to their kids' education. Today most parents are caught, just as we all are, in the great changes of our times, and most are as perplexed as the rest of us about what to do. Parents all want the best for their children, including the best education possible. Yet today it is far from clear what that means. Parents hear of and see a number of often-controversial educational changes being undertaken in their children's classrooms, and it is not surprising that a number of them should ask, "Why all the changes? Is partnering really what my kid needs to succeed and get to college? Why can't my kid be educated in the same way I was?"

It is part of the partnering teacher's job to help parents recognize just how much the world has changed, and with it their children. Partnering teachers need to help parents understand that to meet the needs of the future (both society's and their children's), 21st century students require a different type of education than their parents got—even if the parents think they got a good one.

Both partnering students and partnering teachers need strong parental support in order to get the job done. Here, therefore, are my recommendations to partnering teachers regarding parents:

- Involve your students' parents as much as you can. Try thinking of them as your students as well, that is, as people you are educating. It would be great for the school to hold an open house where the partnering work can be discussed; perhaps you can hold one for your students' parents. When you do this, have teachers, students, administrators, and parents around for a question-and-answer session with the audience.
- Use as much technology as you can to communicate to parents what you are doing, in whatever language(s) they speak. Partnering students can help make short videos to explain what you are doing, which you can share online (if parents have access), via CD, or even via students' cell phones. Your students can set up a multimedia blog or newsletter of their work and show it to their parents at home (if there is a computer) or at the library. As digital TVs achieve higher penetration, they can be used to play these as well.
- Feel free to share parts of this book (and other books supporting partnering) with your students' parents, and try to get copies put in the school and local public libraries. Encourage parents to read about partnering and the changes in 21st century students and learning.
- Encourage your students to share their positive classroom experiences frequently with their parents, and their enthusiasm, once it emerges. You can even, as a project, have simulated conversations with parents and talk with your students about how they might answer their parents' objections, if they have any. It is their children's enthusiasm for school that will ultimately be the strongest persuader.
- Invite parents, as appropriate, to come into your classroom, either in person or virtually, and to participate on student teams.

A Checklist for Parents of Partnering Students

Finally, consider handing out to parents a checklist of what they can do to help their children and letting them self-assess how well they are helping their children learn. This checklist might consist of an overall self-assessed grade, plus separate grades in the following areas:

- Listening to their children
- Helping their children
- Encouraging their children

- Participating in parent-teacher meetings and other parent events
- Sharing their knowledge by coming to school and talking with students

There might also be a place in such an evaluation (or as a separate exercise) for students to write or say, "Here's what I wish I got more of/less of from my parent."

ASSESSING SCHOOLS' PROGRESS

How do we evaluate a partnering school? First, of course, we have to acknowledge that the standard (and increasingly standardized) ways of evaluating schools aren't going to go away and that partnering schools will be evaluated using the same criteria as all others. But that, in fact, is good news because we can expect to see a number of positive results as a school moves more and more toward partnering as a full-time pedagogy. These include the following:

1. Rising test scores—when partnering is done correctly, students will be (1) happier with what they are doing; (2) more engaged in their own learning; (3) clearer, through the guided questions, about what they need to know; and (4) practicing many more skills on their own and with their peers, and therefore will be more effective learners

2. Much more quality student work to post and be proud of—online and off

3. Teachers sharing successes and working together much more than in a traditional school

4. Much better teacher-student relations—essentially those of partners

When implemented well, partnering schools and classrooms should consistently be among the very best.

ASSESSING OUR NATION'S PROGRESS, AND THE WORLD'S

Much has been made recently about America "falling behind" other countries in education. I am not sure I totally agree, either with the diagnosis or with some of the proposed solutions. The comparisons seem to depend on rankings on supposedly comparative tests and on less than desirable graduation rates in U.S. high schools and colleges.

While both of these measures are useful data, they do not tell the whole story and—much worse—they lead to wrong prescriptions about what to do about education. To understand why, ask yourself the following questions:

- Will the United States (or any country) be better off in 2050 with a population that is confident that it can compete on international tests, or a population well versed in 21st century tools for problem solving—a population that knows that it can, in any situation, figure out the right thing to do, get it done, do it with others, do it creatively, and continually get better?

- Will the United States (or any country) be better off in 2050 with a population that can read and write at a ninth-grade level (assuming we could ever attain that, which is highly unlikely) and in which every person has at least an associate's degree (ditto), or with a population that is confident that it can make our increasingly complex digital machines do what they need (i.e., can program at some level) and is highly entrepreneurial?

Being "behind" truly depends on what you measure. As Steven Johnson pointed out recently in an article in *Time,* the United States is responsible for just about all of the Internet innovations in recent years.[26] So in some important areas, we have been and continue to be ahead, and being behind in other areas, such as learning the old-fashioned "school" stuff, may not matter. That depends, of course, what students do instead of learning it, but it is very important that we come to grips with the fact that the things we are required to teach today may not be the things our students need for the future at all, and most of it (likely 80 percent by the Pareto rule) almost certainly isn't.

And finally, why do we insist on measuring learning nation by nation, rather than measuring the world as a whole? Such an approach only encourages competition and fighting, and neglects and discourages the "world" learning that the technologies of the 21st century are so quickly enabling. Education is an area in which we should all be cooperating, trying hard to raise the level not just for Americans, but for every child in the world.

Part III

Safety and Policy Matters

CHAPTER NINE

Policies, Procedures, and Contracts

Communicating Expectations to Teachers, Students, and Parents

Aimée M. Bissonette

A middle school has a zero-tolerance, "no-cell-phones-in-the-classroom" policy. Students are permitted to have cell phones at school but must keep them turned-off and in their lockers except for before and after school and during lunch. A few students have parents deployed overseas with the military. Because those parents have little control over when they can call their children, the principal has made an exception and allowed their children to keep cell phones with them in class, as long as they are set on vibrate. The parent of another student is in prison and can only call her child during school hours. The principal has made an exception for this child as well. Several parents learned about the exceptions the principal has made for these children and are now demanding that their children also be allowed to have their cell phones in the classroom.

A high school without a written policy on student organization web pages is experiencing an increase in the number of requests for dedicated space on the district web page from various student groups so that they can create web pages for their clubs and teams. The school has granted similar requests in the past to the football and baseball teams. Those teams created web pages and posted their rosters, schedules, and league standings. However, the most recent request for space is of some concern to the principal. The request is from the high school's gay-straight alliance, a group of students without official high-school club status.

A middle-school teacher moonlights as a stand-up comic at a local comedy club. By all reports, the teacher's routine is quite funny, but it includes a number of off-color jokes about fictional students and life as a public school teacher. Members of the school board have met and discussed the matter. They understand that the teacher has the right to pursue stand-up comedy, but they wonder what, if any, restrictions they can require him to place on his routine.

A cceptable use policies (AUPs), bullying policies, parent permission slips, photographic releases, disciplinary procedures—all of these, and more, are used by schools to define the rights and responsibilities of students, teachers, and staff. Although they vary in form, length, and content, all are contracts and all are binding on the members of the school community.

Contracts, in essence, establish the *private law* developed by and between parties to address specific situations and relationships. Contracts allow parties to create their own rules of the game. Parties can use contracts to define the terms under which they will work together. Parties also can change those terms (i.e., can amend their contracts) if changing the terms makes sense in light of changing circumstances. It is the flexibility of contracts that makes them ideally suited to handling technology issues, particularly those issues relating to student, teacher, and staff use of school computers and the school Internet system.

CONTRACT LAW

At first blush, the term *contract* may bring to mind multipage, form business agreements, thick with fine print and boilerplate language. But school handbooks, school policies, even simple parent permission slips are all contracts. In fact, school policies may be the most widely used contracts between schools and the members of their school communities. Well-crafted policies lay out expectations, define rights and responsibilities, describe procedures, and detail the remedies available if the policy is violated. Policies allow administrators to use contract-law principles to create a type of private law that governs the school community.

Contracts can be customized to address particular situations and to serve the needs of different groups. For example, a school district may draft one district-wide Internet use policy for its students but, within that policy, may prescribe different disciplinary sanctions for violations of the policy based on the grade level of potential offenders. As another example, a school district with a long-standing antibullying policy may, based on its finding of an increase in offensive text messaging and e-mailing among students, amend its policy to include a prohibition against cyberbullying. Contract law allows school leaders to tailor school rules to their particular school settings.

School leaders craft the policies they think are appropriate (often with the assistance of legal counsel), put students and parents on notice of the school's contract terms by publishing and distributing the policies, and require parents and students to return signed permission or acknowledgment forms before student privileges are granted. School policies, in essence, become the law of the school district, albeit a flexible kind of law that can be revisited and amended as needed to fit the ever changing needs of the school district. In the first example above, for instance, the middle school has a written policy relating to cell phones. It appears, though, that given the increase in military deployments in recent years, the policy may need to be modified. The flexibility of contract law permits this.

School AUPs are the primary vehicles for establishing private law for school communities on the issues of use of school computers and the school Internet system. AUPs vary greatly from school to school. They are all similar, though, in that they lay out the terms and conditions surrounding the use of school computer and Internet resources; describe student, teacher, and staff privileges; prescribe rules of behavior; and identify the consequences for violating those rules. They can be customized to provide varying privileges depending on user age, grade level, or user status (student versus teacher) and can require participation in mandatory training before user privileges are extended. Perhaps most notably, they can be revisited and amended as often as the school deems necessary, which makes it possible to incorporate new technology.

>
>
> ### Resource Alert!
>
> A sample AUP is included in Resource B in this book. Additional online resources relating to AUPs and policy drafting guidelines are also included at the end of this chapter.

The district in the second example needs to amend its AUP. Given the increasing number of requests, the district must establish a policy relating to student organization web pages. Consultation with legal counsel will reveal that the district essentially has three options: (1) It can draft a policy that establishes viewpoint-neutral standards for student organization web pages (i.e., standards that require that posted material relate specifically to organization activities and programs); (2) it can draft a policy that prohibits student organization web pages entirely; or (3) it can draft a policy that permits student organization web pages, with the only restriction being that the web pages must comply with district communication rules and school rules. Once the district has determined the direction it wants to go, it can proceed with amending its AUP.

School records retention policies also are contracts. Records retention policies address the storage, retention, and destruction of electronic records created and stored on school computers and Internet systems. These records include student grade reports, attendance records, standardized test scores, and other student-specific information, as well as information related to the school as a whole.

Records retention policies are even more important now, because of a December 2006 change to the Federal Rules of Civil Procedure. Although electronic records have been used as evidence in lawsuits for over a decade, the change to the Federal Rules formalized the status of electronic records in federal lawsuits. A school's failure to preserve electronic records necessary to a lawsuit can now result in harsh sanctions against the school and its legal counsel. These sanctions can include financial penalties, exclusion of witnesses or pleadings, adverse inference instructions, dismissals, and default judgments.

Because, under the amended rules, schools no longer can allow haphazard storing or purging of electronic records, a contract law solution must be crafted. Schools, working with legal counsel, need to draft records retention policies appropriate for their schools and policies that fit their schools' needs and operating plans, while still providing adequate direction and protection for the information technology (IT) professionals charged with records oversight. Just as with the AUPs above, the policies drafted by different schools likely will vary from school to school. The flexibility of contract law is necessary for this scenario in which the law is expected to continue to evolve.

Throughout the earlier chapters of this book, there are references to a variety of school policies. Chapters 1 and 2 discuss the need for policies on cyberbullying, as well as specific policies regarding the use of electronic devices like cell phones and digital recording devices. Chapter 3 discusses the need to address teacher off-campus speech via policy and provides a sample employee blogging policy. Chapter 4 discusses the need for policies that address student privacy and data security. Chapter 5 discusses filtering and the need for policies that describe the rights and responsibilities of students, teachers, and staff with regard to accessing inappropriate materials. Chapter 6 discusses copyright and the need for an updated copyright compliance policy. These are just a few examples of policies school leaders will be charged with drafting for their schools.

THE ROLE OF THE SCHOOLS

There are a number of things schools must do if they want the policies they draft to be effective. The first is that school leaders need to frankly acknowledge the legal risks in today's 21st century-classroom environment. Legal claims relating to school computer and Internet use can arise even in the absence of intentional wrongdoing. School leaders need to identify all the foreseeable risks to students, teachers, and staff and take reasonable precautions to minimize those risks.

Schools also need to establish and communicate clear boundaries to all members of the school community. Part of this communication is that the school Internet system exists for a limited educational purpose. Schools should emphasize that the school Internet system is primarily intended for students, class assignments, and staff professional-development activities.

As part of the communication effort, schools must be prepared to provide educational programming for students as well as professional-development training for teachers and staff regarding appropriate use of school computers and the school Internet system, student and Internet privacy issues, appropriate monitoring of student Internet use, and appropriate measures to take when issues or concerns arise. In fact, with regard to the third issue above, the school board's concerns about what the teacher may say in his stand-up comic routine may be resolved via education. The teacher very likely could make small adjustments to his stand-up comedy act that would alleviate the school board's concerns about student privacy and teacher off-duty speech without negatively affecting the quality of his act.

Schools should also establish a policy describing the recommended chain of command for reporting incidents. In tandem with this policy, schools may want to craft age-appropriate tests students must pass before being granted a "license" to participate in less-structured Internet activities, such as online chat rooms and social-networking sites.

Five-Step Plan for Drafting School Policy

1. *Collect data.* Review existing school policies and identify the gaps in those policies. Identify the objectives for the new/revised policy. Gather data from educational associations, publications, other schools, and legal sources relating to the new/revised policy.

2. *Solicit input.* Invite teachers, staff, parents, and other stakeholders to provide comments regarding the content and structure of the new/revised policy.

3. *Draft the new/revised policy.* Refer to your particular school's procedures to determine who will be charged with drafting and what procedures should be followed.

4. *Circulate the draft of the new/revised policy.* Solicit feedback from members of the school community.

5. *Approve and disseminate the new/revised policy.* Refer to your particular school's procedures to determine the necessary approval process. Disseminate the approved policy to parents and ensure that the new policy is included in print and hard-copy student handbooks. Communicate news of the approved policy to other members of the school community.

Finally, schools need to acknowledge their role in educating parents about computer and Internet issues. Schools need to communicate early and often with parents, beginning with fall mailings and open houses and continuing through the school year as events occur or new technology is incorporated. Schools must keep parents apprised of how students are using the Internet in the classroom. They also need to advise parents that, although the district monitors student use of the system at school, parents still need to discuss individual family values with children. Most important, schools need to obtain parent consent before allowing student use of the school's computer and Internet system.

Sample Policy Language: Parents' Responsibility

I. Outside of school, parents bear responsibility for the same guidance of Internet use as they exercise with information sources such as television, telephones, radio, movies, and other possibly offensive media. Parents are responsible for monitoring their student's use of the school district system and of the Internet if the student is accessing the school district system from home or a remote location.

II. Parents will be notified that their students will be using school district resources/accounts to access the Internet and that the school district will provide parents the option to request alternative activities not requiring Internet access. This notification should include:

   (a) A copy of the user notification form provided to the student user.

   (b) A description of parent/guardian responsibilities.

   (c) A notification that the parents have the option to request alternative educational activities not requiring Internet access and the material to exercise this option.

   (d) A statement that the Student Online Acceptable Use Consent Form must be signed by the user, the parent or guardian, and the supervising teacher prior to use by the student.

   (e) A statement that the school district's acceptable use policy is available for parental review.

Source: Internet Acceptable Use and Safety Policy (Policy 524), Edina Public Schools.

CONCLUSION

The flexibility of contract law makes it ideal for establishing the parameters of the school community. Contracts can take the form of any number of common school documents and can be customized to meet nearly any situation. Acceptable use policies are the most common kind of contract used by schools. Other contracts include student handbooks, photo releases, and permission forms. Schools should take care in drafting contracts by thoroughly researching their options, anticipating potential problems, soliciting input from members of the school community, and consulting legal counsel. Once finalized, school contracts should be revisited regularly.

Checklist Regarding Policies and Procedures

Has your district done the following?

☐ **Made an assessment of legal risks arising from use of classroom technology?** School leaders need to identify all the foreseeable risks to students, teachers, and staff arising from the uses of technology in its classrooms. This book gives an overview of the many issues schools may encounter. Schools should communicate with legal counsel with regard to their specific technology uses and practices to assess any legal implications. Policy contracts should be drafted to address any potential issues identified.

☐ **Communicated clear expectations and boundaries with regard to all uses of technology in the classroom?** It is important that users of school technology resources know that the resources are for limited educational purposes. Schools should emphasize that the school Internet system is primarily intended for students, class assignments, and staff professional-development activities.

☐ **Enlisted student, staff, and parent input in drafting school technology contracts?** Enlist school technology stakeholders in the review and drafting of technology contracts. Parent, student, teacher, and staff participation will more accurately define actual practices and generate greater acceptance of final policies.

☐ **Established training requirements and policy acceptance procedures prior to allowing use of technology resources?** It is important that schools obtain acknowledgment from students, parents, and staff that they have familiarized themselves with school expectations with regard to computer and Internet use and that they accept the terms and conditions of use as stated in school technology contracts. Schools may also establish training requirements regarding appropriate use of school technology resources prior to allowing users access to such resources.

❑ **Incorporated parent education into your school's technology strategy?** Schools should communicate their technology policies and expectations to parents at every opportunity. New school year mailings and open houses provide opportunities to apprise parents of school technology policies. Schools should also advise parents of the need to discuss their family's values and expectations with regard to Internet use inside and outside the school setting.

❑ **Established a chain of command for reporting incidents?** It is important that school technology-use policies have clear, simple procedures for reporting, monitoring, and resolving incidents involving potential violations of school technology contracts.

Online Resources

Acceptable Use Policies: A Handbook. Virginia Department of Education. Division of Technology.

http://www.doe.virginia.gov/VDOE/Technology/AUP/home.shtml

Acceptable Use Policies for Internet Use.

http://www.media-awareness.ca/english/resources/special_initiatives/wa_resources/wa_teachers/backgrounders/acceptable _use.cfm

Internet Acceptable Use Policy Guidelines.

http://www.education-world.com/a_curr/curr093.shtml

Internet Acceptable Use Policy Template, Mississippi State Auditor's Office.

http://www.osa.state.ms.us/downloads/iupg.pdf

Network Montana Project Internet Acceptable Use Policy Template.

http://www.auditnet.org/docs/internet_acceptable_use_policy_t.htm

Resource

Sample Acceptable Use Policy

[DISTRICT] ACCEPTABLE USE OF COMPUTERS, COMPUTER NETWORKS, AND INTERNET RESOURCES

A. Introduction

The use of [District] computers, computer network, and Internet resources is a key element of the curriculum and instruction in [District]. The [District] computer network is intended for educational purposes. [District] expects that staff will incorporate appropriate use of computer network and Internet resources into the curriculum and will provide guidance and instruction to students as to their uses.

Despite its tremendous educational potential, the Internet also presents the potential for security vulnerabilities and user abuse. For safety purposes, [District] employs both an Internet filter and firewall. [District] maintains compliance with the Children's Internet Protection Act (CIPA). The board expects all employees and students to abide by the [District] Acceptable Use of Computers, Computer Networks, and Internet Resources Procedures set forth below. Failure to follow the guidelines will result in disciplinary action. [District] is not responsible for ensuring the accuracy or usability of any information found on external networks.

Parent(s)/guardian(s) will be given the opportunity to determine their child's access to the Internet when they first begin school in [District], Grade 3, Grade 6, and Grade 9. [District] will not be responsible for any and all claims arising out of or related to the usage of this interconnected computer system.

B. Access

1. [District] offers Internet access for staff and student use. This policy sets forth the online acceptable use procedures for all staff and students using the district's computers and network. This acceptable use policy applies to all technologies capable of

accessing, inputting or extracting information/data from the district's computer network, electronic mail (e-mail), and Internet.

2. Students and employees shall have access to Internet World Wide Web information resources through their classroom, library, or school computer lab.

3. Students and their parent(s)/guardian(s) must sign an Acceptable Use Consent Form to be granted access to the Internet via the [District] computer network.

4. A signature will be required when they first begin school in [District], Grade 3, Grade 6, and Grade 9. Parent(s)/guardian (s) can withdraw their approval at any time.

5. The school district shall provide each employee, where appropriate, an e-mail account.

6. Students shall be provided limited educational access to a classroom/library e-mail account upon request of their classroom teacher for completion of curriculum-related assignments.

7. The use of the school district system and access to use of the Internet is a privilege, not a right. The school district reserves the right to limit or remove any user's access to the school district's computer system, equipment, e-mail system, and Internet access at any time for any reason. Depending on the nature and degree of the violation and the number of previous violations, unacceptable use of the school district system or the Internet may result in one or more of the following consequences: suspension or cancellation of use or access privileges; payments for damages and repairs; loss of credit and/or reduction of grade; discipline under other appropriate school district policies, including suspension, expulsion, exclusion, or termination of employment; or civil or criminal liability under other applicable laws.

C. Educational Purpose

1. The [District] computer network has not been established as a public access service and is not an "open" or "limited open" forum. The term "educational purposes" includes, but is not limited to, information management, classroom activities, media-center projects, educational research, career development, and curriculum activities using computers and Internet resources.

2. The [District] computer network has not been established as a public access service or a public forum. [District] has the right to

place reasonable restrictions on the material accessed or posted through the system into the intranet, e-mail, websites, and list server. Students and employees are expected to follow the rules set forth in this policy and the law when using the [District] computer network. The network will be monitored by staff to ensure educational utilization.

3. Students and employees may not use the [District] computer network for noneducational commercial purposes. This means that no products or services may be offered, provided, or purchased through the [District] computer network, unless such products or services are for a defined educational purpose and such activity has been preapproved by [District].

4. The [District] computers may not be used for political lobbying. It may be used to communicate with elected representatives and to express opinions to them on political issues.

D. Your Rights and Responsibilities

1. Free Speech

   Student right to free speech is set forth [District Policy], which applies also to communication on the Internet. The [District] computer network is considered a limited forum, similar to the school newspaper, and, therefore, the district may restrict speech for valid educational reasons. The district shall not restrict speech on the basis of a disagreement with the opinions expressed.

2. Search and Seizure

   a. Students and employees should not expect any privacy in the contents of personal files on the district system. Administrators and faculty may review files and messages to maintain system integrity and ensure that users are acting responsibly.

   b. The district may examine all information stored on district technology resources at any time. The district may monitor staff and student technology usage. Electronic communications, all data stored on the district's technology resources, and downloaded material, including files deleted from a user's account, may be intercepted, accessed, or searched by a district administrator or designees at any time.

   c. Routine maintenance and monitoring of [District] computer system may lead to discovery that this policy or the following policies or laws have been violated: school board policy dealing with student conduct and district discipline, school board policy dealing with student civil and legal rights and responsibilities, board policy on staff activities, and/or federal, state, or local laws.

d. An individual search shall be conducted if there is reasonable suspicion that this policy, school board policies, and/or the law have been violated. The investigation shall be reasonable and related to the suspected violation.

e. Parent(s)/guardian(s) of students have the right at any time to request to see the contents of student's e-mail files.

3. District Employees

Rights, responsibilities, and duties of district employees as they relate to e-mail and Internet use are governed by the [District] Board of Education Policies and Procedures and the master agreements between the district and the employee bargaining units. Employees may be disciplined or terminated for violating the district's policies, regulations, and procedures.

4. Due Process

a. The district shall cooperate fully with local, state, or federal officials in any investigation related to any illegal activities conducted through [District] computer network.

b. In the event there is a claim that employees or students have violated this policy or other Board policy in use of the [District] computer network, they shall be provided with a written notice of the suspected violation and an opportunity to present an explanation as defined in school board policy for students and bargaining agreements for staff.

c. If the violation also involves a violation of other provisions of school board policy, it shall be handled in a manner described in school board policy which deals with dismissal, including suspension, exclusion, and expulsion. Additional restrictions may be placed on use of individual Internet accounts, or could result in suspension, expulsion, and/or financial liability.

E. Unacceptable Uses

The following uses of the [District] computer network are considered unacceptable:

1. Personal Safety

a. Students and employees shall not post or provide personal contact information about themselves or other people on the Internet. Personal contact information includes a student's or employee's home address or telephone number, a student's school address, and an employee's work address. It is not a violation of this policy to include the school's return address on outgoing e-mail communications.

b. Students shall not agree to meet with someone contacted or met online without parent's approval. Parent(s)/guardian(s) should accompany students to approved meetings.

c. Students shall promptly disclose to their teacher or other school employee any message received that is inappropriate or causes discomfort.

2. Illegal Activities

a. Students and employees shall not attempt to gain unauthorized access to [District] computer network or to any other computer system through [District] computer network or go beyond authorized access. This includes attempting to log in through another person's account or access another person's files. These actions are illegal, even if only for the purposes of "browsing."

b. Students and employees shall not make deliberate attempts to disrupt the computer system or destroy data by spreading computer viruses or by any other means. These actions are illegal, and criminal prosecution and/or disciplinary action will be pursued.

c. Students and employees shall not use the [District] computer network system to engage in any act that is illegal; that facilitates gambling; or that violates any local, state, or federal statute.

d. Students and staff shall not use the Internet or the district's computer network to harass or threaten the safety of others.

e. Misuse of the computer equipment or network including, but not limited to, deletion or violation of password protected information, computer programs, data, password or system files; inappropriate access of files, directories, Internet sites; deliberate contamination of system, unethical use of information, or violation of copyright laws is prohibited.

3. System Security

a. Employees are responsible for their individual e-mail accounts and should take all reasonable precautions to prevent others from being able to use their accounts. Under no condition should staff provide their login identity and/or passwords to another person.

b. Students shall immediately notify a teacher or the system administrator if they have identified a possible security problem.

Students should not look for security problems, because this may be construed as an illegal attempt to gain access. Under no conditions should students provide other students with their login identity and/or network password.

c. Students and employees shall avoid the inadvertent spread of computer viruses by following the district virus protection procedures when downloading software or bringing disks into the school.

d. Students who gain access to teacher computer files, directory, programs, and website without permission from a teacher will be disciplined as defined in the student handbook.

e. The district will assign specific staff with security, management, and account responsibilities associated with the district's Internet resources and network accounts.

f. Tampering with the district's computer security system, and/or applications, and/or documents, and/or equipment, will be considered vandalism, destruction, and defacement of school property. Please be advised that it is a federal offense (felony) to break into any security system. Financial and legal consequences of such actions are the responsibility of the user and/or student's parent or guardian.

4. Inappropriate Language

a Restrictions against inappropriate language apply to public messages, private messages, and material posted on web pages.

b. Students and employees shall not use obscene, profane, lewd, vulgar, rude, inflammatory, threatening, or disrespectful language.

c. Students and employees shall not post information that could cause damage or a danger of disruption.

d. Students and employees shall not engage in personal attacks, including prejudicial or discriminatory attacks, based on a person's race, gender, sexual orientation, religion, national origin, or disability, or engage in any other harassment or discrimination prohibited by school district policy or by law.

e. Students and employees shall not harass another person. Harassment is persistently acting in a manner that distresses or annoys another person. If students or staff are told by a person to stop sending them messages, they must stop.

f. Students and employees shall not knowingly or recklessly post false or defamatory information about a person or organization.

5. Respect for Privacy

   a. Students and employees shall not repost a message that was sent to them privately without permission of the person who sent them the message.
   b. Students and employees shall not post private information about another person on the Internet. This does not prohibit staff from discussing private student information with each other or with a student's parent or guardian via e-mail, in conformance with the Data Practices Act [cite], Student Privacy Act [cite], and applicable school district policies.

6. Respecting Resource Limits

   a. Students and employees shall use the system only for educational and career development activities and limited, high-quality self-discovery and [District] curriculum activities.
   b. Students and employees will have access to limited space on their school's computer server. Student ability to download files shall be limited by mediacenter and school policy. Users are responsible for making backup copies of the documents and files that are critical to their use.
   c. Students and employees shall not post chain letters or engage in spamming. (Spamming is sending an annoying or unnecessary message to a large number of people.)
   d. Students shall not deliberately or knowingly delete another student's or employee's file.
   e. Students and employees shall only use software, including but not limited to e-mail applications and web browsers, that is supplied by the school district. Employees and students shall not install hardware or software on the school district's computer system without express permission of the director of media and technology services.

7. Plagiarism and Copyright Infringement

   a. Students and employees shall not plagiarize works that are found on the Internet. Plagiarism is taking the ideas or writings of others and presenting them as if they were yours.
   b. Students and employees shall respect the rights of copyright owners. Copyright infringement occurs when one inappropriately reproduces a work that is protected by a copyright. If a work contains language that specifies appropriate use of that work, follow the expressed requirements. If unsure whether or not work can be used, request permission from the copyright owner. Copyright law can be very confusing; ask media specialists for guidance as needed.

8. Inappropriate Access to Material

   a. Students and employees shall not use the [District] computer network to access material that is profane or obscene (pornography), contains viruses, network hacking programs, or similar programs that advocate illegal acts, or that advocates violence or discrimination towards other people (hate literature).

   b. If students mistakenly access inappropriate information, they should immediately tell their teacher, media specialist, or another district employee. This will protect them against claims that they have intentionally violated this policy.

   c. Parent(s)/guardian(s) should instruct students if there is additional material that they think it would be inappropriate for them to access. The district fully expects that students shall follow their parent's instructions in this matter.

   d. Educators will monitor student use of the Internet in schools and will take reasonable measures to prevent access by students to inappropriate materials on the Internet and World Wide Web and restrict access to materials harmful to students.

   e. The district will monitor the online activities of employees and students, and operate technology protection measures (filtering/blocking devices or software) on all computers on the district's computer network as required by law. The filtering/blocking software will attempt to protect against access to visual depictions that are obscene, harmful to students, and child pornography, as required by law. Invasion or disabling of the filtering/blocking device installed by the district, including attempts to evade or disable, is a violation of the acceptable use policy.

F. Limitation of Liability

The school district does not assume and, hereby, expressly disclaims liability for the misuse of its computers, equipment, e-mail, and Internet programs that violate this policy or any applicable law. The district makes no guarantee that the functions or the services provided by or through the district system shall be error-free or without defect. The district is not responsible for any damage suffered through the use of its computer system, including but not limited to, the loss of data, interruptions in service, the accuracy or quality of information obtained through or stored in the system, damages or injuries from improper communications, damage to property used to access school district computers or online resources, or financial obligations resulting from the use of school district resources.

10

Preventing Cyberbullying

Sameer Hinduja and Justin W. Patchin

My child struggles with her weight. In whom she thought were two of her best friends she confided her weight during a sleep over and the next day it was posted on their Bebo site. How cruel can kids be? Anyhow, I see profanity and slams every day on the Internet while kids are so-called "chatting," as a parent my kids know that I am going to step in and read what is going on at any given minute. More should do so.

—Submitted anonymously

One of the questions we are asked most often when we speak with school professionals, parents, and the media is "How can cyberbullying be prevented?" Indeed, some of you have picked up this book solely to figure out the answer to that important question. We devote this chapter to identifying a number of practical approaches that we believe can decrease the frequency of online harassment among youth. While there is no magic bullet to deal with it, there are a number of informed steps that can minimize the likelihood of adolescent aggression in cyberspace. Moreover, the advice in this chapter should equip you not only to prevent cyberbullying but also to lay the groundwork for when you must respond to cyberbullying (see Chapter 7).

Some suggest that the only way to prevent cyberbullying and some of the other negatives associated with adolescent Internet use is to forbid kids from going online. To be sure, this is the least appropriate course of action. Think about it for a moment. Would you agree that visiting and touring Washington, D.C., would be a fantastic learning opportunity for students? Sure it is: The war memorials, presidential monuments, and governmental buildings are all great places for kids to see and come to appreciate.

Maybe you would like to take the students in your class or school to the nation's capital for a tour. Well, how would you go about it? You certainly wouldn't just drop them off at the steps of the White House and say, "Have fun!" You know that in addition to all of the wonderful educational opportunities in Washington, D.C., there are many things you wouldn't necessarily want your students to see: violence, prostitutes, homeless people, drunkards, gang members, and so forth. That urban environment holds a number of dangers; in fact, Washington, D.C., has one of the highest crime rates in the United States. Still, that doesn't mean we should prohibit our students from visiting the city and taking advantage of its historical, political, and cultural attractions.

The Internet should be approached in the same manner. It contains in its seedier corners many things we just don't want our kids to see: foul language, hateful and prejudiced speech, pornography, bomb-making instructions—and the list goes on. The Internet also has many potential dangers: sexual predators, kidnappers, and others with malicious or perverse intent who may want to bring harm to children. Just as we wouldn't leave our kids alone to explore Washington, D.C., we shouldn't leave them alone to explore the Internet without supervision, guidance, and explicit instruction. It is critical to provide them with a clear road map and framework for staying safe and being responsible online and to check in on them regularly to make sure they are following through.

Eventually, all children will be exposed to things in cyberspace that are problematic. What they do at that point depends on the instruction they have received and the habits they have developed. The time, energy, and effort you put in toward this end will pay great dividends in the lives of the youth in whom you invest. While it is not a lost cause to talk to adolescents about appropriate Internet use when they are 17 or 18 years old, so much should be done earlier. We encourage introducing this topic as early as possible—and definitely before they start exploring the Internet alone. We find that between fifth and seventh grade, students begin to use computers and the Internet more often and for more varied purposes, and we have spoken with elementary school children who are vastly more proficient than their teachers and parents. You may not have taught them how to use a computer and the Internet, but they seem to have learned it somewhere.

Kids will undoubtedly become well versed with technology at an increasingly younger age as we move forward in the 21st century. What is encouraging is that adults have a great deal of influence and can meaningfully shape behavior at these earlier ages. You may know from experience that this influence lessens as youth approach the teenage years, so it is vital to step in as soon as possible. This simply means *now*, if it hasn't happened already. We believe that they'll not only hear you speak but actually listen to what you are saying.

A comprehensive strategy to prevent cyberbullying, or any other form of adolescent aggression, requires the cooperation of a number of important stakeholders. Parents, teachers, law enforcement officers, other community leaders, and children themselves all have a role to play. None of these players will be able to do it by themselves. This chapter will detail the steps you can take to help prevent cyberbullying and other adolescent problems that arise with the utilization of technology. We first turn our attention to the role of the educator, whose responsibilities include formally assessing the current level of cyberbullying, educating students and staff, establishing clear rules, utilizing the expertise of students, maintaining a safe and respectful school culture, installing monitoring and filtering software, implementing and evaluating formal anticyberbullying programming, and educating parents.

THE EDUCATOR'S ROLE IN PREVENTING CYBERBULLYING

Assessment

The first proactive step you can take is to assess the level of cyberbullying occurring in your school and the impact it is having on the student body and educational environment. Determining the current state of online behaviors among your school population can best be accomplished through an anonymous survey of students and staff. In fact, this should be done on a regular basis so that trend data can be reviewed to determine whether certain problems are improving or worsening over time. There are a number of general concepts specific to cyberbullying that your assessment instrument should attempt to address (see Box 10.1).

Box 10.1 Sample Assessment Questions

- Does cyberbullying occur among students at this school?
- How big a problem is it?
- Have you ever been the victim of cyberbullying?
- Have you ever been afraid to come to school because of something somebody said to you online?
- Have you ever cyberbullied another student?
- If so, why did you do it?
- What should teachers do help prevent cyberbullying?

It is important that you clearly define what *cyberbullying* is to the students so they understand the kinds of behaviors that you are interested in. For example, in our surveys, we inform respondents that "Cyberbullying is when someone repeatedly makes fun of another person online or repeatedly picks on another person through e-mail or text message or when someone posts something online about another person that they don't like." Just asking them if they have been *cyberbullied*, without clearly describing what it is, can lead to confusion among students and make interpreting the results difficult.

If the assessment is coordinated districtwide, numbers can be broken down by school, demographic characteristics (e.g., age, gender, race), region, special populations, and any number of other variables and even compared and contrasted with districtwide data on the general makeup and distribution of students. This analysis can be very instructive in identifying exactly which schools or groups require the most support, education, and resources to deal with cyberbullying. To get you started, we have included a copy of the cyberbullying survey questions we constructed and used when collecting our data from middle schoolers in 2007 (Resource F). Of course, this instrument can be modified to suit your school population.

Additionally, your school may want to consider partnering with a local college or university to help with the collection, analysis, interpretation, and presentation of these data. University faculty generally have experience conducting assessments and can assist in all aspects of the project. In addition, other resources are available, both online and in print, that provide more specific guidance for administrators about how to conduct a thorough assessment. Barbara Trolley, Connie Hanel, and Linda Shields (2006), for example, provide a number of practical recommendations toward this end in their book *Demystifying and Deescalating Cyber Bullying in the Schools.*

Educate Students and Staff

It almost goes without saying that school districts must educate both students and staff about the harmful nature of online aggression. School administrators should take the time to learn about these issues and pass this important information along to teachers and counselors. As an example, the district could convene a staff meeting related to youth Internet safety and bring a specialist in to speak on the topic, provide actual case studies, and summarize the latest research findings.

After being so equipped, teachers and counselors need to pass this information on to students. Teachers should take time to discuss cyberbullying in their classrooms when they discuss broader issues of bullying and peer harassment. They should proactively engage students in conversations about a variety of negative online experiences and possible solutions. For instance, teachers can use vignettes or even real examples of cyberbullying to illustrate its harmful nature and point out that what is written or disseminated online is equally as damaging as face-to-face bullying (or worse). A few sample vignettes are presented in Box 10.2, and others are provided in Resource C of this book. We believe these aptly portray real-life cyberbullying situations and prompt productive, ongoing discussions as to what to do (and how to do it).

Box 10.2 Cyberbullying Scenarios

Scenario #1

A girl had her picture taken, which made her feel uncomfortable. Later that week, her friends tell her that the picture has been posted on another student's blog. What should the girl do? Should she fight back?

Scenario #2

A boy has written a poem for his crush and decided to e-mail it to her. The girl then e-mails it to all of her friends on her buddy list. The next day at school, all of the kids are making fun of him and his poem. What should the boy do? Is using e-mail always safe?

Scenario #3

A teacher notices that during computer lab, one student is not using the computer. The teacher approaches this girl and asks her why. The girl does not speak up right away and nervously looks around the room. Then she replies that she does not feel like using the computer today. However, the teacher notices that a few of the other students are looking over and laughing. What should the teacher do? Is the teacher to assume that the girl is being bullied online? If the teacher finds out that cyberbullying is taking place, what should she do next?

Scenario #4

A boy has brought his camera phone to school one day. He is using the phone to take pictures of other students in the class. The next day, the teacher sees that some of the students are threatening to beat up the little boy. The teacher then finds out that the boy posted pictures of students on the web and was making fun of them. What punishment should the little boy get? Should the other students be punished as well for fighting? What should the school do to prevent this sort of thing from happening?

Scenario #5

Two boys at school are teasing each other during lunch time. They are calling each other names and laughing at one another. Both boys are punished, and the teacher thinks that the fighting has stopped. Rather than fight at school, however, the students have actually started an online fight. One boy created an entire web page to make fun of the other. The boy who is on the website has told his parents. Now the parents have come to the teacher asking why and what is going on. What should the teacher recommend to the parents? What should the teacher do while the students are at school?

Moreover, we recommend that schools sponsor an assembly or presentation on a regular basis that provides information for the school community about safe and responsible Internet use and "netiquette" (network or online etiquette). To make these presentations more vivid and true-to-life, we recommend showing hard-hitting video clips related to cyberbullying that are freely available online. For example, the National Crime Prevention Council (www.ncpc.org/cyberbullying) has created public service announcement videos that powerfully portray the real-world harm that online aggression can inflict. The students to whom we have shown these videos are visibly moved as the message sinks in. Repeatedly piquing the consciences of youth about questionable or deviant behavior seems to make them more sensitive to the issues at hand and more apt to "think twice" before making an unwise decision. They should also be deterred to some extent after being reminded of the potential consequences that follow rule breaking and that virtually all forms of wrongdoing online leave a digital footprint that aids in identifying the perpetrator(s).

Several nonprofit organizations have also developed curricula that a school can utilize to educate staff and students about the nature and consequences of cyberbullying. For example, the Anti-Defamation League (ADL) recently launched a nationwide initiative, entitled "Cyberbullying: Understanding and Addressing Online Cruelty," which includes lesson plans for elementary, middle, and secondary school levels. The organization also offers interactive workshops for middle and high school staff. More information about the ADL's cyberbullying programming can be found at www.adl.org.

The Ophelia Project, a nonprofit organization that works with schools to create safer social climates to reduce aggression among students, also provides trainings and workshops for schools about cyberbullying. Their work focuses on combating relational and other nonphysical forms of aggression by promoting emotional well-being and helping youth develop healthy peer relationships. More information can be found at www.ophe liaproject.org. Finally, i-SAFE (www.isafe.org) has created an extensive Internet safety curriculum for K–12 youth classrooms and also works to educate community members through comprehensive outreach programs. We encourage you to check out the available materials at these websites and see which best meet your goals.

Have Clear Rules Regarding the Use of Computers and Other Technological Devices

When we were in seventh-grade "shop" class, we remember spending several weeks at the beginning of the school year studying the safety practices and procedures associated with the power tools before being allowed to use them. Before being permitted to drive a car a couple of years later, we were required to take a comprehensive driver's education course and pass both a written exam and a road test. Society recognizes that power tools and automobiles can be dangerous if used inappropriately or irresponsibly, so we take the time to educate students about the inherent dangers in their operation.

The same approach should be taken before students are allowed to use computers and the Internet at school. Youth cannot be expected to exercise complete wisdom. They need to be taught how to use technology responsibly. Just as there are rules for using power equipment, there should also be clear rules about what is expected when using computers. As long as students know the rules, they cannot plead ignorance if and when they are caught violating them. They should also know the potential consequences for any wrongdoing. (This is discussed in more detail in the next chapter).

Every school district should have a comprehensive Acceptable Use Policy (AUP) governing the use of technology provided by or used in the schools. The Computer Crime and Intellectual Property Section of the U.S. Department of Justice provides a model AUP, which schools can adapt for their needs. The policy includes detailed information about the safe and responsible use of computers and the Internet and provides suggestions for discipline, supervision, and monitoring. Parents and students must read and sign the AUP (thereby indicating agreement with its terms) at the beginning of every school year. That way, all parties are aware of the policy and the potential consequences associated with any violations of its terms. Interested readers are encouraged to go to www.cybercrime.gov and search for "school acceptable use policy."

In addition to a broad policy, it is also beneficial to post specific principles to guide the behavioral choices of students on computers at school. In Box 10.3, we list several specific rules that educators might consider posting near the workstations in a computer lab or classroom. At the bottom of the list, we also recommend specifying certain websites and software applications that are forbidden at school (e.g., MySpace, AOL Instant Messenger, Google Talk, and Second Life).

In addition to classroom computer use, students need to know which (if any) portable electronic devices are allowed on campus, as we are seeing a surge in the number of youth who possess laptop computers, smartphones (e.g., iPhones, Blackberrys, Sidekicks), and other portable electronic devices that are web enabled in some capacity. Coupled with the increasing number of cell phones that provide Internet access, the possibilities for cyberbullying incidents are exponentially rising.

Accordingly, schools must have a clearly defined policy regarding all portable electronic devices. Some schools have simply elected to ban all such devices from campus. These actions have lead to criticism by some parents, who say they need to be able to contact their kids in the case of an emergency. It can also be very difficult to enforce a complete ban without searching all students as they enter the school each day. A better approach would be to have clearly specified guidelines for when and where the devices are allowed and what will happen if a student is caught using a device at a prohibited time or place. Box 10.4 lists some rules you may want to consider.

Box 10.3 Rules for Classroom Computer Use

I understand that using the school computer is a privilege that is subject to the following rules:

1. I am allowed to use computers for approved, educational purposes only.

2. I will only play games authorized by my teacher.

3. I will not alter computer settings or damage computer equipment.

4. I agree never to write or post anything online that I would not want my teacher or parents to see.

5. I will not use the computer to bring harm to anyone else.

6. I will not type profanity or otherwise offensive language.

7. If I receive harassing messages or accidentally view any offensive or pornographic content, I will report it to my teacher immediately.

8. I will use the Internet to search only areas appropriate to the school curriculum.

9. I agree not to download install software, shareware, freeware, or other files without obtaining permission from my teacher.

10. I will only save material in my personal folder appropriate for educational use.

11. I will only alter my own files and documents.

12. I will not plagiarize from the Internet.

13. If I ever feel uncomfortable about an experience online, I will immediately tell my teacher. I understand that my teacher is willing to help me and will not punish me as long as these rules are followed.

14. I will not agree to meet with anyone I have met online without parental approval. If anyone wants to meet with me and makes me uncomfortable, I will bring it to the attention of an adult I trust.

15. I will not share any of my passwords (my school network account, my e-mail account, my social networking site account, etc.) with anyone else.

16. I will not use a proxy to attempt to access websites or other forms of Internet content and communications technology that have been blocked from my school network. I will also report any instances of other kids using a proxy.

17. I am prepared to be held accountable for my actions and for the loss of computer privileges if these policies are violated.

List of prohibited websites and software applications:

We would also like to emphasize here that when portable electronic devices are confiscated, schools should not overstep their bounds and search their contents, even when there is a clear violation of school policy.

This is best left either to parents or to law enforcement, who know when the circumstances call for such an intrusion of privacy. Schools should limit their actions to seizing but not searching these devices.

Box 10.4 Sample Rules for Portable Electronic Devices at School

Portable electronic devices include but are not limited to laptops, cell phones, personal data assistants, portable electronic games, digital audio players, digital cameras, and wristwatches.

1. Students must have all portable electronic devices turned off during the school day.

2. No portable electronic device may be visible during the school day.

3. Students are not allowed to use any device to photograph or record (either in audio or video format) another person on school property at any time without that person's permission.

4. Portable electronic devices are not allowed in any classroom, bathroom, or locker room.

5. Any unauthorized portable electronic devices will be confiscated. The student's parent or guardian must come to school to recover the device for the student.

6. Any confiscated portable electronic device may be searched by parents or law enforcement as necessary.

7. Students who violate this policy may also be subject to disciplinary action as noted in the Student Handbook.

All schools also have (or should have) policies on the books that prohibit bullying incidents and outline their disciplinary consequences. Administrators must take the time to review and revise them to ensure that they cover cyberbullying behaviors that negatively affect the school environment (see Chapter 5). This policy should be disseminated at the beginning of the school year so that parents and students understand what behaviors are within the disciplinary reach of the school. It may also be instructive to highlight particular situations that have resulted in disciplinary actions (examples from within the district or elsewhere). As Paul R. Getto, policy specialist for the Kansas Association of School Boards, says,

The schools need to promote a safe and friendly environment for all students, teachers and other staff, all of whom can be subjected to bullying in many forms, including cyberbullying. Simply passing policies which prohibit bullying is not, in our opinion, going to accomplish the desired results. Bullying in any form, regardless of the media used, is wrong, destructive, and potentially a problem for students and, in some cases, teachers, if they fear for their peace of mind or their safety while in school.

The importance of clear policies is illustrated in a recent example from Florida. In 2007, a middle school student recorded and subsequently uploaded to the Internet (www.youtube.com) video footage of one of her teachers in class and included a profanity-filled caption. Even though there was no substantial disruption of or interference with the school's educational mission, utilization of school-owned technology, or threat to other students, it was within the bounds of the administration to have her transferred to an alternative school, because the school policy expressly forbids the recording of teachers in the classroom.

The policy stated, in part, that "Any student who uses an article disruptive to school to inappropriately photograph, audiotape, videotape or otherwise record a person without his/her knowledge or consent will be subject to disciplinary action." We applaud this school for being progressive and forward-thinking enough to have formulated and included such a policy within its conduct manual. It is imperative that other schools and school districts do the same so that the simple and clear violation of a policy prohibiting certain behavior can serve as the basis for punitive sanctions (including changes of placement) by a school on a student.

Utilize the Expertise of Students Through Peer Mentoring

Parents and teachers can get up and preach, but if they hear it from another kid, they will remember it.

—Parent from California

The concept of peer mentoring generally involves older students advising and counseling younger students about issues affecting them. Since younger adolescents tend to look up to (and seek to emulate) older adolescents, this dynamic can be exploited to teach important lessons about the use of computers and communications technology. Peer mentoring has been fruitful in reducing traditional bullying and interpersonal conflict within schools (Miller, 2002) and, as such, should be considered in a comprehensive approach to preventing cyberbullying as well. Accordingly, newer cohorts of students can learn from the wisdom of adolescents who have already experienced online aggression and have figured out effective ways to deal with it. This wisdom may sink in more quickly and deeply since it comes from peers rather than adults, as kids have the tendency to tune out adults when being taught certain life lessons (can you relate to that?). On a larger scale, these efforts can significantly and positively affect the social climate within the school community, benefitting youth and their families, teachers and staff, and the community as a whole. As Mike Tully (2007), a noted school law attorney, points out: "Never overlook the possibility of using students themselves as agents of change" (p. 6).

The basic purpose of peer mentoring is to employ older students to change the way younger students think about the harassment or mistreatment of others in certain situations. Mentors can also be utilized to help younger students appreciate the responsibility and risks associated with the use of computers, cell phones, and the Internet. Overall, the goal is to encourage youth to take responsibility for the problem and to work together in coming up with a solution. It also seeks to foster respect and acceptance of others—no matter what—and to get kids to see how their actions affect others and how they can purposefully choose behaviors that promote positive peer relations.

> *I have started to talk to other children who have had a similar experience and try and help them because they are going through the same thing that I went through and it helps to talk to people who understand. I tell them to be brave and not to worry because everything will be OK.*
>
> —Student from England

Highly adaptable, depending on your needs, peer mentoring can be accomplished in a number of ways. For example, one-on-one sessions might take place where a high schooler is called in to meet with a middle school victim to offer support and help. Or high school students could regularly talk to groups of middle schoolers in the cafeteria during lunch. A few high school students could also organize a presentation for small classroom-sized (20+) middle school groups. Finally, skits can be presented in auditoriums or cafeterias by high schoolers for assemblies of younger students. All of these interactions can be comprised of one or more activities. Box 10.5 lists several messages that can be communicated to the school community using trained student mentors. Over time and as needed, additional formal and informal lessons—as well as continued interaction between the high school mentors and the middle school mentees—can occur.

A number of nonprofit organizations have also developed materials to help teach students to be ambassadors in Internet education. For example, i-SAFE, discussed earlier in this chapter, offers an i-MENTOR Training Network. This program consists of six online videos that educate older youth about Internet safety issues and how to talk to other students about the lessons. The program is designed for students in 5th through 12th grade who are interested in becoming Internet Safety Leaders in their school. The Ophelia Project, also discussed above, has a "Creating a Safe School" mentorship program that "empowers older students as trained

Box 10.5 Mentor Messages

Schools can utilize older students to convey a number of important messages of Internet safety and responsibility to younger students, including the following:

- Reiterating that they are not alone in experiencing victimization and the resultant pain, rejection, humiliation, and loneliness
- Encouraging them to speak up and not remain silent when confronted with cyberbullying
- Sharing one or more highly relatable vignettes or stories about cyberbullying
- Explaining the "language" of cyberbullying, including the relevant terms and technology
- Describing positive ways in which conflict between peers can be de-escalated or resolved
- Using role-playing examples to get students thinking about the various ways to address a cyberbullying situation
- Providing an opportunity to discuss and answer any questions, clarify any confusion, and reinforce how to deal with cyberbullying problems

mentors to their younger classmates and model positive social interaction and courageous intervention" (The Ophelia Project, 2006, ¶ 4). We encourage you to check out these programs to learn more about creating a safer school climate by utilizing student mentors.

Maintain a Safe and Respectful School Culture

School culture can be defined as the "sum of the values, cultures, safety practices, and organizational structures within a school that cause it to function and react in particular ways" (McBrien & Brandt, 1997, p. 89). Overall, it is critical for educators to develop and promote a safe and respectful school culture or climate. A positive on-campus environment will go a long way in reducing the frequency of many problematic behaviors at school, including bullying and harassment. In this setting, teachers must demonstrate emotional support, a warm and caring atmosphere, a strong focus on academics and learning, and a fostering of healthy self-esteem.

In our research, we found that students who experienced cyberbullying (both those who were victims and those who admitted to cyberbullying others) perceived a poorer climate or culture at their school than those who had not experienced cyberbullying. Youth were asked whether they "enjoy going to school," "feel safe at school," "feel that teachers at their school really try to help them succeed," and "feel that teachers at their school care about them." Those who admitted to cyberbullying others or who were the target of cyberbullying were less likely to agree with those statements. As you can see from Chart 10.1, the difference may not seem like much, but it is statistically meaningful. While we don't know whether a poor school climate *caused* cyberbullying behaviors (or was the result of them), we do know that the variables are related.

Chart 10.1   Cyberbullying and School Climate

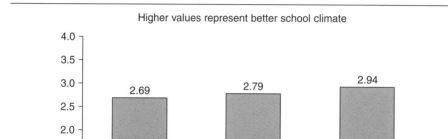

In addition, strategic efforts to promote bonding among students should be in place, as this is related to personal, emotional, behavioral, and scholastic success. Toward this end, we often champion what can be termed a "respect policy" or "honor code" when working with schools. For example, one with which we are familiar reads as follows (North High School, 2005):

Respect is the cornerstone of our relationships with each other. We are committed to respecting the dignity and worth of each individual at North High School and strive never to degrade or diminish any member of our school community by our conduct or attitudes. We benefit from each other. Our diversity makes us strong. (¶ 1)

The goal of such a statement is to specify clearly to students and staff alike that all members of the school community are expected to respect each other and that such respect should govern all interpersonal interactions and attitudes among students, faculty, and staff on campus (and hopefully off campus as well). Respect policies serve as reference points against which every questionable thought, word, and deed can be measured and judged. Every instance of harm between individuals lacks a measure of respect for the victim, including those that occur through the use of electronic devices.

Apart from their inclusion in policy manuals, respect policies should be disseminated within school materials to both students and parents and posted visibly in hallways and classrooms. While one might wish that students would automatically and naturally treat each other (and the adults in their lives) with respect, we know that in reality this does not always happen. As such, the respect policy reminds them of a standard that has been set and will be enforced.

It is also crucial that the school seeks to create and promote an environment where certain behaviors or language simply is not tolerated—by students and staff alike. In a school with a positive culture, students know what is appropriate and what is not. In these schools, there are a number of behaviors that the community as a whole would agree are simply "not cool." It isn't cool to bring a weapon to school. It isn't cool get up in the middle of class and walk out of the classroom. It isn't cool to assault a teacher physically. It isn't cool to use racial slurs. Certain behaviors are simply not acceptable in the eyes of both adults and youth.

We hope that with education and effort, cyberbullying will someday be deemed "not cool." This ideal may be wishful thinking, but it is worth pursuing. All forms of bullying, no matter how minor, need to be condemned—with the responsible parties disciplined. If teachers deliberately ignore minor (or even serious) bullying because they just don't want to deal with it, what message does that send to the students? Students need to see that their teachers, counselors, and administrators take these behaviors seriously.

Install Monitoring and Filtering Software

The Children's Internet Protection Act (CIPA), passed in 2000, requires that public schools (and libraries) install filtering software on computers that have access to the Internet if they want to remain eligible for federal funding assistance. Filtering software blocks Internet content that is deemed inappropriate for children (e.g., violent or pornographic material). This is typically done in two ways: site blocking and content monitoring.

Site blocking filters typically prohibit computer users from accessing websites designated as inappropriate (those on a "black list"). Alternatively, some site blocking filters only allow users to access sites that have been preapproved (those on a "white list"). Both approaches usually do not block instant messaging, e-mail, peer-to-peer (P2P) applications, or other software that may pose problems or threats.

Content monitoring, on the other hand, generally uses a key word-blocking approach. Here, data are analyzed against a library of user-defined words and phrases deemed unfitting. The software then blocks that data regardless of the Internet application (or medium) through which it comes. In addition, most software programs allow users to block specific categories that identify certain types of websites. Box 10.6 lists some of the common website categories that one school district blocks so that students and staff cannot access these types of sites from school computer labs.

Box 10.6 WebSite Categories Commonly Blocked by Schools

- Abortion
- Adult/Mature
- Auctions
- Blogs/Newsgroups
- Chat/Instant Messaging
- E-mail
- Gambling
- Games
- Hacking
- Humor/Jokes
- Illegal Drugs
- Illegal/Questionable
- Nudity

- Online Games
- Peer-to-Peer (P2P)
- Personal/Dating
- Pornography
- Proxy Avoidance
- Remote Access Tools
- Sexuality/Alternative Lifestyles
- Social Networking
- Spyware Effects/Privacy Concerns
- Spyware/Malware Sources
- Streaming Media/MP3s
- Violence/Hate/Racism
- Weapons

Most school districts use hardware and software firewalls and filters to block access to social networking websites (e.g., MySpace and Facebook), third-party e-mail services (e.g., Hotmail and Yahoo), instant messaging software programs (e.g., AOL Instant Messenger and MSN Messenger), and P2P file sharing programs (e.g., KaZaA, LimeWire, eDonkey, and BitTorrent) from school computers. Nevertheless, it is still relatively easy to access these sites and programs from school if the student knows where to go and how to do it.

Specific websites—called "proxies"—are popping up every day that redirect individuals to sites that have been "blacklisted," or prohibited by hardware or software rules at school. Basically, an adolescent can access MySpace (for example) at school through his or her web browser—even if it is blocked by the school network administrators—by first accessing another website (such as www.leafdrink.com), inputting "www.myspace .com" into a web page form field, and then being rerouted to that site (thereby circumventing a direct connection to MySpace and bypassing the block or filter). The proxy serves as an intermediary site (that is not prohibited) from which a user can access a prohibited site, because the school network has allowed a connection to the proxy site. (It is virtually impossible to block all of these types of sites!) Finally, instant messaging software programs can be run off of a pocket USB drive (also known as a flash, thumb, or key drive) that a student brings to school and plugs into his or her computer. Those programs can also use a proxy site to reroute a connection to the proper instant messaging network, even if traditional access and use of such programs is restricted.

We all know that the Internet is a great instructional tool but that its content varies in quality and appropriateness. While schools are able to evaluate text books and library books carefully before approving them for school use, this remains a difficult task when dealing with material from the Internet. Filtering and blocking software is unfortunately limited in its utility and is primarily a reactive measure that serves more as a short-term solution to the problem of inappropriate Internet use among adolescents. A more proactive approach is required, involving the creation of a safe school culture, educational initiatives, formal assessment, and systemic programming affecting multiple stakeholders. In keeping with this philosophy, Nancy Willard (2003), the director of the Center for Safe and Responsible Internet Use, aptly points out: "By developing a comprehensive approach to address such concerns, schools can help young people develop effective filtering and blocking systems that will reside in the hardware that sits upon their shoulders" (p. 4).

Implement and Evaluate
Formal Anticyberbullying Programming

We also suggest that school officials actively work to develop and implement an antibullying curriculum that includes training modules on online aggression. Before implementation, it may once again be helpful to partner with researchers from a nearby university so that a scientific evaluation of the programming can occur to determine its worth. Very little is currently known about what works to educate youth about cyberbullying and online safety; even less is known about what works in responding to cyberbullying. At this early stage, it is important to try a variety of different approaches, starting with those with demonstrated success at preventing traditional bullying (for example, the Olweus Bullying Prevention Program [Olweus, Limber, & Mihalic, 1999b]). This curriculum can be supplemented with netiquette lessons covering the unique features of online communication and responsibility.

Whatever approach you decide to take, it is essential to conduct a formal and systematic evaluation of its merits so that others can learn from your experience. A thoughtful and well-designed evaluation is crucial for securing funding for more antibullying initiatives and for convincing others of the utility of the program—especially given the fiscal and organizational constraints currently facing most districts. Remember that a program is only as good as the quality of its evaluation.

Educate Parents

As educators, you have a unique platform from which to reach the parents of your students about these important issues. As such, it is important for you to pass along information to parents regarding adolescent use of electronic devices—thereby partnering with them in promoting positive online experiences among youth. For example, a letter can be sent to encourage them to do their part (see Box 10.7).

Box 10.7 Sample Letter From School to Parents

Dear Parents:

We wanted to send this brief letter home to let you know about some of the activities that students are involved in when using computers, cell phones, and other electronic devices. As you may have heard, many adolescents have reported experiencing "cyberbullying." Cyberbullying is when students use computers, cell phones, or other electronic devices to repeatedly harass or mistreat another person.

We have no reason to believe that this is a greater problem in our district than others, and we want to keep it that way. We are taking a number of important steps to help prevent cyberbullying, including educating the school community about its harmful nature. We have also recently updated our district policy and Student Handbook to reflect the changing nature of adolescent aggression. We have informed students and are now letting you know that we will discipline any cyberbullying that negatively affects the school environment or infringes upon the rights of others.

We encourage you to talk with your child about these issues. It is also important that you monitor their behavior to make sure they are responsibly using computers and cell phones. We are doing our part at school and trust that you will do your part at home so that we can jointly reduce the likelihood that cyberbullying will become a problem in our community.

Feel free to contact us if you have any questions or concerns.

Sincerely,

A newsletter can also be distributed to parents on a regular basis, updating them on new developments in the way kids are using and abusing technology. For example, the newsletter might make parents aware of new websites that teens are frequenting or innovative ways that youth are circumventing Internet safeguards on home computers. In addition, we recommend sponsoring regular community events to discuss issues related to Internet safety and cyberbullying. Through these initiatives, school personnel and parents can work together in addressing the inappropriate behaviors that will inevitably arise. After reading this book, you (yes, you!) should consider giving a presentation to parents after school or at a PTA meeting. You are now much better informed than the majority of adults out there, and you can do your part by working to educate those around you.

This school is an elementary school (K–5), so our prevention has been educating the parents about cyberbullying and encouraging them to be involved with their child's web page access and content. We have also

asked students to come forward if they experience cyberbullying that
would have an impact on the school community.

—Principal from Florida

As a final point concerning the role of educators, an increasing amount of information is available across the Internet about cyberbullying. On our website, www.cyberbullying.us, we provide a large number of downloadable resources that you can distribute in electronic or hardcopy format to fellow administrators, staff, teachers, counselors, parents, and youth as needed. There are no restrictions on their dissemination, and we are frequently creating and uploading new resources as we continue to study the problem and work with those affected. For quick reference, some are included in Resource B of this book; however, they are cleanly formatted and suitable for distribution as PDF files on our website. In addition, we provide a multitude of web links related to online aggression so that you can learn more from other professionals who are doing great work in this area.

THE PARENT'S ROLE IN PREVENTING CYBERBULLYING

It was an argument with my two best friends. I had fallen out with both
of them for many reasons. Since we had been best mates, I put up with lots
of rubbish. I was sick of it and wanted to get out of the pain and trouble
I had been through. So once I had got out of it I thought I would be free. But
no. They continued to harass me. Via e-mail, MSN, text messages. Made
me feel very lonely and depressed. It was just before the summer holidays,
so during them I was pretty much on my own all the time. Parents at
work all day and since they were my best mates who I used to do every-
thing with, I didn't really have anyone to see. They had turned everyone
against me you see. So I got into depression and it was absolutely horrid.
My parents were extremely supportive and helpful, I can't thank them
enough. But no matter how great they can be, there is always the fact that
you're on your own in the rest of the world—that is saddening.

—15-year-old girl from the United Kingdom

The anecdote above underscores the fact that parents cannot protect their children from everything wrong, bad, or evil in this world. However, there is much that they *can* do. They can engage their kids in a dialogue about the relevant issues, venture into cyberspace with them, and informally or formally monitor their electronic activities. Cumulatively, these efforts should demonstrate to youth that the adults in their life actively care about their online safety.

Communication Is Key

First and foremost, it is important for parents to develop an open dialogue with their children so they feel comfortable approaching them if confronted with an unpleasant online experience. It's often difficult to talk about these issues at first, but it is essential. As discussed earlier, our research suggests that only a minority of teens who experience cyberbullying tell their parents (or other adults). Much of this lack of openness relates to the youth's perception that they will be blamed or will lose their computer, cell phone, or Internet privileges. Conveying to them that you will patiently listen to their problem or situation and respond in a nonjudgmental and responsible manner is essential in cultivating and preserving an open line of communication.

> *Bullying boils down to communication. Teach your kids to communicate with you about the small stuff and they'll tell you about the big stuff too.*
>
> —Mother from Minnesota

If parents are unsure of how to bring up these issues with those under their care, we have provided some sample "scripts" to help get the conversation started (Resource C). These examples can demonstrate the ease with which the topic of cyberbullying can be discussed and the most productive, noncritical ways of doing so. Research has consistently identified the utility of ongoing discussions by parents, caregivers, or teachers with children about their online interactions and activities (Berson et al., 2002; Ybarra & Mitchell, 2004). Says Suzanne Stanford, CEO of My Internet Safety Coach (as cited in Writer, 2006),

> Often, kids are afraid to tell their parents for fear that their computer will be taken away or that their parents will make the situation worse. What they don't realize is that unless the bullying stops immediately, it can escalate and leave permanent psychological scars. (¶ 9)

Essentially, there must exist a crystal-clear understanding about what is appropriate and what is not with respect to online activities. Toward that end, we have created an "Internet Use Contract," which can be used as is or as a template to create your own custom contract (Resource D). Its purpose is to promote a trusting relationship between parents and children when it comes to the latter's use of computers and the Internet. Both parties agree to abide by certain mutually acceptable rules of engagement and indicate their acceptance and understanding of those rules with their signatures at the bottom of the form. To remind the child of this pledged commitment, we recommend that this contract be posted in a highly visible place (e.g., next to the computer). Just as in the "Rules for Classroom

Computer Use" detailed above, a parent should also specify which websites and software applications are prohibited.

In addition to implementing and enforcing rules for computer use, parents should consider corresponding rules for cell phones. Resource E provides a sample "Family Cell Phone Use Contract" that parents can adapt and utilize. The point to emphasize is that having a cell phone is a privilege (like computers) that can be revoked for misbehavior. That said, it is also important for parents to realize that they need to give their kids some space with respect to their communications with others. Parents should resist constantly hovering over their child when that child is text messaging friends and should not go through the phone's text message logs when it is unattended (unless there is a serious cause for concern). Instead, they should focus on developing a trusting relationship with their children and only invade privacy as a last resort.

Go Online

It is imperative that parents go online with their children. Many adults are intimidated by electronic devices and/or the Internet, which is completely understandable given that we have not grown up with computers like adolescents today have. Nonetheless, this should not prevent parents from exploring the mediums and venues through which youth communicate and interact in cyberspace. In fact, unfamiliar parents can enlist the assistance of their children in getting acclimated with Internet-based activities. Parents should ask their children to show them where they go online and why they like certain web environments. Some youth will be immediately open to this, while others may resist. Parents should be patient and slowly work their way into the online lives of their children. It may take time, but it will pay dividends down the road.

Once online with their kids, parents can casually inquire further about the technologies and websites: Why are they so popular? What do you and your friends do on these sites or with this software? Can everyone see the messages you send or post? Do you really "know" everyone with whom you are communicating? Who are "BBallDude19" and "foxyFLgal"? What sort of pictures or video have you posted online? Parents must remember to keep an open mind and resist knee-jerk reactions of a condemning or criticizing nature. Once parents have a trusting relationship with their children, they will be able to influence their Internet behaviors accordingly.

Box 10.8 provides several additional questions to help get the proverbial ball rolling. Expressing interest in their cyberspace experiences without criticizing or condemning their activities online paves the way for a long-term positive relationship with the adolescents in your life. Responses to these questions should serve to bring about deeper discussion about issues related to cyberbullying and online harassment, and will open the door for parents to the online worlds in which their kids are living.

Box 10.8 Questions to Ask Youth About Cyberbullying

1. What websites do you usually go onto?

2. What sites are your friends into these days?

3. What is your favorite website?

4. What do you do on these sites?

5. Do you ever go online at your friend's house?

6. Have you ever been contacted by someone online that you didn't know?
   a. What did they want?
   b. What did you do?
   c. How did you respond?

7. Do you know what cyberbullying is?

8. How do you keep yourself safe online?

9. Have you ever received a text message from someone that made you upset?
   a. Do you know who it was?
   b. How did you respond?

10. Has anyone at school ever talked with you about using the computer responsibly?

At some point, further probing may be warranted. For example, parents might seek to determine the tendency of their child to rationalize cyberbullying given a specific circumstance or situation. Then, they can point out the faulty reasoning in those decision-making processes so that the youth's behavioral choices are not swayed by emotion or opportunity. To be sure, it is impossible for parents to protect and watch over their children at all hours of the day and night. Still, it is possible through a combination of these efforts to instill in them safe Internet practices that will guide their online (and consequently even offline) activities.

The Earlier the Better

Developing safe Internet practices very early on in the lives of children is essential to ensure that they internalize those habits as their computer and Internet proficiency grows. Kids these days become technologically adept at a very early age (see the tech-savvy youngster in Figure 10.1), and parental guidance is of the utmost importance in teaching them to use electronic devices in responsible ways. Moreover, it will be much easier for parents to insist upon going online with their children at 8 or 9 years of age than when they are 15 or 16. Positive habits instilled at an early age will pay dividends in their decision-making processes later in life. To be sure, developing appropriate belief systems and behavioral choices is a much more valuable and enduring approach than simply threatening them with punishments for particular rule violations.

Figure 10.1   Educate Youth From an Early Age

SOURCE: Photo courtesy of Christine Sellers.

Monitor Their Activities

We also feel that it is key for parents to monitor their children closely when they are on the computer. Most parents and guardians realize this; recent data show that 73 percent keep the home computer in an open family area—either purposefully or inadvertently providing at least casual surveillance of the online activities of youth at home (Lenhart, Madden, & Hitlin, 2005). Relatedly, we believe it is a bad idea to put an Internet-enabled computer in the privacy of your child's bedroom (though a computer unconnected to the Internet is not expected to be a problem).

> *I would never bully online because it hurts. Also, if the kids had half a brain they would consider that a parent is monitoring it like mine do.*
>
> —13-year-old girl from Massachusetts

Another solution to be considered is the installation and use of monitoring software programs. Since parents cannot watch over their child's online activities all of the time, they may want to consider employing specialized software to do the job. A number of commercial software programs are on the market that can help in this regard. Some allow adults to block access to certain websites, while others only allow the computer user to access specified sites (as discussed above). Still others track all the places computer users go when connected to the Internet.

We certainly support using these programs as a part of a comprehensive approach to online safety and responsibility, but it is naive to think that these software programs alone will keep kids safe or prevent them from bullying others or accessing inappropriate content. Indeed, some research has shown that filtering software and the specification of Internet usage rules is not significantly related to a decreased chance of Internet harassment victimization (Ybarra & Mitchell, 2004).

Other research has determined that 54 percent of parents use some type of Internet filter, 62 percent check up on the websites their children visit, and 64 percent have specified rules for the time their children spend online (Lenhart et al., 2005). Even with filters, proactive inquiries, and rule setting, motivated youth can easily find a way to visit objectionable websites or participate in inappropriate online behavior. They may go to a friend's house, the library, or a local coffeehouse with free wireless Internet access. They may even learn to subvert the hardware and software filters that responsible adults have implemented, as previously discussed. This is why software alone is often insufficient.

Many parents use parental controls at home, which is a great first step. But relying solely on parental controls can provide a false sense of security since many children access the Internet from various locations. It is crucial that children, parents and educators are informed and well-versed as to potential risks our children may face online.

—Jace Galloway, Internet
Safety Coordinator from Illinois

Use Discretion When Spying

If parents choose to use filters and tracking software, we encourage them to tell their children about it. Not only will this act as a deterrent, but parents can then explain *why* they have chosen to incorporate such controls on the computer. It is important for parents to communicate to their children that there are people in cyberspace intent on causing harm and that the software will help to keep them protected.

Some parents with whom we speak are adamant that it is perfectly acceptable—if not demanded—that they covertly and surreptitiously spy on their children's Internet activities. Of course, parents ultimately decide what they think is appropriate in monitoring the online behaviors of the youth in their household. However, if parents do this without informing their children, there is a significant risk of damaging any positive relationship that exists between them. At that point, children may no longer trust their parents at all, which means they will not confide in them about problems they are having—online or offline. We strongly believe that parents should be honest and upfront with their children at all times.

THE STUDENT'S ROLE IN PREVENTING CYBERBULLYING

Responsibility for youth safety online should largely be shared among the adults that serve this population, because it appears that the problem of cyberbullying would quickly grow out of hand if kids were left to their own devices. That said, adolescents can take a number of steps to help protect themselves from victimization. Safeguarding personally identifiable information (rather than heedlessly posting it in public spheres) and being careful with the passwords to their online accounts are the two most vital practices for avoiding victimization at the hands of bullies on the Internet.

Protecting Personal Information

While it seems like common sense, adolescents often need to be reminded that they should never give out their personal information anywhere on the Internet—especially to people they don't know in real life. They may think that the person on the other side of the computer is a friend, but how can they ever know for sure? Even if that person is a friend, there is no way of knowing if someone else in the room is looking over that person's shoulder. Youth should know that anything they reveal about themselves online can (and likely will) be used against them. Cyberbullies can use the personal information to cause a significant amount of emotional harm.

> *I was talking to my friend about something that was bothering me on an e-mail, I sent it to her then the next day another friend of mine had hacked onto my e-mail and took it, and she was the friend that was bothering me, saw it and printed it out, she took it to school with her the next day and showed every one, and it had personal stuff on it, it wasn't just about the person, that was only about 1 line of it. Everyone saw the personal information and teased me for a few days.*

> —12-year-old girl from an undisclosed location outside the United States

Along these same lines, youth should be careful in posting anything to a website that they wouldn't want the entire world to see. We discussed this initially in Chapter 4 when we considered social networking websites. Many kids today enjoy posting pictures or videos on sites like Flickr, Photobucket, YouTube, or MySpace for their friends or family members to check out. They need to understand fully that individuals with malicious motives may also access this content and do with it what they will. For instance, pictures can be downloaded and then manipulated to make it look as though something inappropriate is occurring. Similarly, there have been numerous stories in the news detailing how predators and pedophiles have been able to contact minors based on personal data and digital photos posted on publicly accessible websites or social networking profile pages. Cyberbullies are also easily able to use such content to inflict serious emotional and psychological harm on those who unwittingly, naively, or carelessly post it.

Finally, adolescents must remember that photos, videos, and text cannot be easily deleted from the Internet because of the ease and speed with which digital content is reproduced and archived. Search engines or websites like www.archive.org regularly index (i.e., add to their databases) the contents of web pages across the Internet, including a student's personal web or profile page. After being indexed, the content is retrievable and viewable by others who look for it—*even after it is removed from the original site*. Moreover, people you know (and people you don't know) may have saved the pictures, videos, and text on their own computer hard drives and can repost the material online or send it around to others at any time. Suffice it to say that the permanence factor of anything on the Internet can have significant and long-lasting repercussions for youth who have not been careful or discrete with what they've decided to share with others in cyberspace.

Password Protection

Passwords are necessary to access personal accounts on a computer network. They serve as "authentication" devices and uniquely identify someone as being who they claim to be. Of course, correct authentication prevents others from accessing or altering your personal data. In our current Information Age, passwords are a part of everyday life. However, some users inadvertently make themselves vulnerable to cyberbullying by exposing or carelessly distributing their password.

> *A guy from school changed my MSN e-mail password, I still can't get into my account. He also threatens to beat me up if don't break up with my girl friend.*
>
> —16-year-old boy from Kentucky

Many youth simply don't see the risk in telling others their password. In our school assemblies to students, we ask how many of them know their best friend's computer password, and (perhaps not surprisingly) a majority of the hands are raised. To be honest, this is very alarming to us. Even if youth are responsible enough not to distribute their passwords deliberately, they might inadvertently expose them to others. Many users leave their passwords on a sticky note next to their computers (in case they forget it!). Someone who visits may see it and remember it for later use.

Why is it important to keep passwords secret? An example will help to illustrate the potential problems. A teenage boy might select a MySpace password that is very difficult to guess, but because it is so difficult, might write it down on a small slip of paper taped underneath his keyboard. When his best friend comes over for a visit, the keyboard might accidentally be dropped—revealing the taped paper and, consequently, the password. If that friendship goes sour, the password could be used by the (ex-) best friend to access the account and then upload humiliating content for everyone to read or see.

As a guidance counselor in my present setting, I have experienced students telling me of problems mentioned over AOL Instant Messenger. Students get on other students' accounts due to the sharing of passwords and then say mean or horrible things as a joke or as intimidation. This can leave a student feeling highly scared to come to school, or even more distraught than normal as a teenager with his or her peer relationships.

—School counselor from Florida

Even if adolescents are extremely careful in never writing down their passwords or disclosing them to others, a password might still be discovered through other means. For example, some Internet content providers have "password hint questions," which allow users to retrieve forgotten passwords to online accounts by responding correctly to the questions presented. If the response is successful, an e-mail is sent to the address associated with the account. Within this e-mail, the current password or a new password is given. One of these password hint questions might be "What is my pet's name?" If someone knows your pet's name and you've used it as a password hint, an e-mail with password information would be sent to the relevant e-mail account. If a person knows how to access *that* e-mail account, access to *other* Internet accounts may be possible. Through this procedure, a person can change the passwords of all of your other online accounts simply by having access to your e-mail and knowing a few facts about you.

Finally, some people use the same password for multiple purposes— school and personal e-mail, MySpace, eBay, PayPal, and many other accounts online. As such, finding out the password to one account can lead to simple access to other accounts. While we are considering cyberbullying in this text, there are obvious risks associated with identity theft when someone commandeers another person's password. Box 10.9 lists some recommendations that everyone—children and adults alike— should follow when creating passwords to web- and software-based accounts.

Box 10.9 Recommendations for Creating a Unique Password

- Use passwords with at least seven characters.
- Use a mixture of upper- and lower-case letters, numbers, and nonalphabetic characters.
- Use first letters of an uncommon sentence, song, poem, quote, etc.
- Use word fragments not found in the dictionary (mihtaupyn).
- Use short words separated by characters (dog%door, candy$trip).
- Use transliteration as seen on vanity license plates (e.g., "Elite One" becomes "El te0nE").
- Use lines from a childhood verse or popular song ("It's 3am, I must be lonely" becomes I3amimbL).
- Use phrases from movies ("May the Force be with you" becomes MtFBwu).
- Use expressions inspired by the name of a city ("Rice-a-Roni, the San Francisco Treat" becomes RaRtSFT).
- Interweave characters in two words ("Play Date" becomes PateDlay).

LAW ENFORCEMENT'S ROLE IN PREVENTING CYBERBULLYING

Law enforcement will undoubtedly need to become involved in responding to serious forms of online aggression (e.g., threats to someone's personal safety or in other situations where a law has been violated), but we also feel they have a role to play in a comprehensive prevention plan. First, educators should invite law enforcement officers or utilize school resource officers in their classroom discussions and schoolwide assemblies about responsible Internet use. Students need to realize that inappropriate online conduct may result in serious legal consequences offline. Second, officers should also discuss the ways in which online deviance is investigated, so students recognize that just about everything is traceable when sent or posted electronically. Using specific examples of cases will also reinforce the seriousness of these situations to many youth.

> I have found that students use the Internet to bully and harass each other. These students particularly use the site MySpace.com. Cyberbullying has become the way kids threaten each other and intimidate each other. Kids feel that they can't be tracked or get in trouble for acts that they're not caught doing so they use the Internet to hide behind, and bully and intimidate other kids.

> —School Resource Officer from Florida

WARNING SIGNS: WHAT TO LOOK FOR

It is often difficult to determine whether behavioral or attitudinal changes in youth are signals of distress or simply the usual "adolescent angst" commonly associated with this often-tumultuous transitional period in their lives. Nevertheless, it is important for educators, parents, and other adults to learn to read the behavior of their students and children so that real problems can be detected, diagnosed, and promptly handled. A number of signals may suggest that a child is experiencing some type of distressing event while online (see Box 10.10). Identifying these indicators may help to minimize the negative emotional and psychological effects of Internet-based harm.

Box 10.10 A child may be a victim of cyberbullying if he or she . . .

- Unexpectedly stops using the computer
- Appears nervous or jumpy when an instant message or e-mail appears
- Avoids answering his or her cell phone in front of you
- Appears uneasy about going to school or outside in general
- Appears to be angry, depressed, or frustrated after using the computer
- Avoids discussions about what he or she is doing on the computer
- Becomes abnormally withdrawn from usual friends and family members
- Is being bullied at school

The most obvious sign that something is going on involves a marked change in the adolescent's computer habits. Students may suddenly stop using the computer or overtly refuse when asked to do something online. If a child has been known to go on the computer every day at school but then unexpectedly goes several days without logging on, this change of behavior may signal an underlying problem. In addition, if a student appears nervous when a new e-mail or instant message arrives or is constantly looking over his or her shoulder when at the computer, this behavior may indicate that something is amiss. If a student seems extraordinarily angry, upset, or depressed, especially when using the computer, those emotions may signal a cyberbullying incident. And if youth try to avoid discussions about what they are doing on the computer or put up emotional walls when questioned about harassment or bullying, a serious problem may be at hand.

Relatedly, adults know that many youth try to avoid having to go to school for a variety of reasons. However, if a teenager adamantly refuses to go and will not discuss why, further probing is essential. From our discussions with victims, we know how difficult it can be to face cyberbullies at school—as well as face the rest of the student body who may know about the electronic harassment. Consider Vada's story from Chapter 1; she likely would be mortified to return to school the next day knowing that everyone had seen the printouts of the web page that Ali had created.

There are also a number of red flags that may indicate that a child is mistreating others in cyberspace (see Box 10.11). If a youth quickly switches or closes screens or programs when you walk by, he or she is probably trying to hide something. In these situations, it may be important for you to restress the rules and let the student know that if he or she gives you reason to be concerned about online activities, you will install tracking software (if you haven't already done so) or restrict Internet access to times when you will be able to supervise and monitor online behavior.

Box 10.11 A Child May Be Cyberbullying Others if He or She . . .

- Quickly switches screens or closes programs when you walk by
- Uses the computer at all hours of the night
- Gets unusually upset if he or she cannot use the computer
- Is using multiple online accounts or an account that is not his or her own
- Laughs excessively while using the computer
- Avoids discussions about what he or she is doing on the computer or becomes defensive

---

Furthermore, parents should be advised that if their children are using the computer during all hours of the night, they may be using it for inappropriate activities. They should put reasonable restrictions on computer use and determine exactly what their children are doing online all night. If the children appear to get unusually upset when their usage is limited, they are likely using it too much. Again, be reasonable. Parents should listen to their children when they tell them what they are doing on the computer and rationally assess whether further restrictions are necessary. Give them the benefit of the doubt but check up on them to make sure they are keeping their end of the bargain.

As another point, parents should be encouraged to learn their children's e-mail addresses and social networking profile names and make clear that the children are not allowed to create multiple online profiles or accounts. They should inquire further if they see that a youth is logged onto what seems to be a different e-mail address or MySpace account. Many youth we speak to admit to that they have a "parent-friendly" MySpace page that they don't regularly use and a completely separate one that they constantly use when interacting with their friends. Obviously, a level of trust must exist so that such outright deception does not occur. Not only does it make it difficult for parents to prevent their child's victimization and assist if something does happen, it also subverts any efforts to create the open line of communication indispensable for a healthy, functional parent-child relationship.

If a young person is laughing excessively while using the computer, or if a group of students is gathered around the computer laughing or giggling, they may be cyberbullying others. If they appear jumpy, nervous, or unwilling to share the humor with you, they are probably doing something they shouldn't be doing. However, there are many appropriate humorous pieces of content on the Internet, so don't jump to conclusions. We all appreciate a hilarious comic or funny video; just ask them to show you what is so funny. In general, avoiding discussions or becoming defensive about what they are doing online is a clear sign that they are engaging in activities that likely don't align with your standards of appropriate behavior, thus meriting further inquiry.

SUMMARY

Educators, parents, students, and law enforcement are all important pieces of the cyberbullying prevention puzzle, as shown in Figure 10.2. Individually, it is difficult for any one person to stop cyberbullying from occurring; together, however, adults can present a formidable force against online cruelty. As this chapter has discussed, teachers must supervise students who are using computers in their classrooms and educate the school community about responsible Internet use and netiquette. School administrators must take online aggression seriously and ensure that policies are in place that allow the school to take action against cyberbullies when their actions substantially and materially affect the learning environment or infringe upon the rights of others (as discussed in Chapter 5).

It is also clear that parents must be educated and encouraged to participate in their child's online experiences—which also involves disciplining unacceptable online behaviors when necessary. Youth need to exercise care when it comes to the personal information they post online and should carefully protect their passwords. Law enforcement officers should

Figure 10.2   Pieces of the Cyberbullying Prevention Puzzle

collaborate with school officials to provide education about Internet safety in a way that conveys to students both that threats using electronic devices will be punished and that help is available if they are afraid for their safety. With all of this said, though, prevention efforts can only do so much. Unfortunately, even the best prevention strategies are not 100 percent effective. The following chapter provides guidance and direction on when and how to respond to cyberbullying incidents when they do occur.

QUESTIONS FOR REFLECTION

1. Do you think it is possible to prevent all forms of cyberbullying completely? If yes, how? If not, why not?

2. Whose responsibility is it to prevent cyberbullying?

3. How can students be used to help prevent cyberbullying?

4. At what age do you think it is appropriate for a youth to have a computer in his or her bedroom?

5. How do you know when someone is being cyberbullied? How do you know when someone is cyberbullying others?

Internet Use Contract

Child Expectations

I understand that using the family computer is a privilege that is subject to the following rules:

1. I will respect the privacy of others who use this computer. I will not open, move, or delete files that are not in my personal directory.

2. I understand that Mom and Dad may access and look at my files at any time.

3. I will not download anything or install programs without first asking Mom or Dad.

4. I will never give out private information while online. At no time will I ever give out my last name, phone number, address, or school name—even if I know the person with whom I am communicating. My screen name will be:_____.

5. I understand that I can use the computer for approved purposes only.

6. I will never write or post anything online that I would not want Mom or Dad to see. I will not use profanity or otherwise offensive language. If I receive messages or view content with offensive language, I will report it to Mom and Dad immediately.

7. I will never agree to meet an online friend in person without first asking Mom or Dad. Dangerous people may try to trick me into meeting up with them.

8. If I ever feel uncomfortable about an experience online, I will immediately tell mom or dad. I understand that Mom and Dad are willing to help me and will not punish me as long as these rules are followed.

Parent Expectations

I understand that it is my responsibility to protect my family and to help them receive the best of what the Internet has to offer. In that spirit, I agree to the following:

1. I will listen calmly. If my child comes to me with a problem related to online experiences, I promise not to get angry but to do my best to help my child resolve the situation.

2. I will be reasonable. I will set reasonable rules and expectations for Internet usage. I will establish reasonable consequences for lapses in judgment on the part of my child.

3. I will treat my child with dignity. I will respect the friendships that my child may make online as I would offline friends.

4. I will not unnecessarily invade my child's privacy. I promise not to go further than necessary to ensure my child's safety. I will not read diaries or journals, nor will I inspect e-mails or computer files unless there is a serious concern.

5. I will not take drastic measures. No matter what happens, I understand that the Internet is an important tool that is essential to my child's success in school or business, and I promise not to ban it entirely.

6. I will be involved. I will spend time with my child and be a positive part of my child's online activities and relationships—just as I am offline.

List of prohibited websites and software applications:

Signed:

Family Cell Phone Use Contract

Child Expectations

1. I acknowledge that using a cell phone is a privilege and, therefore, will not take it for granted.

2. I will not give out my cell phone number to anyone unless I first clear it with my parents.

3. I will always answer calls from my parents. If I miss a call from them, I will call them back immediately.

4. I will not bring my cell phone to school if it is prohibited. If allowed to bring it to school, I will keep it in my backpack or locker and turned off between the first and last bell.

5. I will not use my cell phone for any purpose after _____AM/PM on a school night or after _____AM/PM on a nonschool night, unless approved by my parents.

6. I will not send hurtful, harassing, or threatening text messages.

7. I will not say anything to anyone using the cell phone that I wouldn't say to them in person with my parents listening.

8. I will pay for any charges above and beyond the usual monthly fee.

9. I will not download anything from the Internet or call toll numbers without first asking my parents.

10. I will not enable or disable any setting on my phone without my parent's permission.

11. I will not take a picture or video of anyone without that person's permission.

12. I will not send or post pictures or videos of anyone online without that person's permission.

13. I will not send or post any pictures or videos to anyone without first showing them to my parents.

14. I will not be disruptive in my cell phone use. If my parents ask me to end a call or stop text messaging, I will.

Parent Expectations

1. I will respect the privacy of my child when my child is talking on a cell phone.

2. I will not unnecessarily invade my child's privacy by reading text messages or looking through call logs without telling my child first. If I have a concern, I will express it to my child, and we will look through this material together.

3. I will pay the standard monthly fee for the cell phone contract.

4. I will be reasonable with consequences for violations of this contract. Consequences will start at loss of cell phone privileges for 24 hours and progress according to the seriousness of the violation.

Signed:

11

Top Ten Rules That Govern School Authority Over Student Cyber Expressions

Jill Joline Myers, Donna S. McCaw, and Leaunda S. Hemphill

Although conflicting court decisions have surfaced and jurisdictional variations exist, the following general principles guiding cyber bullying situations have emerged from court precedent:

1. First Amendment provisions apply to public school students.

2. Censorship is permissible if the student expression reasonably suggests a substantial disruption to school activities.

3. Censorship is permissible if the student expression actually interferes with students' rights to educational benefits or substantially detracts from the learning environment.

4. Lewd, vulgar, or profane language is inappropriate in a public educational environment.[1]

5. Reasonable regulations may be imposed with respect to the time, place, and manner of student expressions involving school property, school equipment, or school events.

6. Schools may regulate school-sponsored expression if the expression is viewed as endorsed by the institution.

7. Schools may regulate school-sponsored expression on the basis of any legitimate pedagogical concern.

8. Off-campus expressions may be regulated only when a sufficient nexus to campus is shown.

9. Expression may be restricted if it is reasonably perceived to be inconsistent with the "shared values of a civilized social order."[2]

10. True threats and criminal activity may always be regulated regardless of whether they originated on or off campus.

These Top Ten Rules, like the First Amendment right from which they come, are not absolute. Exceptions exist. Further, the Rules do not exist in a vacuum. The Rules should be viewed within the context of each other and as stand-alones. In general, the Rules provide a strong framework within which school leaders may act.

Rule 1: First Amendment Provisions Apply to Public School Students

Students have First Amendment rights. They have the right to express opinions on controversial topics and maintain individual viewpoints. Students have the right to express themselves freely off campus on their own time. Parents control student expressions off campus. They have not delegated their authority to schools. However, students do not possess unlimited First Amendment rights in public schools. If more than a de minimis connection between the speech and the schools exists, schools have the power and duty to intervene. Schools have the authority to "inculcate the habits and manners of civility."[3] The age, maturity, and cognitive development of both the offender and the audience are critical factors in censoring student speech. More censorship of expression is allowed for younger and less mature students. The school's purpose involves more learning than debate at lower grade levels. *Tinker* and its progeny suggest that students retain First Amendment rights, but those rights are restricted to what is appropriate for the care and tutelage of children.[4]

Rule 2: Censorship Is Permissible if the Student Expression Reasonably Suggests a Substantial Disruption to School Activities

Student expression may be sanctioned if the school can reasonably forecast that the expression will cause a substantial disruption to school activities. The seminal court case, *Tinker*, allows students to make silent, passive, political expressions that do not cause disorder or disturbance at school.[5] It is not permissible to sanction student expression based on a desire to avoid unpleasantness or prevent the expression of unpopular viewpoints. Schools do not need to wait for a disruption to start if they can forecast a disruption. If there is a fore-seeable disruption, schools should attempt to prevent its occurrence.

Disruptions do not need to be profound to justify student sanctioning. There is no need to wait for complete chaos, but there must be more than a mild distraction to the educational environment before schools may act. "There is no magic number of students or classrooms that need to be disturbed."[6] School administrators must be able to provide fact-intensive information about the disruption or the potential disruption before censorship of student expression is permissible. It is not sufficient that students merely talk about the offensive expressions or make general comments about the expressions. Likewise, expressions that make individuals self-conscious or uncomfortable do not justify censorship. However, schools may sanction a student if the expression realistically (1) depicts verbal or graphic violence, (2) threatens or undermines members of the school community, or (3) portends a violent disruption. Animated depictions of attacks on teachers are examples of graphic violence that may justify sanctioning of a student's expression. Undermining the professionalism of school administrators may justify sanctioning when it interferes with the effective operation of the school. Furthermore, most courts allow immediate sanctioning whenever a student makes comments analogous to "going Columbine." The dangers inherent in the school environment necessitate restricting speech threatening school shootings.

Some factors that need to be considered before censorship is permissible are

1. the record of past disturbance,

2. the number of individuals who viewed the expressions,

3. the location where the expressions were viewed or accessed,

4. the manner in which the expressions arrived on campus,

5. the student's intention that the expression impact the school environment, and

6. the necessity for supplementary administrative resources.

A significant connection between the student expression and the school must exist before administrative actions may be taken.

Rule 3: Censorship Is Permissible if the Student Expression Actually Interferes With Students' Rights to Educational Benefits or Substantially Detracts From the Learning Environment

Only expressions that actually impinge on the rights of other students may be censored. The courts do not allow school administrators to censor students' expression at all times, at all places, and under all circumstances. However, the courts do allow administrators to censor expression that inhibits a student from learning or experiencing educational benefits. If a student's expression attacks a core characteristic (race, ethnicity, disability, sexual orientation, or gender), then the expression may be censored if the expression did in fact interfere with a student's right to educational benefits or substantially detracts from the learning environment. Note that expressions that impinge on the rights of other students may be prohibited even when no substantial disruption to student activities is foreseeable.[7]

Rule 4: Lewd, Vulgar, or Profane Language Is Inappropriate in a Public Educational Environment

Schools have the authority to prohibit lewd, offensive, and vulgar student expressions from occurring on campus in public discourse.[8] Schools have the responsibility to prevent students from being subjected to language and material that is inappropriate for their physical and cognitive developmental level. The key factors are (1) the expression actually must occur on school campus and (2) expression must occur before a school audience. Cyber expressions created off campus may not be censored by the school, despite the offensiveness of such expressions. It is the parents' responsibility to monitor off-campus student expressions. Note that no substantial disruption needs to occur before a school may sanction based on this rule.

Rule 5: Reasonable Regulations May Be Imposed With Respect to the Time, Place, and Manner of Student Expressions Involving School Property, School Equipment, or School Events

Student expressions that are appropriate off campus or before some audiences are not always appropriate on school premises or before all students. Schools are not public forums; therefore, school administrators may impose reasonable restrictions of on-campus expressions created by students. Censorship is permissible if it is reasonably related to a pedagogical concern. Thus, schools may establish standards to prevent expressions that are ungrammatical, poorly written, inadequately researched, biased, or prejudiced, or that are expressed in an inappropriate tone. Schools must consider the emotional maturity of their populations in determining whether to disseminate student expressions on potentially sensitive topics. For example, schools may regulate dissemination of expressions that discuss the existence of Santa Claus in elementary schools or that present material that is inappropriate for an immature audience.

Rule 6: Schools May Regulate School-Sponsored Expression if the Expression Is Viewed as Endorsed by the Institution

School officials may more freely sanction school-sponsored expressions than student-initiated expressions. School-sponsored expressions include those created as part of the school curriculum or a school-sponsored activity. The school administrators exercise editorial control over student assignments, school publications, and other school-sponsored expressive activities. Therefore, schools may regulate expressions that bear "the imprimatur of the school."[9]

Rule 7: Schools May Regulate School-Sponsored Expression on the Basis of Any Legitimate Pedagogical Concern

Closely related to Rule 6 is this maxim that authorizes schools to censor student expression for legitimate pedagogical purposes. If there is a significant connection between the school and the student's expression, school administrators may exercise control. School administrators must accept that they may not intervene by sanctioning questionable expressions in cyber space that occur off campus during nonschool hours.

Rule 8: Off-Campus Expressions May Be Regulated Only When a Sufficient Nexus to Campus Is Shown

Only if the sting of the expression significantly impacts the school environment may the school intervene. The line is drawn where the expression disrupts school-related activities. Outside of that line, **the school has no authority**. For example, it is not the school's responsibility or necessarily within its authority to regulate all offensive or sexually suggestive photos posted on a student's social networking sites off campus and during summer break, if there is no reference or link to the school.[10] (Law enforcement and parents have authority over this conduct.) Conversely, it may be within the school's authority to sanction off-campus, online student expression when it violates a school's code of conduct. For example, online photos depicting student athletes drinking alcohol may warrant school administrative restrictions of extracurricular activities.[11] The distinguishing factor separating these two examples is the intimate connection between the campus and the student activity. The further the expression is attenuated from school activities, the less likely that the schools may moderate it.

Rule 9: Expression May Be Restricted if It Is Reasonably Perceived to Be Inconsistent With the "Shared Values of a Civilized Social Order"

School administrators have an affirmative obligation to instill in students the "fundamental values of 'habits and manners of civility' essential to democratic society" and to teach students "the boundaries of socially appropriate behavior."[12] Schools meet this obligation when they allow students to observe freedom of speech firsthand in order to see their constitutional rights at work. This does not mean that schools must allow students to advocate sex, drugs, or alcohol use in public educational institutions. Schools should impart boundaries for socially appropriate behavior.

Rule 10: True Threats and Criminal Activity May Always Be Regulated Regardless of Whether They Originated On or Off Campus

Schools may restrict student expression that falls outside of First Amendment protection, including true threats and criminal conduct. Additionally, schools need not tolerate activities that promote criminal conduct such as illegal drug use. The most difficult concept for school administrators to understand concerns true threats. Only the most egregious expressions fall within the definition of true threats. True threats must communicate a serious, unequivocal intent to harm someone or cause a reasonable person to feel immediately threatened. In today's society, most statements asserting school violence constitute true threats.

Conclusion

"Schools can and will adjust to the new challenges created by . . . students and the Internet, but not at the expense of the First Amendment."[13] Students need to know school boundaries exist, even on the Internet. By applying the **Top Ten Rules** suggested here, school administrators have a framework to assist them in enforcing appropriate boundaries dealing with student cyber expressions.

Notes

1. Hedges v. Wauconda Community School Dist. 118 9 F.3d 1295, 1297–1298 (7th Cir. 1993).
2. Bethel School District No. 403 v. Fraser, 478 U.S. 675, 683 (1986).
3. *Id.* at 681.
4. Vernonia Sch. Dist. 47J v. Acton (94-590), 515 U.S. 656 (1995).
5. Tinker v. Des Moines Independent Community School District, 393 U.S. 503, 508 (1969).

6. J.C. v. Beverly Hills Unified School District, 2010 LEXIS 54481, 44 (C.D. Cal. 2010).

7. Tinker, 515 U.S. at 509.

8. Bethel School District No. 403 v. Fraser, 478 U.S. 675, 681 (1986).

9. Hazelwood School District v. Kuhlmeier, 484 U.S. 260, 270–271 (1988).

10. Associated Press. (2009, November 3). *Ind. teens punished for racy MySpace photos sue high school.* Retrieved from http://www.firstamendment center.org/news.aspx?id=22270.

11. Associated Press. (2008, January 11). *Facebook photos sting Minn. high school studies.* Retrieved from http://www.firstamendmentcenter.org/news .aspx?id=19537.

12. Bethel School District No. 403 v. Fraser, 478 U.S. 675, 681 (1986).

13. Hudson, D. (2008, August). *Cyberspeech.* First Amendment Center. Retrieved June 22, 2010, from http://www.firstamendmentcenter.org// speech/studentexpression/topic.aspx?topic=cyberspeech&SearchString= cyberspeech.

References

Preface

Alexander, B. (2008). Web 2.0 and emergent multiliteracies. *Theory into Practice, 47*(2), 150–160.

Anderson, R., & Dexter, S. (2005). School technology leadership: An empirical investigation of prevalence and effect. *Educational Administrator Quarterly, 41*(1), 49–82.

Darling-Hammond, L., Meyerson, D., LaPointe, M., & Orr, M. T. (2010). *Preparing principals for a changing world: Lessons from effective school leadership programs.* San Francisco: Jossey-Bass.

Dawson, C., & Rakes, G. (2003). The influence of principals' technology training on the integration of technology into schools. *Journal of Research on Technology in Education, 36*(1), 29–49.

Drago-Severson, E. (2004). *Helping teachers learn: Principal leadership for adult growth and development.* Thousand Oaks, CA: Corwin.

Gerard, L. F., Bowyer, J. B., & Linn, M. C. (2010). How does a community of principals develop leadership for technology-enhanced science? *Journal of School Leadership, 20*(2), 145–183.

McLoud, S., & Richardson, J. W. (2011). The dearth of technology leadership coverage. *Journal of School Leadership, 21*(2), 216–240.

Schrum, L., Galizio, L. M., & Ledesma, P. (2011). Educational leadership and technology integration: An investigation into preparation, experiences, and roles. *Journal of School Leadership, 21*(2), 241–261.

Stuart, L. H., Mills, A. M., & Remus, U. (2009). School leaders, ICT competence and championing innovations. *Computers & Education, 53,* 733–741.

Williams, P. (2008). Leading schools in the digital age: A clash of cultures. *School Leadership and Management, 28*(3), 213–228.

Chapter 1

1. Educational writers, from John Dewey to today's Web 2.0 advocates (e.g., Ian Jukes, Alan November, Will Richardson, David Warlick) to advocates of case-, problem-, and inquiry-based learning, have all suggested the need for some form of new partnership between students and teachers, involving much less telling by teachers and much more doing by students.

2. I have heard this from a great number of people, including Dr. Edith Ackermann (a former student of Piaget), Dr. Derrick DeKerchove (a former student of Marshall McLuhan), and many others. I was told by a children's TV executive that "kids getting older younger" was a longtime internal slogan at MTV.

3. Ibid.

4. From the opening sequence of the *Star Trek* television show.

5. Dewey, J. (1963). *Experience and education*. New York, NY: Collier Books. (Original work published 1938.)

6. Johnson, L. F., Smith, R. S., Smythe, J. T., & Varon, R. K. (2009). *Challenge-based learning: An approach for our time*. Austin, TX: New Media Consortium.

7. Boss, S., & Krauss, J. (2007). *Reinventing project-based learning: Your field guide to real-world projects in the digital age*. Washington, DC: International Society for Technology in Education.

8. Tim Rylands in the United Kingdom.

9. Hu, W. (2007, May 4). Seeing no progress, some schools drop laptops. *New York Times*. Retrieved from http://www.nytimes.com/

10. Nicole Cox, instructor, in a report by the Rochester Institute of Technology:

I divided the class into discussion groups of four–six people. Students posted their responses to the readings online within their own group, and then had the opportunity to read the responses from their group "mates." Once they'd read all the responses within their group, they were asked to write a reaction to one other response. . . . There was also a definite improvement in writing skills—again, I think they taught each other. Most groups had at least one student whose writing was actually quite polished (both in content and style), and they would sort of lead by example. Using proper grammar and a more academic tone to make a point somehow makes it seem more valid than one made in all lowercased colloquialisms. I also think a form of "peer pressure" forced students into more vigorous participation. Students whose work was not on par with the work of the other members of the group would sometimes be "shunned"—left out of the discussion. As participation was an important part of a student's grade, those students soon learned the level of acceptable production in order to be considered a viable member of the group. (Retrieved from http://online.rit.edu/faculty/blended/final_report.pdf)

11. Mabry Middle School, Mabry, Georgia.

12. Ingo Schiller, parent of two children at Newsome Park Elementary School, in Newport News, Virginia. Curtis, D. (2001, November 11). Real-world issues motivate students. *Edutopia*. Retrieved from http://www.edutopia.org/magazine

Chapter 2

Anderson, C. (2006). *The long tail: Why the future of business is selling less of more*. New York: Hyperion.

Bridgeland, J. M., DiIulio, J. J., Jr., & Morison, K. B. (2006). *The silent epidemic: Perspectives of high school students*. Washington, DC: Civic Enterprises, LLC. Retrieved May 14, 2008, from http://www.civicenterprises.net/pdfs/thesilentepidemic3-06.pdf

Kurzweil, R. (2005). *The singularity is near: When humans transcend biology.* New York: Penguin.

National Association of Manufacturers. (2005). *2005 skills gap report—a survey of the American manufacturing workforce.* Washington, DC: Author.

National Governors Association. (2005). *An action agenda for improving America's high schools.* Washington, DC: Achieve, Inc., and National Governors Association. Retrieved May 14, 2008, from http://www.nga.org/Files/pdf/0502ACTIONAGENDA.pdf

Nearly half of Texas students entering college now must take remedial classes. (July 7, 2006). *Houston Chronicle,* p. B1 [Electronic version]. Retrieved July 7, 2006, from http://www.chron.com/disp/story.mpl/metropolitan/4029961.htm

Pink, D. H. (2001). *Free agent nation: The future of working for yourself.* New York: Warner Books.

Schlechty, P. C. (1997). *Inventing better schools: An action plan for educational reform.* San Francisco: Jossey-Bass.

Trump, J. L. (1959). *Images of the future: A new approach to the secondary school.* Urbana, IL: Commission on the Experimental Study of the Utilization of the Staff in the Secondary School, National Association of Secondary School Principals.

Chapter 3

Ackerman, R., & Mackenzie, S. (2006). Uncovering teacher leadership. *Educational Leadership 63*(8), 66–70.

Adamy, P., & Heinecke, W. (2005). The influence of organizational culture on technology integration in teacher education. *Journal of Technology and Teacher Education, 13*(2), 233–255.

Bai, H., & Ertmer, P. (2008). Teacher educators' beliefs and technology uses as predictors of preservice teachers' beliefs and technology attitudes. *Journal of Technology and Teacher Education, 16*(1), 93–112.

Bartunek, J. M., Greenberg, D. N., & Davidson, B. (1999). Consistent and inconsistent impacts of a teacher-led empowerment initiative in a federation of schools. *The Journal of Applied Behavioral Science, 35*(4), 457–478.

Bauer, J. (2005). Toward technology integration in schools: Why it isn't happening. *Journal of Technology and Teacher Education, 13*(4), 519–546.

Bogler, R. (2005). The power of empowerment: Mediating the relationship between teachers' participation in decision making and their professional commitment. *Journal of School Leadership, 15,* 76–98.

CDW-G. (2007). *Teachers talk tech: Fulfilling technology's promise of improved student performance.* Retrieved May 3, 2009, from http://newsroom.cdwg.com/features/feature-06-26-06.html

Consortium for School Networking (CoSN). (2001). *A school administrator's guide to planning for the total cost of new technology.* Washington, DC: Author.

Crawford, A. R., Chamblee, G. E., & Rowlett, R. J. (1998). Assessing concerns of algebra teachers during a curriculum reform: A constructivist approach. *Journal of In-service Education, 24,* 317–327.

Danielson, C. (2006). *Teacher leadership that strengthens professional practice.* Alexandria, VA: Association for Supervision and Curriculum Development.

Danielson, C. (2007). The many faces of leadership. *Educational Leadership, 65*(1), 14–19.

DuFour, R. (2004). Schools as learning communities. *Educational Leadership, 61*(8), 6–11.

Fullan, M. (1993). Why teachers must become change agents. *Educational Leadership 50*(6), 12–17.

Fullan, M. (2007). *Leading in a culture of change* (Rev. ed.). San Francisco: Jossey-Bass.

Glassett, K. F. (2007). *Technology and pedagogical beliefs of teachers: A cross case analysis.* Unpublished doctoral dissertation, University of Utah—Salt Lake City.

Hall, G. E., & Hord, S. M., (1987). *Change in schools: Facilitating the process.* Albany: State University of New York Press.

Heflich, D. A., Dixon, J. K., & Davis, K. S. (2001). Taking it to the field: The authentic integration of mathematics and technology in inquiry-based science instruction. *Journal of Computers in Mathematics and Science Teaching, 20*(1), 99–112.

Henderson, J. (2008). Providing support for teacher leaders. *Education Update, 50*(10). Retrieved April 30, 2009, from http://www.ascd.org/publications/newsletters/education_update/oct08/vol50/num10/Providing_Support_for_Teacher_Leaders.aspx

Hernandez-Ramos, P. (2005). If not here, where? Understanding teachers' use of technology in Silicon Valley schools. *Journal of Research on Technology in Education, 38*(1), 35–46.

Horsley, D. L., & Loucks-Horsley, S. (1998). Tornado of change. *Journal of Staff Development, 19*(4), 17–20.

Jonassen, D. (1997). Instructional design models for well-structured and ill-structured problem-solving learning outcomes. *Educational Technology Research and Development, 45*(1), 65–94.

Kirschner, P. A., & Erkens, G. (2006). Cognitive tools and mindtools for collaborative learning. *Journal of Educational Computing Research, 35*(2), 199–209.

Kongrith, K., & Maddux, C. D. (2005). Online learning as a demonstration of type II technology: Second-language acquisition. *Computers in the Schools, 22*(1), 97–111.

Leithwood, K., Louis, K. S., Anderson, S., & Wahlstrom, K. (2004). *Review of research: How leadership influences student learning.* Minneapolis: Center for Applied Research and Educational Improvement; Toronto: Ontario Institute for Studies in Education; and New York: The Wallace Foundation. Retrieved November 7, 2008, from http://www.wallacefoundation.org/SiteCollection Documents/WF/Knowledge   Center/Attachments/PDF/ReviewofResearch-LearningFromLeadership.pdf

Lieberman, A., & Miller, L. (2004). *Teacher leadership.* San Francisco: Jossey-Bass.

Little, J. W. (1982). Norms of collegiality and experimentation: Workplace conditions of school success. *American Educational Research Journal, 19*(3), 325–340.

Louis, K. S., & Kruse, S. D. (1995). *Professionalism and community: Perspectives on reforming urban schools.* Thousand Oaks, CA: Corwin.

Manouchehri, A., & Goodman, T. (2000). Implementing mathematics reform: The challenge within. *Educational Studies in Mathematics, 42*, 1–34.

Martin, L., & Kragler, S. (1999). Creating a culture of teacher professional growth. *Journal of School Leadership, 9*(4), 311–320.

Marzano, R. J., Waters, T., & McNulty, B. A. (2005). *School leadership that works: From research to results.* Alexandria, VA: Association for Supervision and Curriculum Development.

Nir, A. E., & Bogler, R. (2008). The antecedents of teacher satisfaction with professional development programs. *Teaching and Teacher Education, 24*(2), 377–86.

Norris, C., Sullivan, T., Poirot, J., & Solloway, E. (2003). No access, no use, no impact: Snapshot surveys of educational technology in K–12. *Journal of Research on Technology in Education, 36*(1), 15–28.

Poole, B. (2006). What every teacher should know about technology. *Education World.* Retrieved April 30, 2009, from http://www.education-world.com/a_tech/columnists/poole/poole015.shtml

Prouty, D. (n.d.). Top 10 ways to be a successful technology coordinator. *The Snorkel.* Retrieved May 9, 2009, from http://www.thesnorkel.org/articles/Top10.pdf

Reeves, D. B. (2006). *The learning leader: How to focus school improvement for better results.* Alexandria, VA: Association for the Supervision of Curriculum Development.

Riel, M., & Becker, H. J. (2008). Characteristics of teacher leaders for information and communication technology. In J. Voogt & G. Knezek (Eds.), *International handbook of information in primary and secondary education* (pp. 397–417). New York: Springer.

Rogers, E. M. (2003). *Diffusion of innovations* (5th ed.). New York: Simon & Schuster.

Sadker, M., & Sadker, D. (2005). *Teachers, schools, and society.* New York: McGraw Hill.

Sandholtz, J. H., & Reilly, B. (2004). Teachers, not technicians: Rethinking technical expectations for teachers. *Teachers College Record, 106*(3), 487–512.

Schmoker, M. J. (2001). *The results fieldbook: Practical strategies for dramatically improved schools.* Alexandria, VA: Association for the Supervision of Curriculum Development.

Schrum, L. (1999). Technology developments for educators: Where are we going and how do we get there? *Educational Technology Research and Development, 47*(4), 83–90.

Schrum, L., Skeele, R., & Grant, M. (2002–2003). Revisioning learning in a college of education: The systemic integration of computer based technologies. *Journal of Research on Technology in Education, 35*(2), 256–271.

Semich, G., & Graham, J. (2006). Instituting teacher leaders in technology: A personal approach to integrating technology in today's classroom. In C. Crawford, D. Willis, R. Carlsen, I. Gibson, K. McFerrin, J. Price, et al. (Eds.), *Proceedings of Society for Information Technology and Teacher Education International Conference 2006* (pp. 3608–3611). Chesapeake, VA: AACE.

Shanker, A. (1996). Quality assurance: What must be done to strengthen the teaching profession? *Phi Delta Kappan, 78,* 220–224.

Somech, A. (2002). Explicating the complexity of participative management: An investigation of multiple dimensions. *Educational Administration Quarterly, 38*(3), 341–371.

Somech, A., & Bogler, R. (2002). Antecedents and consequences of teacher organizational and professional commitment. *Educational Administration Quarterly, 38*(4), 555–577.

Southwest Educational Development Laboratory (SEDL). (2008). Professional learning communities: What are they and why are they important? *Issues . . . About Changes, 6*(1). Retrieved April 30, 2009, from http://www.sedl.org/change/issues/issues61/attributes.html

Tate, J. S., & Dunklee, D. R. (2005). *Strategic listening for school leaders.* Thousand Oaks, CA: Corwin.

Testerman, J. C., Flowers, C. P., & Algozzine, R. (2002). Basic technology competencies of educational administrators. *Contemporary Education, 72*(2), 58–61.

Chapter 4

Rinehart, G. (1993). *Quality education: Applying the philosophy of Dr. W. Edwards Deming to transform the educational system.* New York: McGraw-Hill.

Chapter 5

Baron, N. (2008). *Always on: Language in an online and mobile world.* New York: Oxford University Press.

Buckingham, D. (2007). *Beyond technology: Children's learning in the age of digital culture.* Cambridge, England: Polity Press.

Burbules, N., & Callister, T. (2000). *Watch IT: The risks and promises of information technologies for education.* Boulder, CO: Westview Press.

Ito, M., Horst, H. A., Bittanti, M., boyd, d., Herr-Stephenson, B., Lange, P. G., Pascoe, C., J., & Robinson, L. (with Baumer, S., Cody, R., Mahendran, D., Martínez, K., Perkel, D., Sims, C., & Tripp, L.). (2008). *Living and learning with new media: Summary findings from the Digital Youth Project.* The John D. and Catherine T. MacArthur Foundation Report on Digital Media and Learning. Download the report at http://digitalyouth.ischool.berkeley.edu/report

Jenkins, H. (with Clinton, K., Purushotma, R., Robison, A., & Weigel, M.). (2006). *Confronting the challenges of participatory culture: Education for the 21st century.* The John D. and Catherine T. MacArthur Foundation. Retrieved August 18, 2007, from http://digitallearning.macfound.org.

MacArthur Foundation. Re-Imagining learning in the 21st century. http://tiny.cc/teachtech_1_2

Moll, L., Amanti, C., Neff, D., & Gonzalez, N. (1992). Funds of knowledge for teaching: Using a qualitative approach to connect homes and classrooms. *Theory Into Practice, 31*(2), 132–141.

Pew Research Center. (2010). *Millennials: A portrait of generation next. Confident. Connected. Open to Change.* (P. Taylor & S. Keeter, Eds.). Retrieved March 24, 2010, from http://pewresearch.org/millennials.

Street, B. (1995). *Social literacies.* London: Longman.

Chapter 6

Atwell, N. (1998). *In the middle: New understandings about writing, reading, and learning* (2nd ed.) Portsmouth, NH: Heinemann.

Barton, D., & Hamilton, M. (1998). *Local literacies: Reading and writing in one community.* London: Routledge.

Brown, D. (1999). Promoting reflective thinking: Preservice teachers' literacy autobiographies as a common text. *Journal of Adolescent & Adult Literacy, 42,* 402–410.

Brownlow, K. (1969/1976). *The parade's gone by*. Berkeley, CA: University of California Press.

Burke, J. (2000). *Reading reminders: Tools, tips, and techniques*. Portsmouth, NH: Heinemann.

Garmston, R. J., & Wellman, B. M. (1992). *How to make presentations that teach and transform*. Alexandria, VA: ASCD.

Kist, W. (2000). Beginning to create the new literacy classroom: What does the new literacy look like? *Journal of Adolescent and Adult Literacy, 43,* 710–718.

Kist, W. (2003). Student achievement in new literacies for the 21st century. *Middle School Journal, 35*(1), 6–13.

Kist, W. (2005). *New literacies in action: Teaching and learning in multiple media*. New York: Teachers College Press.

Koch, K. (1970). *Wishes, lies, and dreams: Teaching children to write poetry*. New York: HarperCollins.

Kress, G. (2003). *Literacy in the new media age*. London: Routledge.

Loomans, D., & Kolberg, K. (1993). *The laughing classroom*. Tiburon, CA: H.J. Kramer.

McLaughlin, M., & Vogt, M. (1996). *Portfolios in teacher education*. Newark, DE: International Reading Association.

Romano, T. (1995). *Writing with passion: Life stories, multiple genres*. Portsmouth, NH: Boynton/Cook.

Romano, T. (2000). *Blending genre, altering style: Writing multigenre papers*. Portsmouth, NH: Boynton/Cook.

Schofield, A., & Rogers, T. (2004). At play in fields of ideas. *Journal of Adolescent & Adult Literacy, 48,* 238–248.

Taba, H. (1967). *Teacher's handbook for elementary social studies*. Reading, MA: Addison-Wesley.

Wilhelm, J. D. (1997). *You gotta be the book: Teaching engaged and reflective reading with adolescents*. New York: Teachers College Press.

Chapter 7

Collier, A. (n.d.). Why technopanics are bad. *ConnectSafely*. Retrieved August 12, 2009, from http://www.connectsafely.org/Commentaries-Staff/why-technopanics-are-bad.html

Cummins, J. (1979). Cognitive/academic language proficiency, linguistic interdependence, the optimum age question and some other matters. *Working Papers on Bilingualism, 19,* 121–129.

Goodwin-Jones, R. (2005). Emerging technologies: Skype and podcasting: Disruptive technologies for language learning. *Language Learning and Technology, 9*(3), 9–12.

Johns, K. M., & Tórrez, N. M. (2001). Helping ESL learners succeed. *Phi Delta Kappa, 484,* 7–49.

National Clearinghouse for English Language Acquisition and Language Instruction Educational Programs, U.S. Department of Educaiton. (n.d.). *Frequently asked questions*. Retrieved August 11, 2009, from http://www.ncela.gwu.edu/faqs/

The Partnership for 21st Century Skills. (2004). *Framework for 21st century learning*. Retrieved August 12, 2009, from http://www.21stcenturyskills.org/index.php?option=com_content&task=view&id=254&Itemid=120

Pink, D. (2006). *A whole new mind*. New York: Riverhead Trade.

Stanley, G. (2006). Podcasting: Audio on the Internet comes of age. *TESL-EJ, 9*(4). Retrieved August 21, 2009, from http://www-writing.berkeley.edu/TESL-EJ/ej36/int.html

Svedkauskaite, A., Reza-Hernandez, L., & Clifford, M. (2003, June 24). *Critical issue: Using technology to support limited-English-proficient (LEP) students' learning experiences.* North Central Regional Education Laboratory. Retrieved August 11, 2009, from http://www.ncrel.org/sdrs/areas/issues/methods/technlgy/te900.htm

Teachers of English to Speakers of Other Languages. (2006). *PreK–12 English language proficiency standards.* Alexandria, VA: Author.

Teachers of English to Speakers of Other Languages. (1996–2007). *Technology standards for language learners.* Alexandria, VA: Author. Retrieved August 21, 2009, from http://www.tesol.org/s_tesol/sec_document.asp?CID=1972&DID=12051

Thorne, S., & Payne, J. (2005). Evolutionary trajectories, Internet mediated expression, and language education. *CALICO, 22*(3), 371–397.

SUGGESTED READINGS

Blake, R. J., (2008). *Brave new digital classroom: Technology and foreign language learning.* Washington, DC: Georgetown University Press.

Dudeney, G. (2007). *The Internet and the language classroom (Cambridge handbooks for language teachers).* NY: Cambridge University Press.

Green, T. D., Brown, A. H., & Robinson, L. K. (Eds.). (2007). *Making the most of the Web in your classroom: A teacher's guide to blogs, podcasts, wikis, pages, and sites.* Thousand Oaks, CA: Corwin.

Leu, D. J., Diadiun Leu, D., & Coiro, J. (2004). *Teaching with the Internet K–12: New literacies for new times.* Norwood, MA: Christopher Gordon.

November, A. (2001). *Empowering students with technology.* Thousand Oaks, CA: Corwin.

November, A. (2008). *Web literacy for educators.* Thousand Oaks, CA: Corwin.

Pitler, H., Hubbell, E. R., Kuhn, M., & Malenoski, K. (2007). *Using technology with classroom instruction that works.* Alexandria, VA: Association for Supervision and Curriculum Development.

Ramirez, R., Freeman, Y. S., & Freeman, D. E., (2008). *Diverse learners in the mainstream classroom: Strategies for supporting ALL students across content areas—English language learners, students with disabilities, gifted/talented students.* Portsmouth, NH: Heinemann.

Solomon, G., & Schrum, L. (2007). *Web 2.0: New tools, new schools.* Eugene, OR: International Society for Technology in Education.

HELPFUL WEBSITES

Classroom 2.0: http://www.classroom20.com

Connect Safely.org—a forum for parents, teens, experts to discuss safe socializing on the fixed and mobile Web: www.connectsafely.org

EFL and Web 2.0—an excellent online college course on a wiki page designed to teach EFL and ESL students the basics of using different Web 2.0 technologies: http://eflcourse.wikispaces.com

IALLT (International Association for Language Learning Technology): http://iallt.org

Integrating Technology Into the ESL/EFL Classroom—a series of lesson ideas with links to videos: http://integrate-technology.learnhub.com/lessons

International Society for Technology in Education: http://www.iste.org

Langwitches—a helpful blog with links and tutorials for teaching languages through technology: http://langwitches.org/blog

NCELA (National Clearinghouse for English Language Acquisition and Language Instruction Educational Programs): http://www.ncela.gwu.edu

SafeKids.com—Internet safety and civility for kids and parents: http://www.safekids.com

Social Networks and the Web 2.0 Revolution (blog post and video): http://www.teachingenglish.org.uk/blogs/nik-peachey/social-networks-web-20-revolution

Chapter 10

Berson, I. R., Berson, M. J., & Ferron, J. M. (2002). Emerging risks of violence in the digital age: Lessons for educators from an online study of adolescent girls in the United States. *Journal of School Violence, 1*(2), 51–71.

Lenhart, A., Madden, M., & Hitlin, P. (2005). *Teens and technology: Youth are leading the transition to a fully wired and mobile nation.* Retrieved August 2, 2005, from http://www.pewinternet.org/pdfs/PIP_Teens_Tech_July2005Web.pdf

McBrien, J. L., & Brandt, R. S. (1997). *From the language of learning: A guide to education terms.* Alexandria, VA: Association for Supervision and Curriculum Development.

Miller, A. (2002). *Mentoring students and young people: A handbook of effective practice.* London: Kogan Page.

North High School. (2005). *Respect policy.* Retrieved September 21, 2007, from http://www.north.ecasd.k12.wi.us/respect/respect.pdf

Olweus, D., Limber, S., & Mihalic, S. F. (1999b). *Bullying prevention program: Blueprints for violence prevention; Book nine.* Boulder: Center for the Study and Prevention of Violence, Institute of Behavioral Science, University of Colorado.

The Ophelia Project. (2006). *CASS: Creating a Safe School,*™ Retrieved May 30, 2008, from http://www.opheliaproject.org/main/cass.htm

Trolley, B., Hanel, C., & Shields, L. (2006). *Demystifying and deescalating cyber bullying in the schools: A resource guide for counselors, educators, and parents.* Bangor, ME: Booklocker.com.

Tully, J. M. (2007). *The outer limits: Disciplining students without getting sued.* Retrieved November 3, 2007, from http://uacoe.arizona.edu/wren/documents/The_Outer_Limits_Disciplining_Cyber-Mischief_Without_Getting_Sued.pdf

Willard, N. E. (2003). *Safe and responsible use of the Internet: A guide for educators.* Retrieved January 20, 2007, from http://www.csriu.org/onlinedocs/pdf/srui/entire.pdf

Writer, G. (2006). *Cyber bullies: What you and your kids need to know now.* Retrieved July 11, 2006, from http://www.phillyburbs.com/pb-dyn/news/291–07112 006–682108.html

Ybarra, M. L., & Mitchell, K. J. (2004). Online aggressor/targets, aggressors and targets: A comparison of associated youth characteristics. *Journal of Child Psychology and Psychiatry, 45,* 1308–1316.

CORWIN

A SAGE Company

The Corwin logo—a raven striding across an open book—represents the union of courage and learning. Corwin is committed to improving education for all learners by publishing books and other professional development resources for those serving the field of PreK–12 education. By providing practical, hands-on materials, Corwin continues to carry out the promise of its motto: **"Helping Educators Do Their Work Better."**